IMAGES of America

LULING

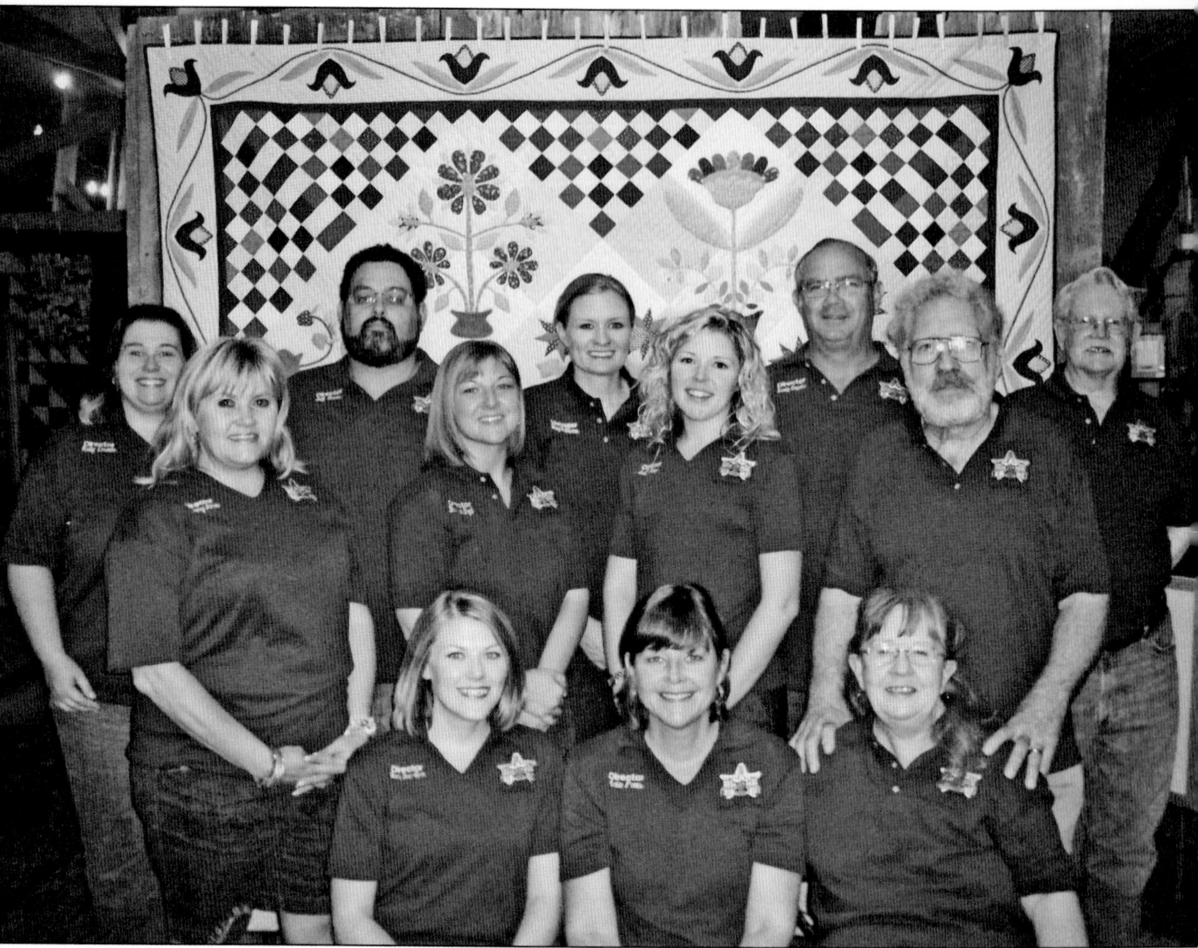

Pictured on Luling's Main Street are, from left to right, (first row) Mandy Dean-Knotts, Ada Potts, and Pat Parsons; (second row) Tammy James, Sharolynn Boyd, Jessica Knotts, and Chuck Parsons; (third row) Kelly Loredo, Jeff Davis, Misty Pendley, Randy Engelke, and Riley Froh. Kelly Allen is not pictured. (Courtesy Wayne Pendley.)

On the Cover: Davis Street is shown between Walnut Street and Pine Street. Most of these edifices in business in the early 1920s still stand today, although some have changed drastically. The three-story building at left was the historic Walker Brothers and Company store. Today it is the home of the Central Texas Oil Patch Museum, the Watermelon Thump, and the chamber of commerce. Davis remains Luling's principal street. (Courtesy Caldwell County Genealogical and Historical Center.)

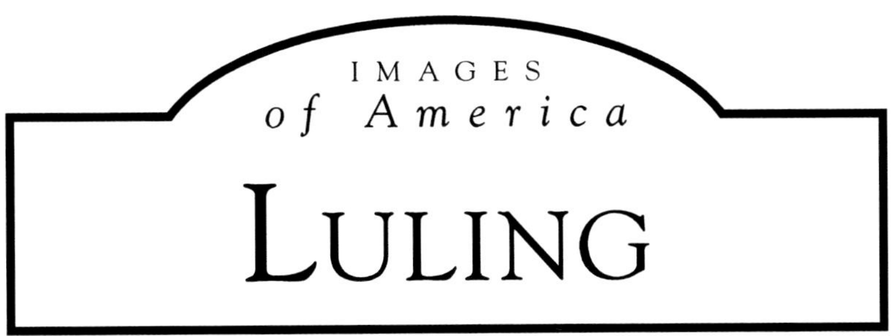

Chuck Parsons and Luling Main Street

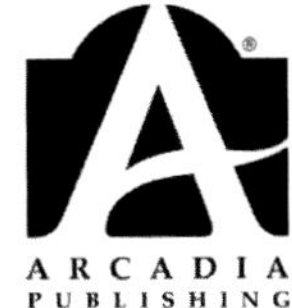

ISBN 978-0-7385-7145-4

Published by Arcadia Publishing
Charleston, South Carolina

Printed in the United States of America

Library of Congress Control Number: 2008942877

For all general information contact Arcadia Publishing at:
Telephone 843-853-2070
Fax 843-853-0044
E-mail sales@arcadiapublishing.com
For customer service and orders:
Toll-Free 1-888-313-2665

Visit us on the Internet at www.arcadiapublishing.com

Dedicated to the memory of Eva Wilson, longtime editor of the Plum Creek Almanac and protector of Luling history. (Courtesy Caldwell County Genealogical and Historical Society.)

Contents

Acknowledgments

No Arcadia book can be produced in a vacuum. Many have helped substantially with this pictorial Luling project. Among those vital participants are Luling Main Street Board of Directors, Pres. Jessica Knotts, Vice President Tammy James, Secretary/Treasurer Ada Potts, and Historian Mandy Dean-Knotts; Cindy Gonzales; Kelly Loredo; Jeff Davis; Sharolynn Boyd; Pat Parsons; and Luling Main Street manager Misty Pendley. Special thanks are due Luling Main Street board member Kelly Allen and Leona Moore for their tireless work in scanning so many photographs.

Members of the Caldwell County Genealogical and Historical Society (G&H) also assisted in helping locate items and articles in the award-winning *Plum Creek Almanac*. The G&H collections are incomparable for preserving the history not only of Luling but of all Caldwell County. A special thank-you is well earned by Bill Watson, president of the society, and Peggy Engeldow.

Numerous individuals contributed photographs and memories, including Wanda Carter; Bonnie Dredla of the Luling Foundation; Aaron Cooper Dunn, son of Mike and Allison Dunn and grandson of G&H member Joyce Williams, who helped identify camera locations in several old photographs; Randy Engelke, whose collection of early Luling memorabilia is most impressive; Riley Froh, author of "The Toughest Town in Texas" chapter in *The Way West* and the definitive biography of Edgar B. Davis; Meatre D. Harrison; Luling mayor Mike Hendricks; Gilberto and Lupe Guerrero, who provided valuable information on *La Escuela Mexicanna*; Don and Judy Lightsey for many valuable photographs from early-20th-century Luling; Karen McCrary, editor of the *Luling Newsboy and Signal*; Lewis C. Shaw; Johnny Lee Spriggs Jr.; Betty Sue Blackwell Towns, first Watermelon Thump Queen; Betty and Tyson Meneley of Prairie Lea, Texas; and Carol Voigt, director of the historic Central Texas Oil Patch Museum of Luling.

INTRODUCTION

The town of Luling, Texas, is the second-largest community in Caldwell County, 15 miles south of county seat Lockhart at the crossroads of three highways: State Highways 80, 90, and 183. Its excellent barbecue and other popular amenities, such as the historic Central Texas Oil Patch Museum or researching the family tree at the Caldwell County Genealogical and Historical Society Library, have made it a well-known community. Pioneers began to settle in the 1840s along the meandering of Plum Creek. In 1848, the Plum Creek Post Office was opened. Then the Galveston, Harrisburg, and San Antonio Railroad laid its track three miles west of Plum Creek, connecting the newly born community to Columbus in Colorado County. The new site was named Luling after the maiden name of the wife of the railroad builder. A post office was established in 1874, and with the further development of the railroad, the community grew rapidly. Within the first decade of its existence, the population grew to nearly 2,000. Farmers shipped out cotton, cottonseed oil, livestock, and pecans. Further growth followed with a second railroad laying track, the San Antonio and Aransas Pass (the SAAP).

In Luling's history, two names stand out: Thomas Wentworth Pierce and Edgar Byram Davis. One of the main streets is named Pierce Street; the other "main" street is named Davis Street, giving both men recognition for their contribution. T. W. Pierce was a native of Dover, New Hampshire, born there on August 16, 1818. His early years were spent with his father in the business of shipbuilding and development of markets for trade. Early in his life, he realized the value of the railroad, and due to his business acumen, he was named president of the Galveston, Harrisburg, and San Antonio Railroad. The tracks reached the San Marcos River in the fall of 1874. Pierce had purchased land from businessman Joseph Josey and arranged the layout of the city, which he named Luling. Pierce donated land for churches, schools, four city parks, and the Belle Haven Orphanage.

Today's citizens are more familiar with the contribution of E. B. Davis to not only the town of Luling but the state as well. Born February 2, 1873, in Brockton, Massachusetts, with only a high school education, he began making money in the shoe business. More millions were made in the foreign rubber plantations. Always a generous individual, Davis gave away much of these proceeds to friends and associates, then began to manage the oil leases of his brother in Caldwell County. Davis visited Luling for the first time in 1919 and decided that God had directed him to come and change the economic system: instead of depending on the one crop of cotton, he determined there were great amounts of oil that would change the face of Caldwell County. In March 1921, Davis incorporated the United North and South Oil Company. After six dry wells, the Rafael Rios No. 1 gushed on August 9, 1922. Davis became not only a successful oil man but a philanthropist. Most of his wealth he gave away. He died in Galveston, Texas, on October 14, 1951, and is buried at the site of one of his homes. In 1966, the Edgar B. Davis Memorial Hospital was built on the site of his Luling home. His grave site is on the hospital grounds.

—Mike Hendricks, Mayor of Luling

One

The Railroad Comes

The modern city of Luling began in the 1840s. Early settlers began building modest homes along Plum Creek south of the county seat, Lockhart. In 1848, a post office was opened, naturally named Plum Creek. This community and nearby Atlanta may have continued to grow had the railroad traveled farther south. In 1874, the Galveston, Harrisburg, and San Antonio Railroad laid track from Columbus to a point three miles west of Plum Creek. As with so many smaller towns, when the railroad bypassed them, the towns died. People relocated to what became Luling. The dreams of those early settlers were perhaps no different from the dreams of many citizens living here today. They wanted good homes and good schools for their children. They also wanted good churches, whether that was a small tent in a pasture or an imposing edifice with spires reaching toward heaven. These dreams did become reality but not overnight. The end-of-tracks towns also attracted the less desirable types, one of whom was the professional gambler and sometimes-gunfighter Joseph Lowe, aptly called "Rowdy Joe." The raucous saloons and gambling halls operated for a time, but wiser heads soon took over and streets became safe. But tranquility cannot last forever, and things happen, such as the train wreck of 1939. Fire was and remains a constant concern, as evidenced by several severe fires that have cost the community dearly in its loss of tangible history. The tangibles of local history remind us of the men and women who have gone before. Our current activities, such as the Davis Street Quilt Show, the Oil City Car Show, or the annual Meet the Authors event, will hopefully be remembered favorably by later generations.

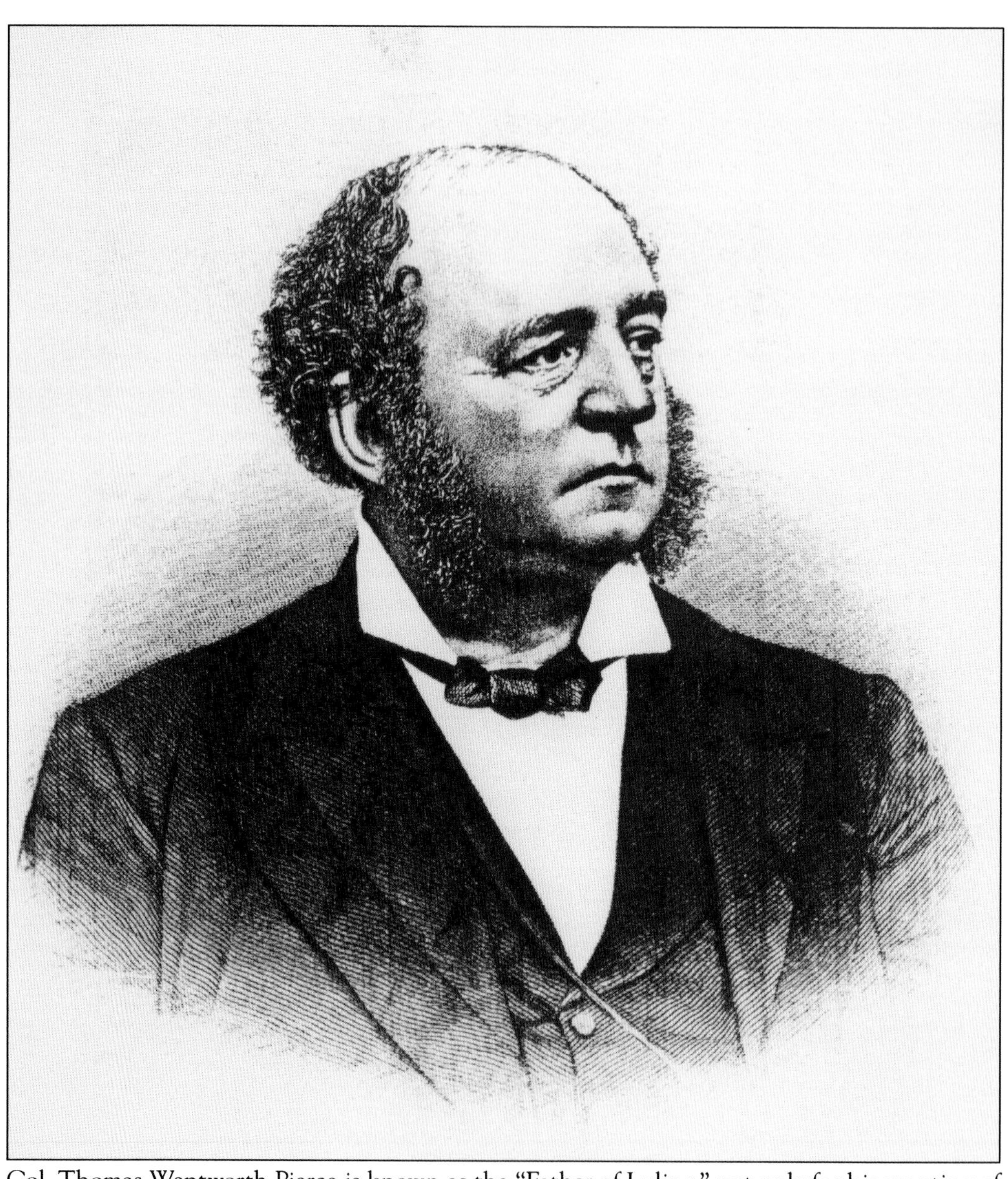

Col. Thomas Wentworth Pierce is known as the "Father of Luling," not only for his granting of property for churches, schools, and city parks, but because of his bringing the railroad to the site that became Luling. Construction of the Galveston, Harrisburg, and San Antonio Railroad was stopped twice, once by the threatened invasion of Mexican troops and later by the American Civil War. With the railroad finally completed through Luling, it continued and joined the Southern Pacific near Pecos. A celebration was held on January 12, 1883, with Colonel Pierce driving the silver spike. With this act, the "Sunset Route" was complete. Pierce, whose name is remembered with the street name, died in Boston in 1885. His will benefited nine towns that his railroad had created: Schulenburg, Flatonia, Marion, Luling, Waelder, Weimer, and Columbus, each receiving $2,000. The towns of Ellinger and Harwood each received $1,000. Funds were also allocated for educational institutions and hospitals. (Courtesy Caldwell County Genealogical and Historical Society, hereafter G&H Society.)

“Rowdy Joe” Lowe earned a reputation over much of the American West. He and his common-law wife, Rowdy Kate, operated gambling houses in Kansas and Texas, including Luling. But Luling’s better citizens ran them both out of town. Rowdy Joe Lowe is shown here in a sober pose, but when Luling was the toughest town in Texas, he appeared much wilder. (Courtesy Western History Collections, University of Oklahoma Library.)

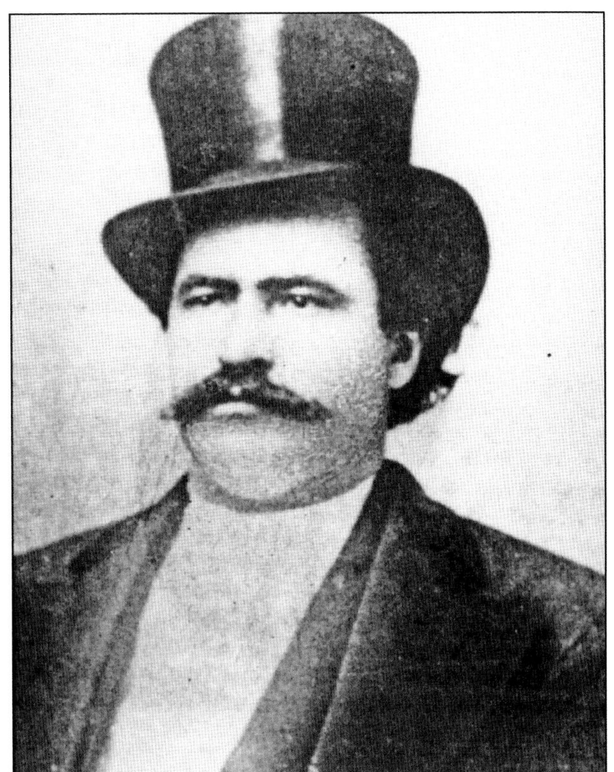

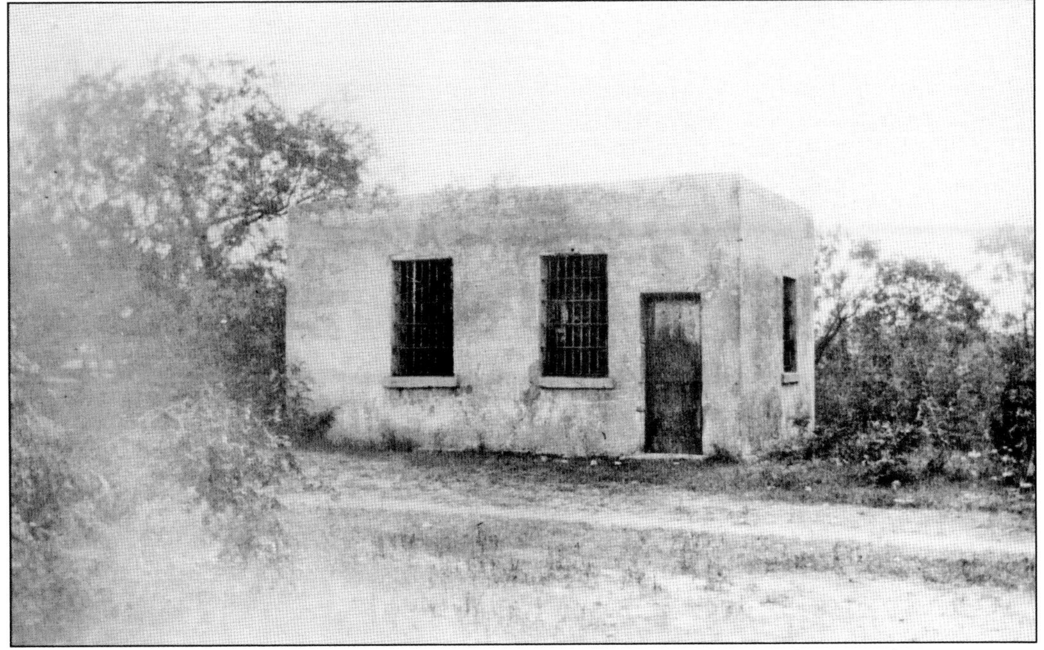

Luling’s early jail held characters as well known as Rowdy Joe Lowe or other now forgotten men who disturbed the peace of Luling’s streets. Built in the early 1880s, it was still in use as late as 1959. The building, since modified, stands at the corner of Laurel and Lamar Streets. It is now the city storage room. (Courtesy Don and Judy Lightsey.)

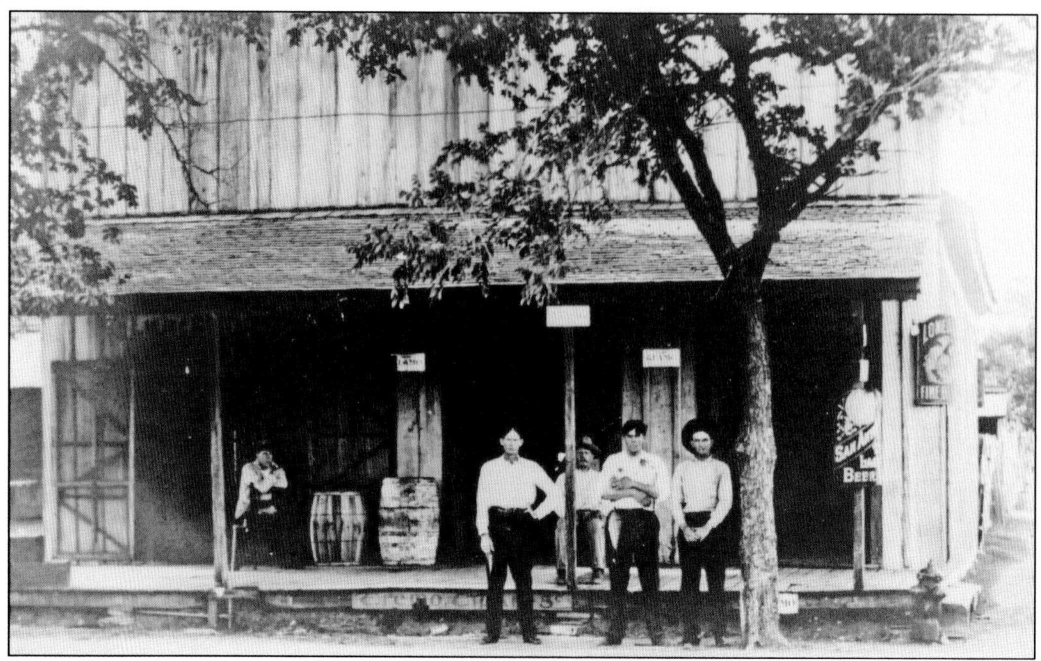

The saloon of L. W. Boyd is shown as it appeared in 1905. The signs reveal that San Antonio beer and Lone Star were among popular brands at the turn of the 19th century. Standing at left is Burrel R. Ussery. The others are identified simply as the Walker brothers. (Courtesy Don and Judy Lightsey.)

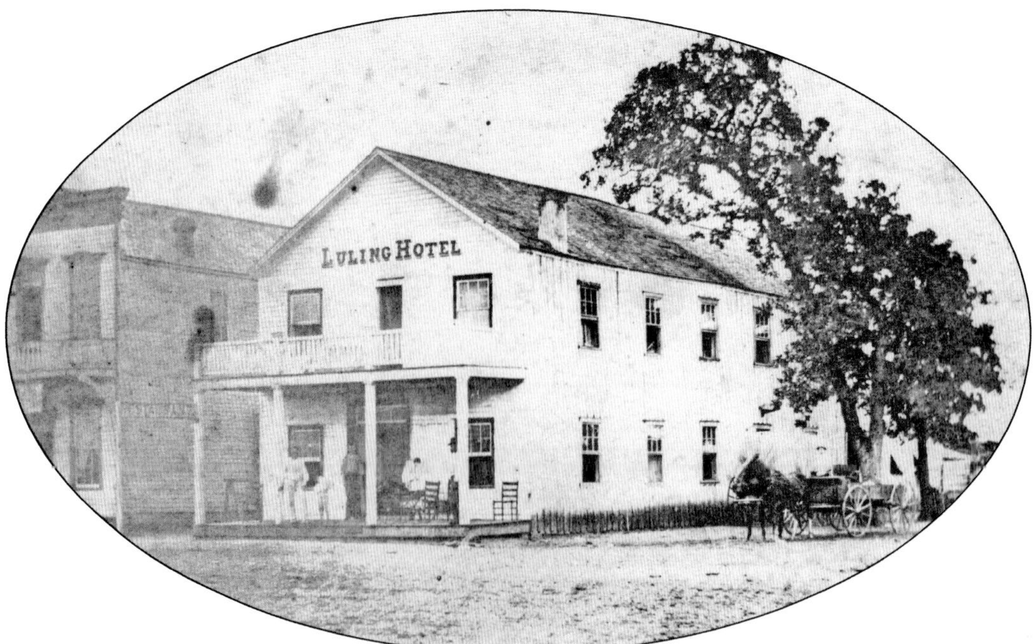

Although undated, this image of the Luling Hotel located at 402 East Pierce Street appears to date from the horse-and-buggy era. It was first operated by P. T. Carter after he emigrated from England to the United States. Robert W. Carter noted that his father had his photography gallery upstairs in the building next door. (Courtesy G&H Society.)

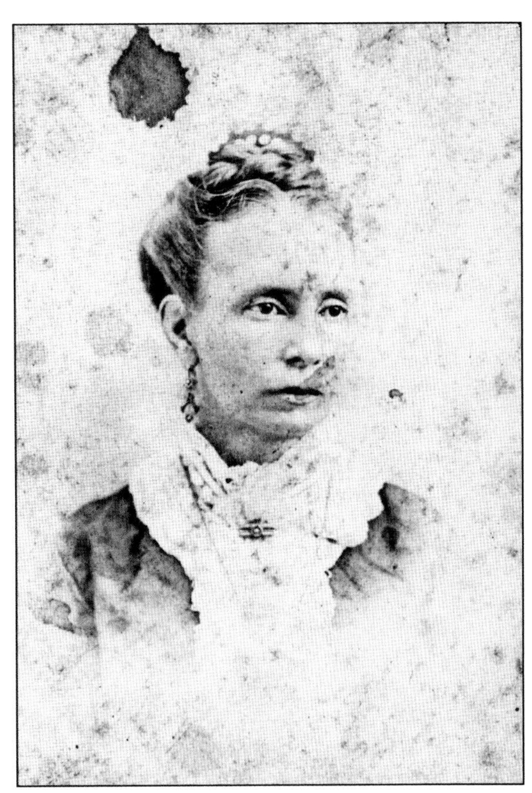

Kosciusco DeWitt Keith and his wife, Mary Jane (McGaffey) Keith, would be forgotten today but for one special reason: they were the parents of the first white girl born in Luling. They were married on December 3, 1857, and first lived at Plum Creek but then *walked* to Luling, arriving in September. Marianne "Annie" Luling Keith was born November 13, 1874. They operated a store in which they also lived. In 1878, K. D. Keith sold his store and lumber yard and moved to San Antonio but moved back to Luling, where he operated a lumber yard. Daughter Annie later moved to Cleburne, Texas, where she worked for the Santa Fe Railroad as bookkeeper for 24 years. Annie died at her San Antonio home on May 14, 1957, and is buried in the Luling Cemetery. (Both courtesy G&H Society.)

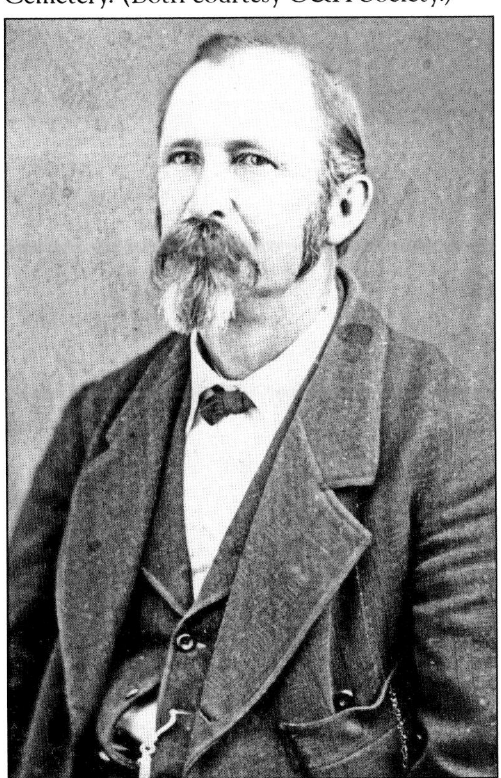

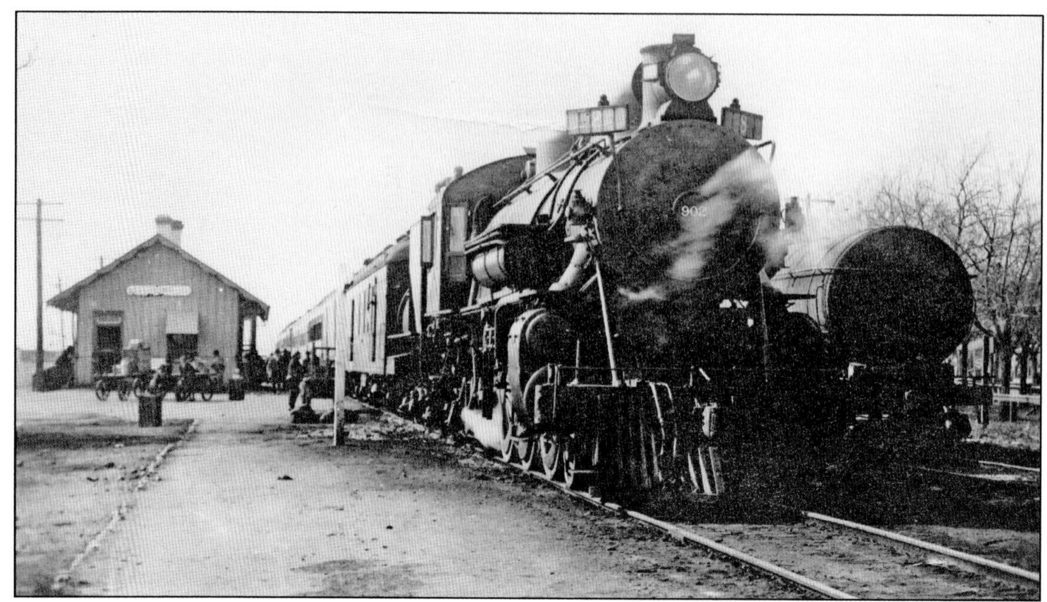

The iron horse of the American West arrived in Luling in 1874. Here is a later engine of the Galveston, Harrisburg, and San Antonio line at the Luling depot. A second line, the San Antonio and Aransas Pass, arrived in 1889. The tracks of the former line still cut through Luling today. (Courtesy G&H Society.)

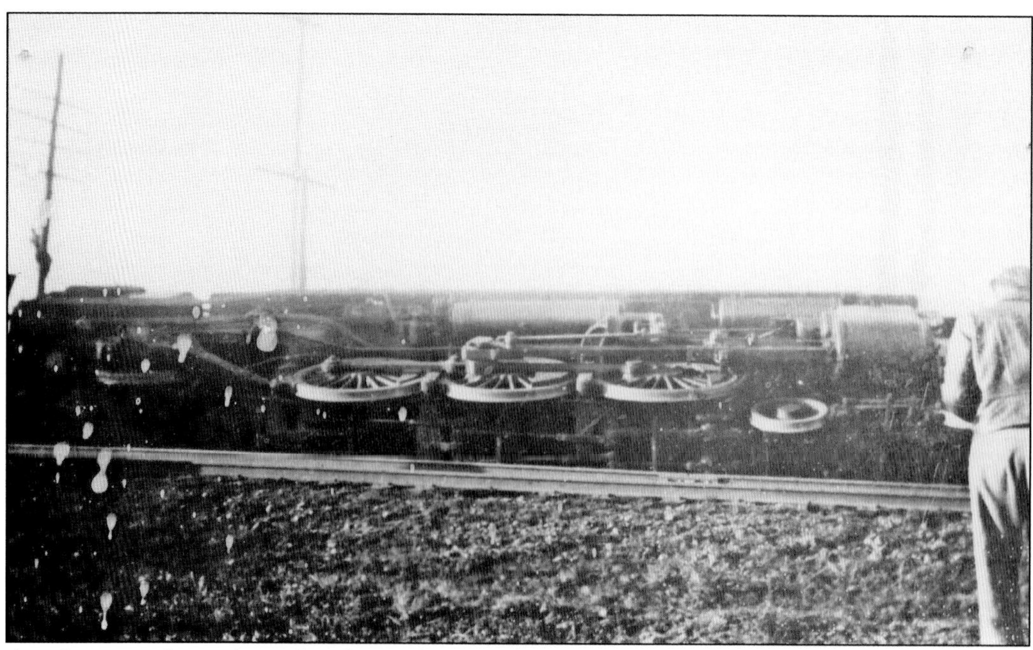

Accidents involving the railroad were fierce and terrifying. One of record occurred in Luling at the corner of Pierce and Ivey Streets. The date was March 29, 1939. The photographer is unknown, but several views show the engine as well as several cars completely off the track. (Courtesy Don and Judy Lightsey.)

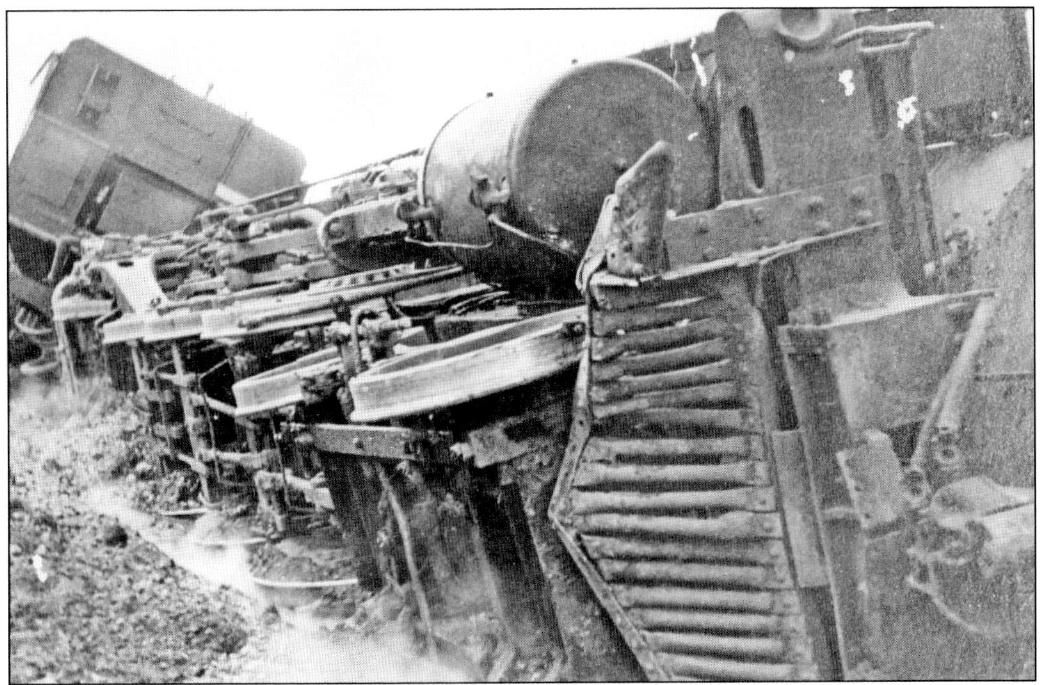

The train wreck at the corner of Pierce and Ivey Streets not only knocked cars off the track but the locomotive as well, shown here on its side. The owner of these original images wrote on the photograph that it happened "in front of John Wilson's house." Today one hears the sound of a train passing through Luling every hour. (Courtesy Don and Judy Lightsey.)

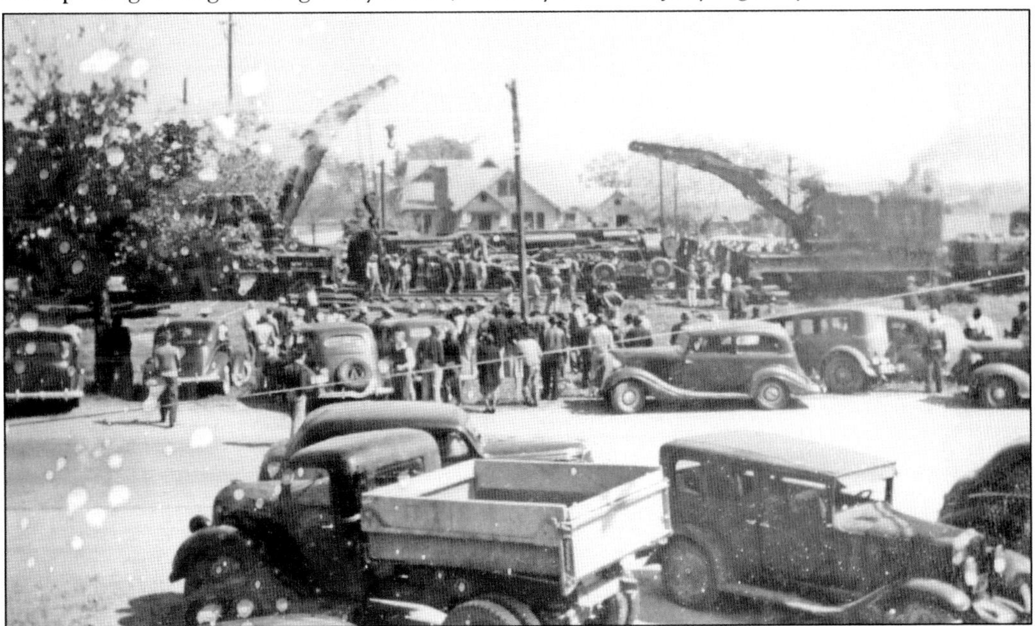

An unusual image shows the cranes working to upright the cars and locomotive knocked off the tracks. Great interest is evident from the number of people watching the activity. Note the automobiles have running boards, which are now basically obsolete. (Courtesy Don and Judy Lightsey.)

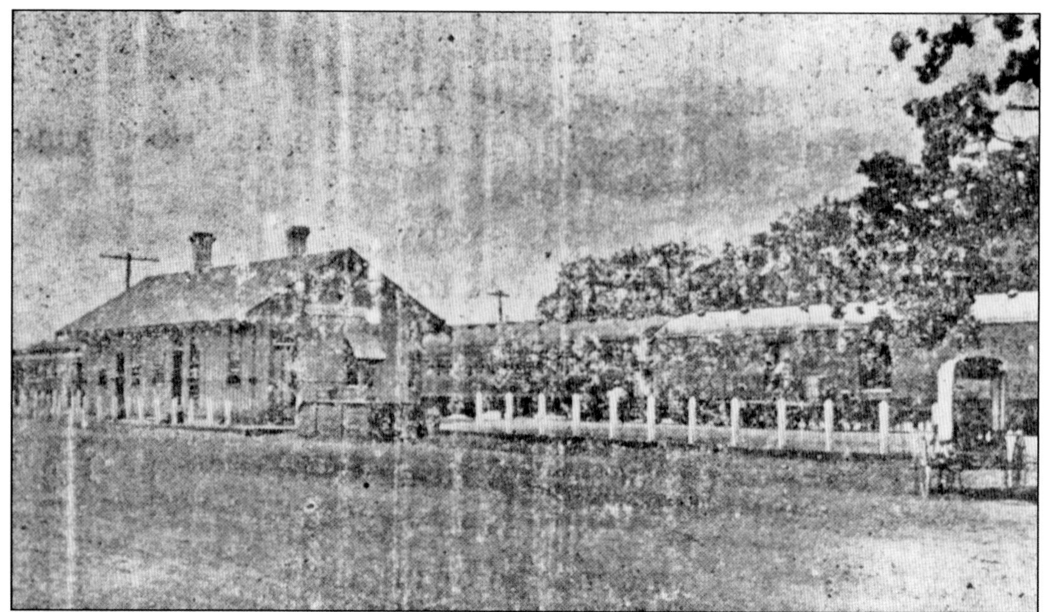

The Galveston, Harrisburg, and San Antonio passenger depot no doubt was comfortable for everyone in its day. Little is known of the interior amenities, but at least the long shed had benches on each side for people to sit on while waiting for the arrival of the train. The horse-drawn hack at right suggests people could be brought to the depot via this "taxi" rather than walking. (Courtesy G&H Society.)

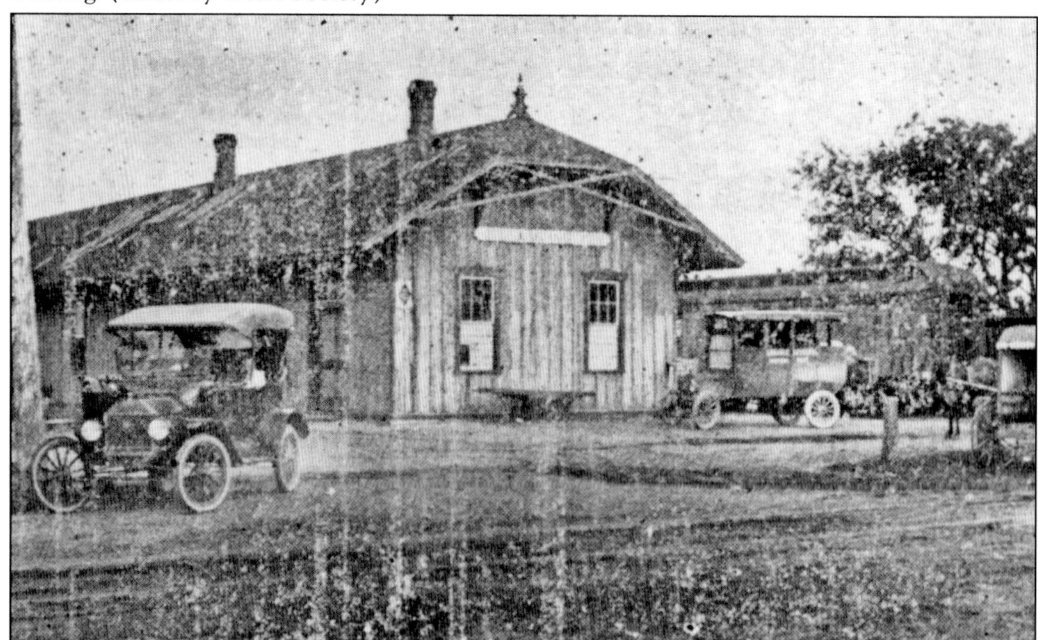

The second railroad to come to Luling was the San Antonio and Aransas Pass, or SAAP. It connected Shiner, Lavaca County, to Caldwell County seat Lockhart through Luling in 1889. Three early agents for the railroad were J. W. Gracey, J. E. Fisher, and H. P. Allen. Among other attractions Luling could also boast of were an opera house, two hotels, and the railroad. (Courtesy G&H Society.)

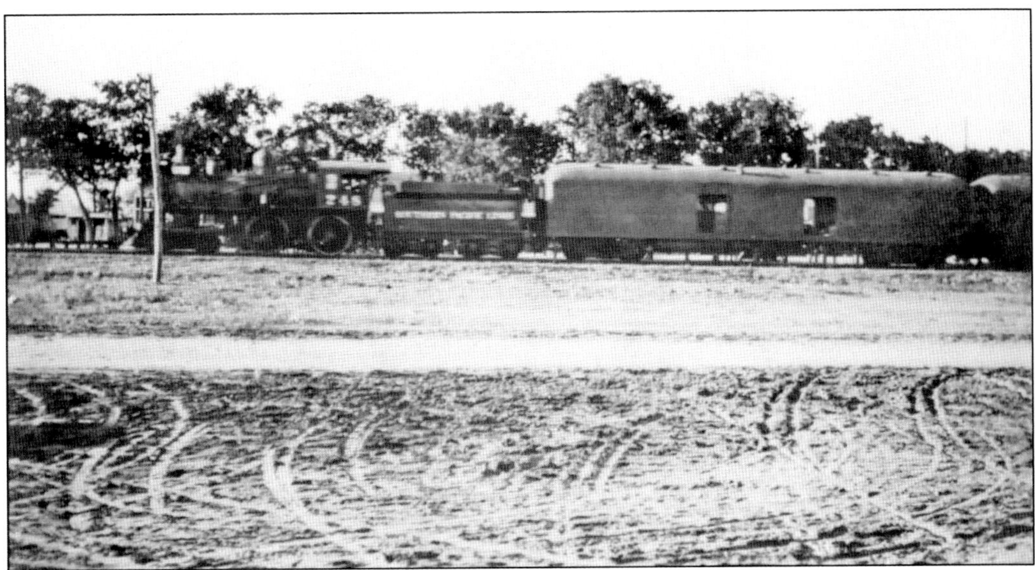

A Southern Pacific train stopped in front of the Carter Photograph Gallery at 506 Pierce Street. This image was made by Luling's photographer, Robert W. Carter. According to notes on the reverse, it was taken with Carter's new camera with a shutter speed of 1/300 of a second. He stood in front of his father's gallery to take the photograph sometime in 1911. (Courtesy G&H Society.)

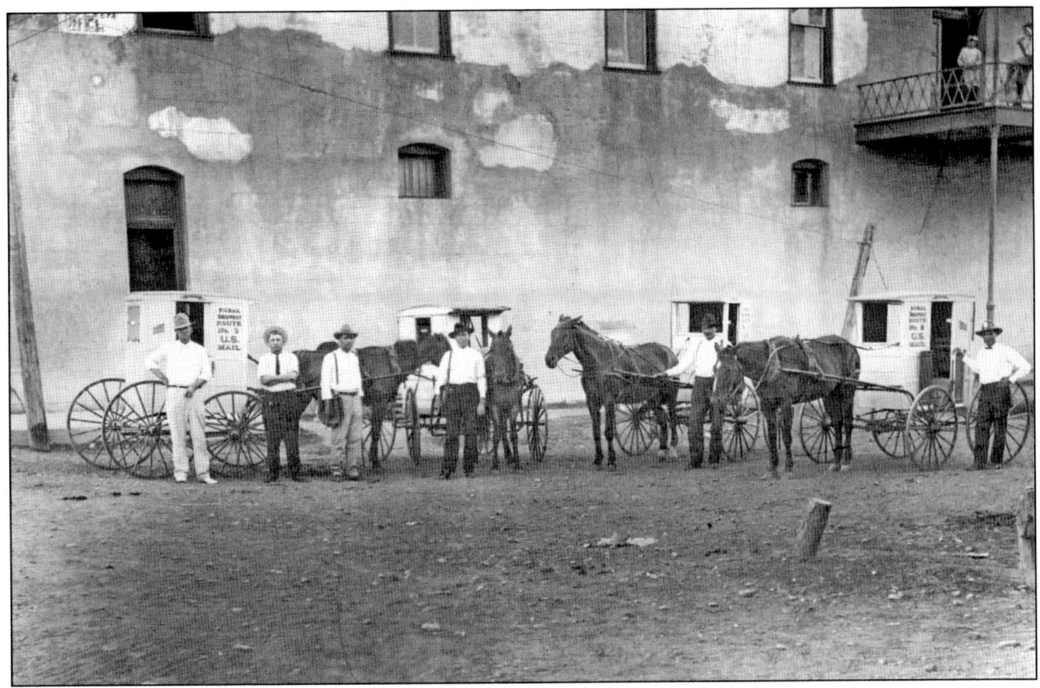

The first post office in this area was established at Plum Creek in 1848. When that community ceased to exist, Luling handled the mail. This undated photograph shows rural mail carriers from the horse-and-buggy days standing in front of the Wilson Hotel. One horse was sufficient to pull the small covered hack. These carriers may have dressed up for the special occasion. (Courtesy G&H Society.)

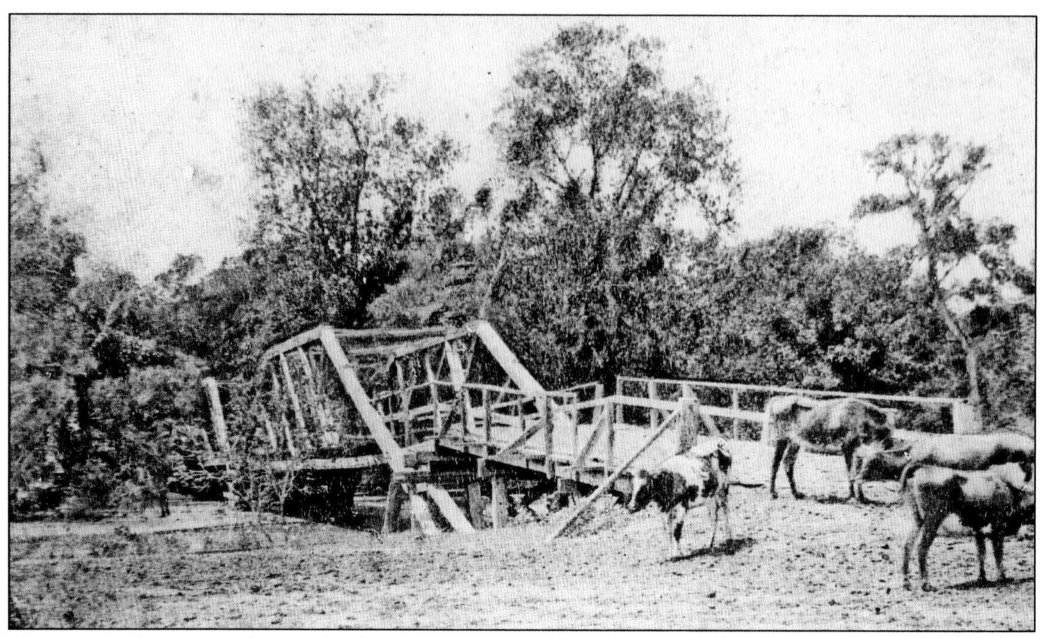

To get to Luling from the south, the early day traveler had to cross this wooden bridge. Although it appears less than solid by today's standards, apparently it was sufficiently strong for the era of the horse and buggy. Available historic records do not reveal the bridge ever collapsing. The San Marcos River forms the county line between Caldwell, Gonzales, and Guadalupe Counties. (Courtesy Don and Judy Lightsey.)

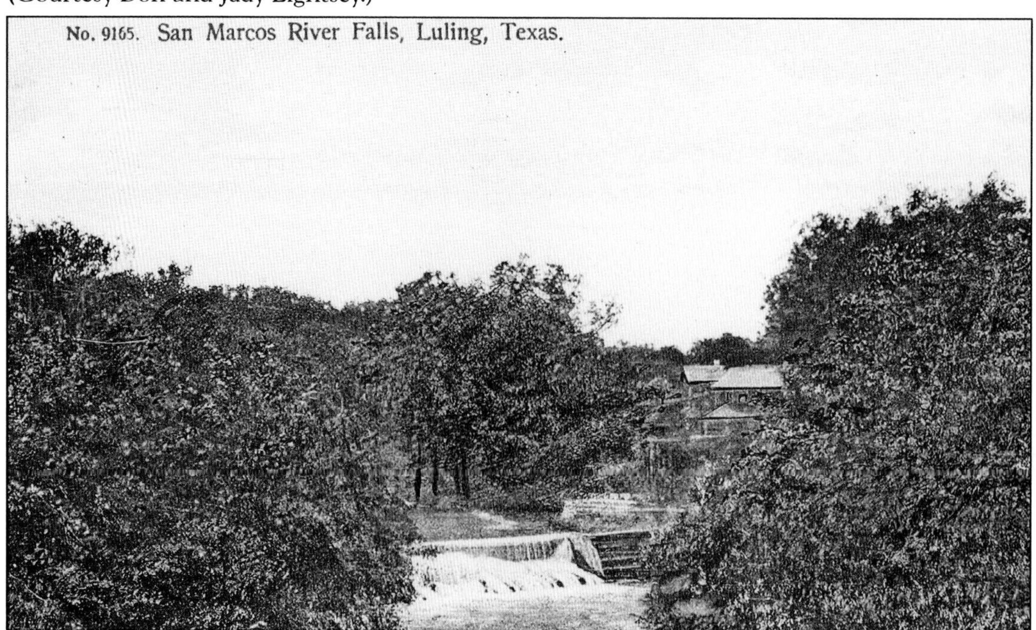

River traffic may have worked at one time, but the San Marcos River falls, shown here in this early photograph, may have restricted much of it. In the background the Zedler Gin and Mill, built by John and James Meriwether, is partially shown. Operated at a loss for several years, it was sold to the Walker Brothers and then to Fritz Zedler, who made it successful. (Courtesy Don and Judy Lightsey.)

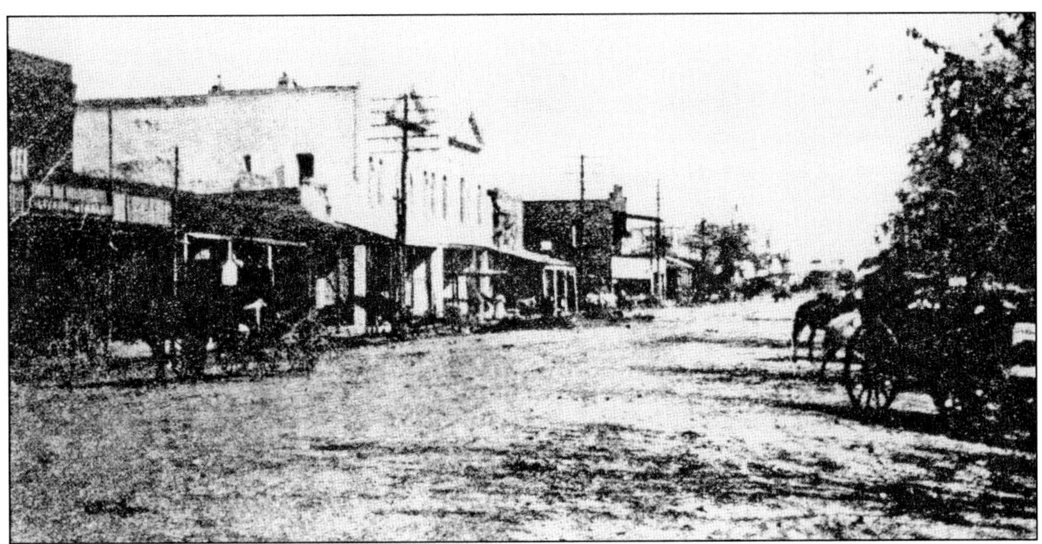

A view of Luling's Davis Street looks east during the era before the automobile was common. Several of these buildings were destroyed or damaged by an arsonist early on July 1, 2000. Among those suffering damage were an antique shop, a graphics shop, and one of four buildings used for the annual Watermelon Thump. A clothing store suffered serious smoke and water damage. (Courtesy G&H Society.)

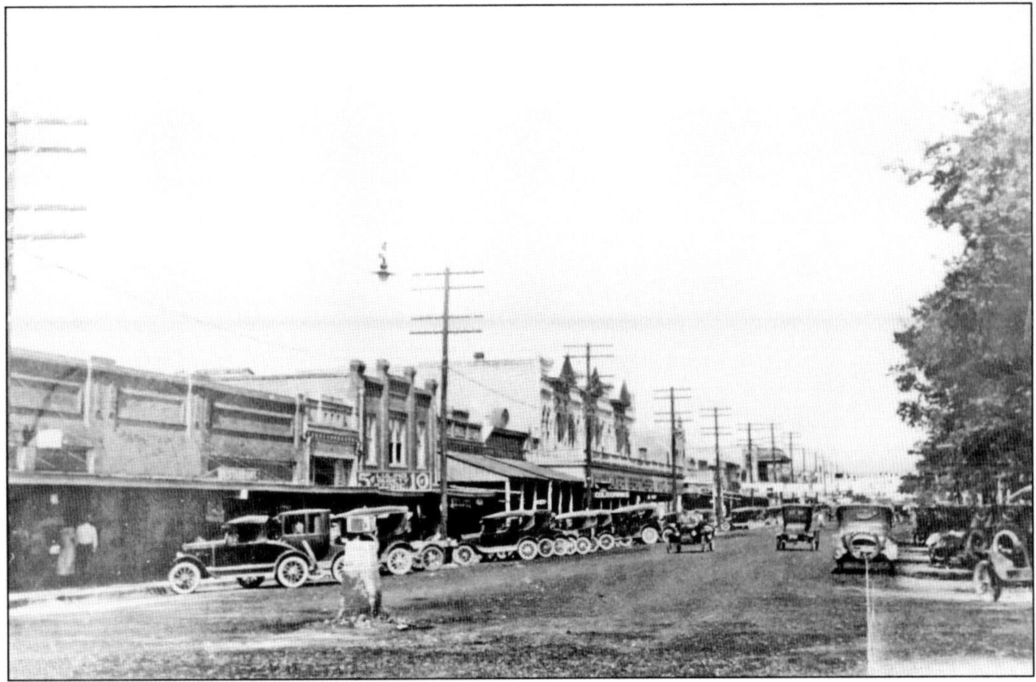

This image was taken on Davis Street between Walnut and Pecan Streets, looking east. Today's businesses, from the corner, are Monte's Bar, empty, Insurance Team and Melinda's Beauty Works (sharing front), Texas Gas Service, the "Spitway" (Championship Watermelon Seed Spitting), *Newsboy and Signal* newspaper, empty, Luling Discount Pharmacy, Walker Building, and empty building. The Spitway is now reserved for the Watermelon Thump Seed Spitting contest. (Courtesy G&H Society.)

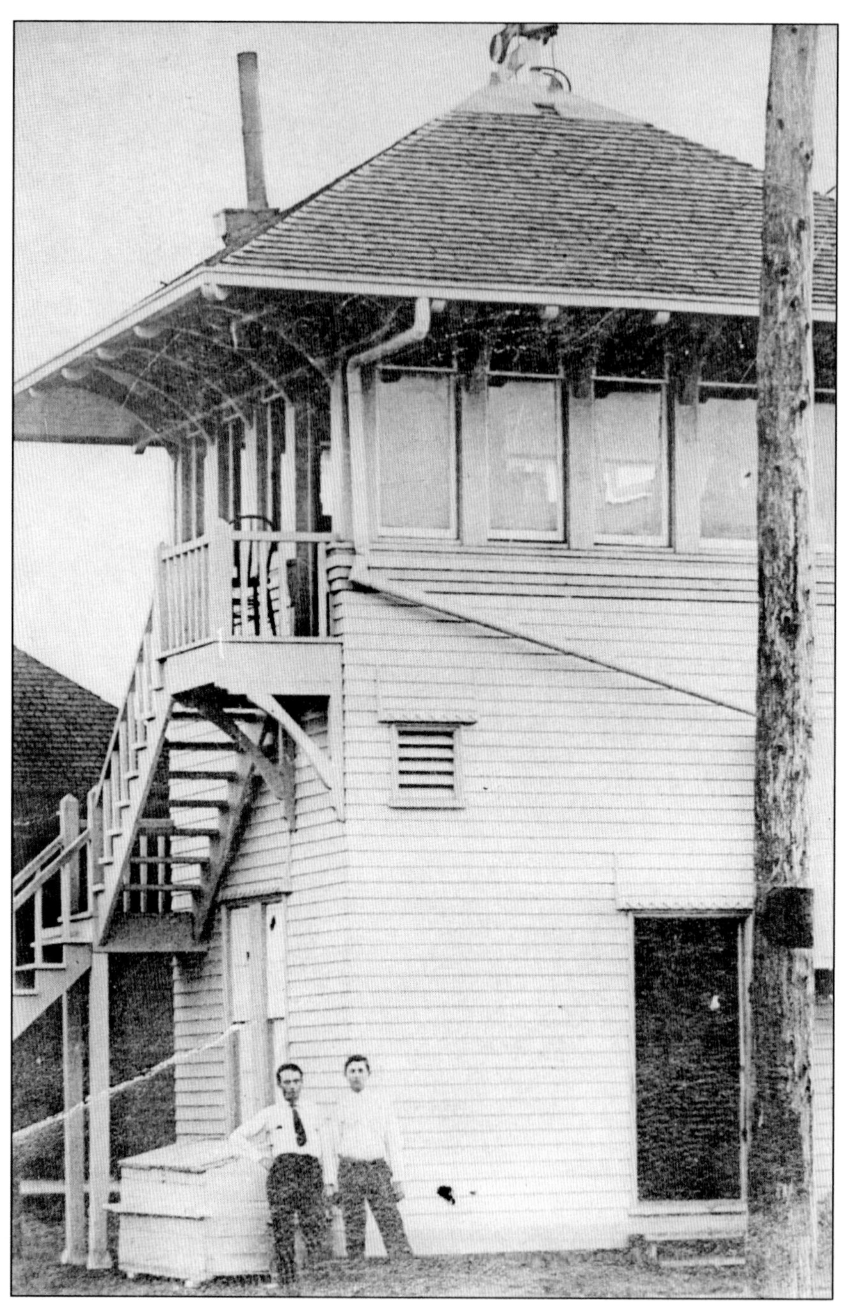

This is an early but undated photograph of the dispatch and switch office for the San Antonio and Aransas Pass Railroad. This building is still located on the corner of Pierce and South Mesquite Streets. The two men, crossing switch operators, are not identified. With the lessening of railroad traffic, the building sat empty for a number of years. One Luling resident contemplated opening the then vacant facility as a bookstore (currently there are no bookstores in Caldwell County) but decided against the business opportunity. In 2008, the building became the home of the E&R Tire Service. It is currently operated by Enrique A. Reyna and remains quite similar to the original, although the front, facing Pierce Street, has been altered slightly. (Courtesy Carol Voigt and the Central Texas Oil Patch Museum.)

Two

Main Street Takes Shape

Shortly after the end of the Civil War, James Knox Walker opened a mercantile store in Prairie Lea, a community only seven miles west of Luling. In 1874, he relocated to Luling. At first, he and brother John P. operated the new business as "J. K. Walker and Brother." A move to the north side, on the corner of Pecan and Davis Streets, was completed in 1883. Later J. K. sold his interest to one E. A. Brackney, and the store then became J. P. Walker and Company. William B. Walker moved from Prairie Lea and bought out Brackney, and the store became W. B. N. and J. K. Walker. In 1889, George C. and W. P. Walker came to Luling, bought out the Cahill hardware store, and formed the G. C. Walker and Company. With J. K.'s death in 1892, and W. B.'s death in 1898, the store became Walker Brothers and Company in 1900. In the earliest years, the store served as a primary mercantile center for customers from Gonzales, Guadalupe, Wilson, and Caldwell Counties. You could buy almost everything in the store: flour, bacon, cloth, molasses, vinegar, and coal oil. Walker's also acted as the middleman in some deals, such as the buying and selling of cotton.

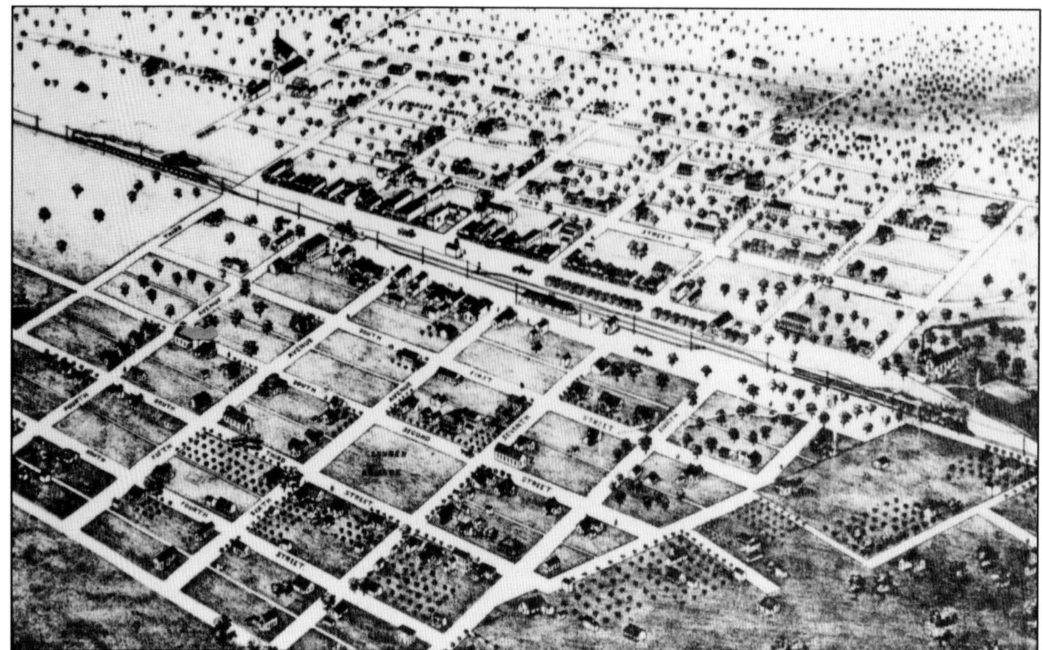

Artist Augustus Koch provided historians with many "bird's-eye views" of Texas communities in the 19th century. This is how Luling appeared in 1881, according to Koch. It took careful measuring and a degree of imagination to provide a view as if it were being viewed from above. Note the railroad cutting the community into the north and south divisions. (Courtesy G&H Society.)

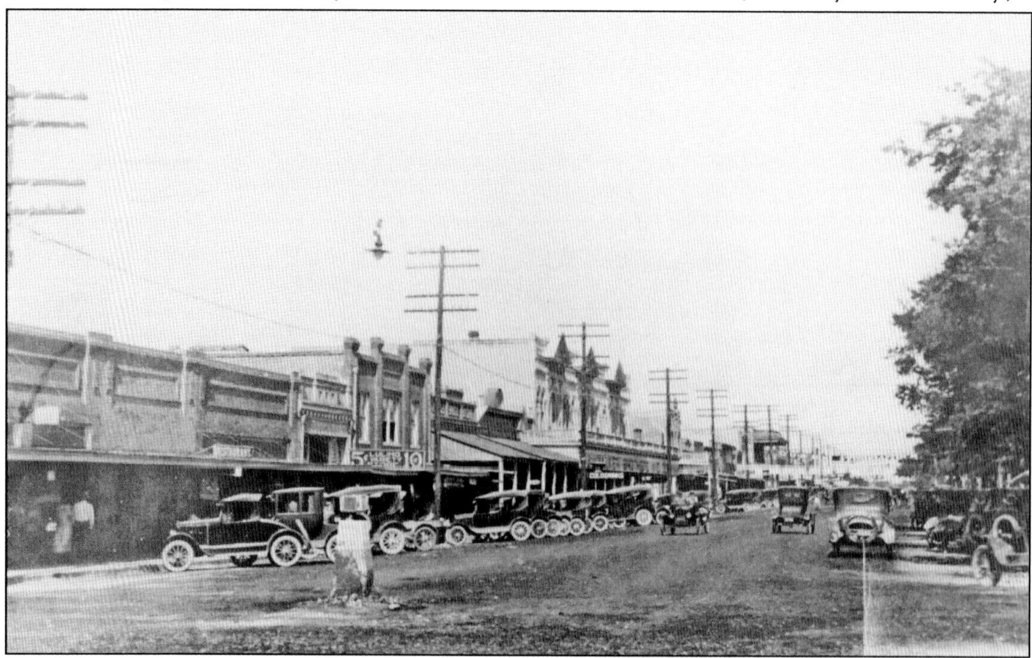

By the time this image was taken, a view of Davis Street dating from the early 20th century, the automobile had replaced the horse and buggy. The streets have now been paved, but the buildings remain essentially the same. The "Keep Right" sign at the left corner reminds the driver to stay on the right side of the street, always good advice. (Courtesy G&H Society.)

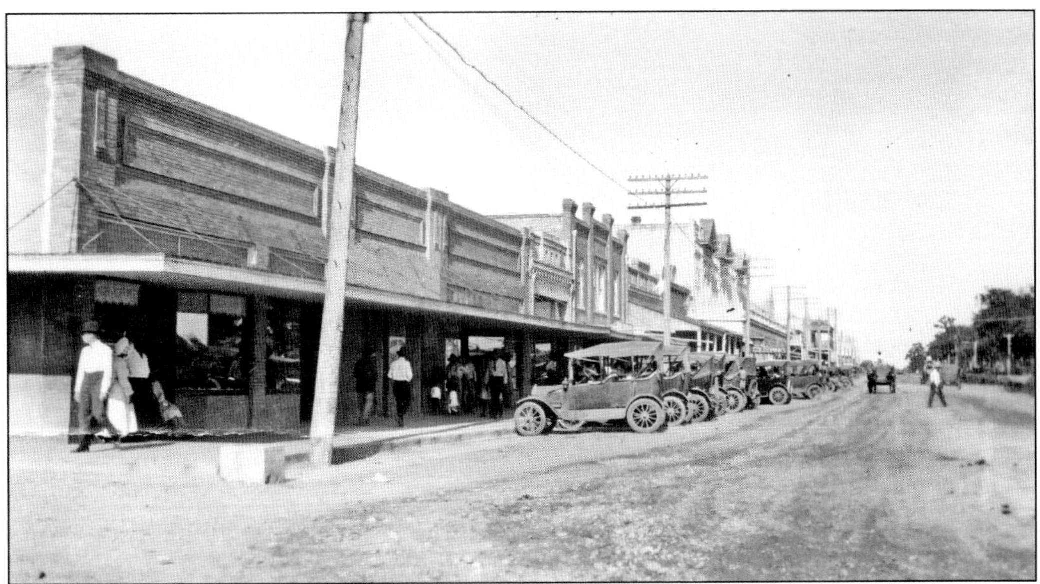

This photograph shows Davis Street looking east in the early days of the automobile. These buildings remain essentially the same, but a number were damaged or destroyed by an arsonist on July 1, 2000. Among those suffering damage were an antique store, a graphics shop, and one of four buildings used for the annual Watermelon Thump. (Courtesy G&H Society.)

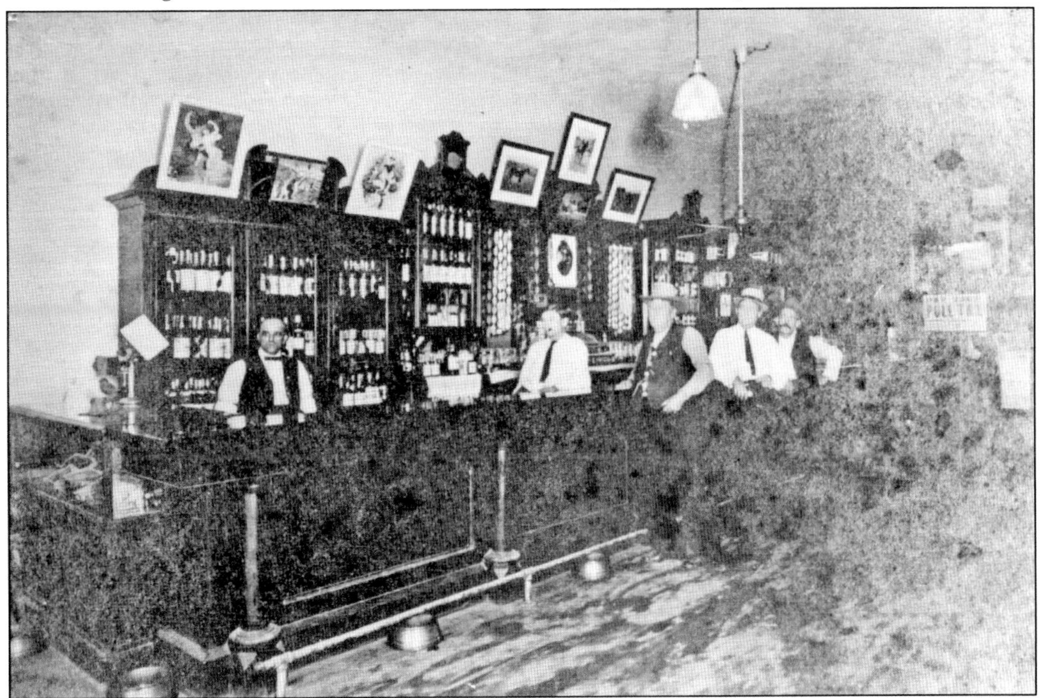

Muenster's Saloon was located near the present-day Dismukes Pharmacy at 511 East Davis Street and was operated by German-born Henry Muenster. The photograph reveals that patrons and bartenders typically wore neckties. The 1900 Caldwell County census shows Muenster as a "Saloon Keeper" with his wife, Sarah, and sons Joseph H. and Roland A. Note the sign on the right for "Poll Tax" and spittoons on the floor. (Courtesy Don and Judy Lightsey.)

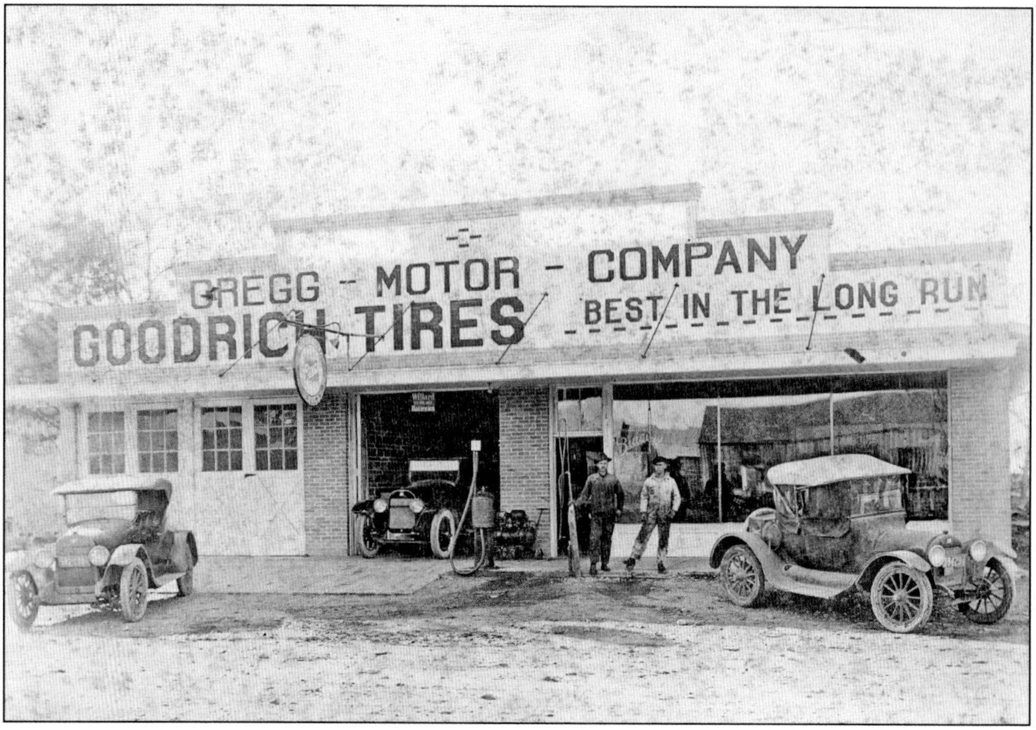

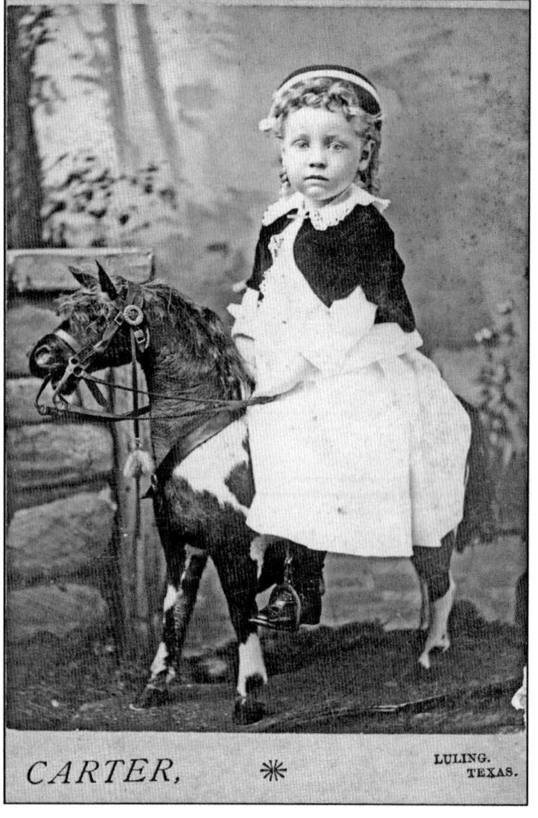

Will Gregg is shown at left in a Carter photograph, mounted on a toy pony and in a dress, which was normal for boys in that era. With a little growing up and the curls shorn off, he was all boy. Born August 9, 1887, the son of pioneers David and Susan Gregg and grandson of Alexander Gregg (the first bishop of the Episcopal Church in Texas), Will "went over the top" in France during World War I and returned a captain of infantry. He then opened the Gregg Motor Company and remained in Luling until his death on July 30, 1960. Although the men are not identified in this photograph, the original photograph indicates Gregg had three mechanics: "Tobe" Milligan, "Mert" Moon, and "Tigle" Holcomb. (Both courtesy G&H Society.)

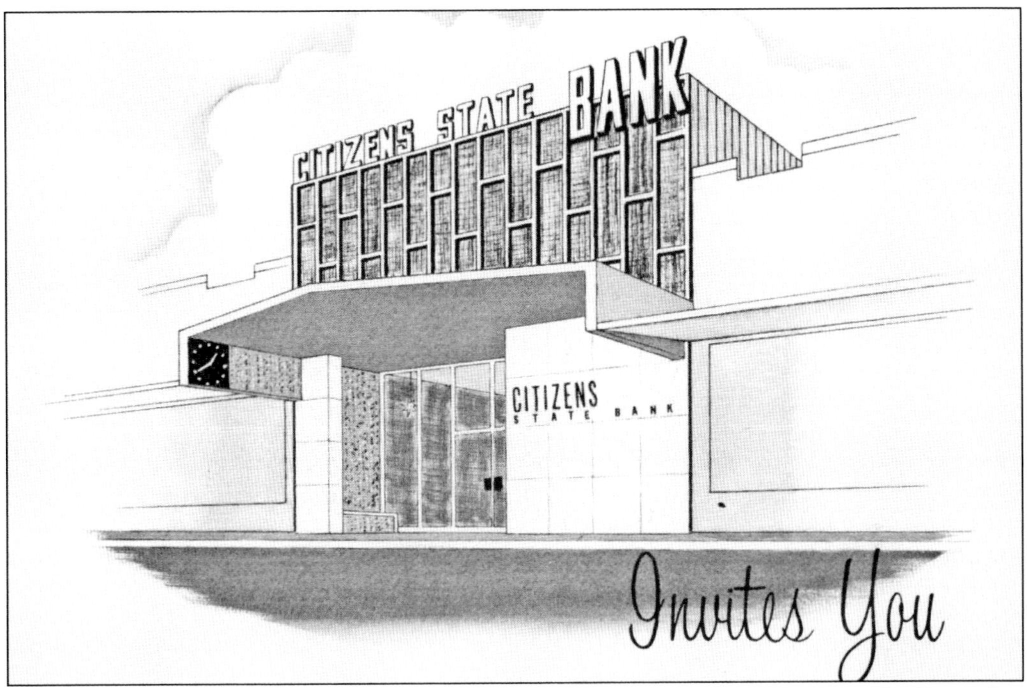

This is an elaborate drawing of the Citizens State Bank, then located where the Dismukes Pharmacy now stands, at 511 East Davis Street. The bank still serves the citizens of Luling but is now located at 200 South Magnolia Street. No indication is given as to the identity of the artist. (Courtesy Linda Wright and the Historic Stanley Theatre Collection.)

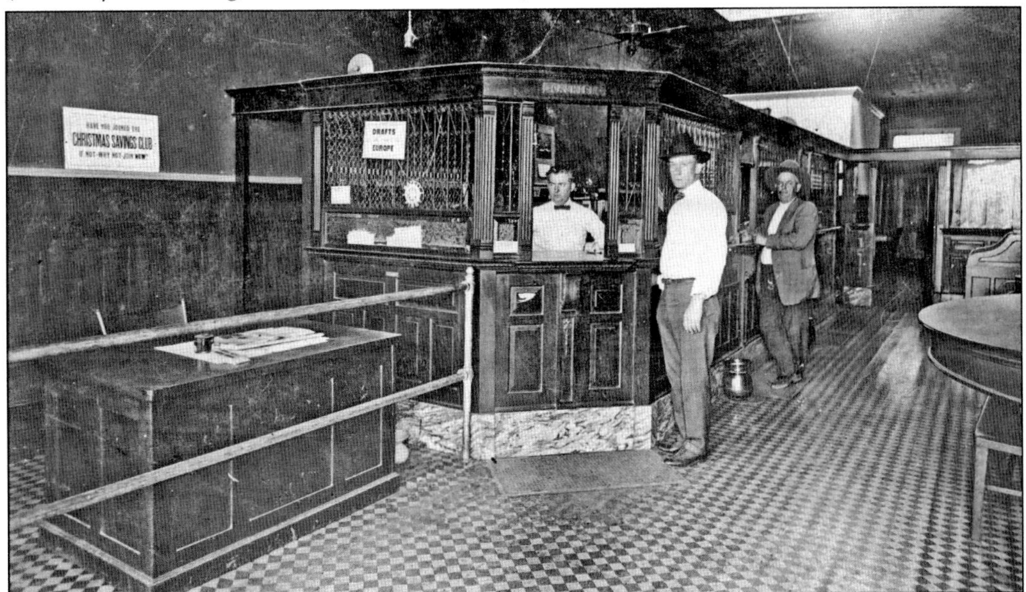

Here is an interior view of the Citizens State Bank when at 511 Davis Street. It was founded by Dr. S. J. Francis (1867–1935). At the time this image was made, Mattie Francis was president, Anna M. Wallace was assistant cashier, Sidney J. F. Francis II was vice president, and O. M. Brown was vice president and cashier. Advertisements in the city directories promised "Safety-Courtesy-Promptness." To call about an account, one would dial "TR 5-2472." (Courtesy G&H Society.)

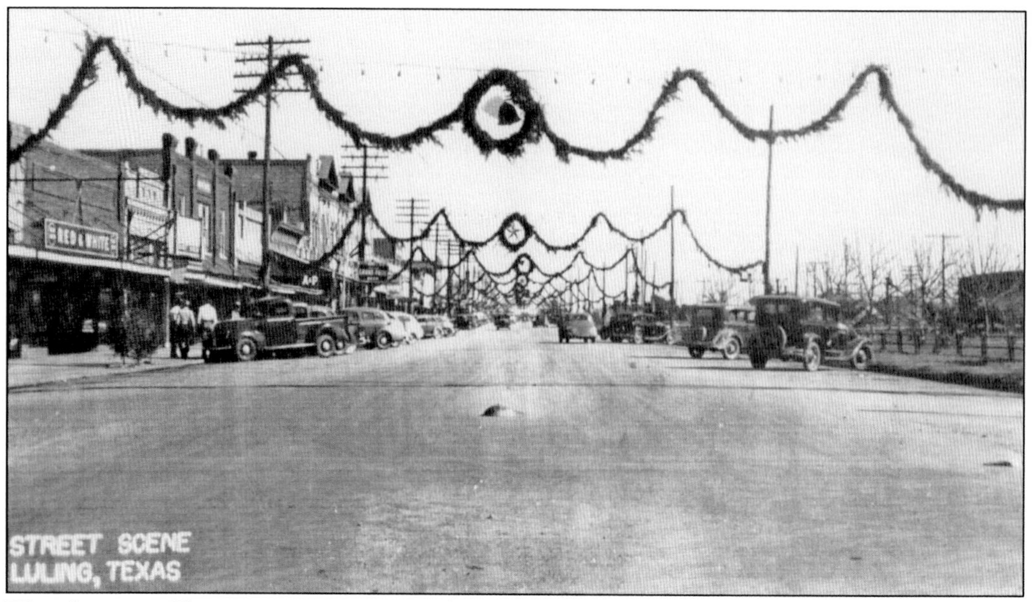

This dramatic Christmas scene is unusual in the respect that the south side of Davis Street, on the right, shows very small trees. Today these are mature and provide shade for parking while shopping in the north side businesses. Judging from the automobiles, the scene is from the late 1920s or early 1930s. The lump in the foreground is an early-day stop sign. This remains there today. (Courtesy G&H Society.)

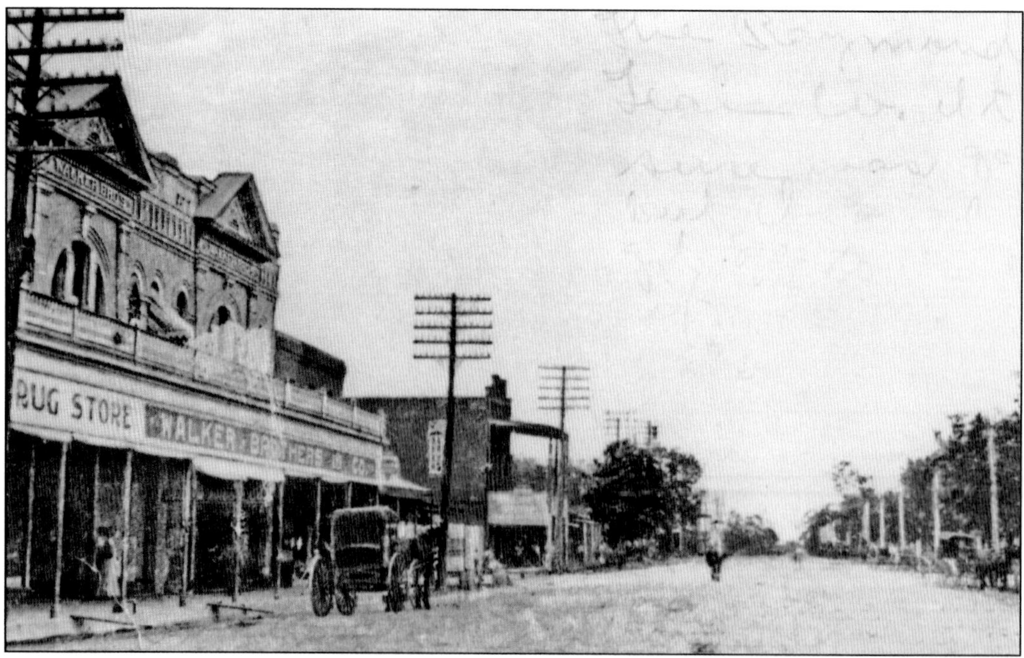

Davis Street, one of two principal streets of Luling, is pictured from the intersection of Davis and Laurel Streets at the dawn of the 19th century. Drastic changes have taken place, although the tall building at far left still stands, now housing the Chamber of Commerce Building in the historic Central Texas Oil Patch Museum. When this photograph was made, the structure was the Walker and Brothers building. (Courtesy G&H Society.)

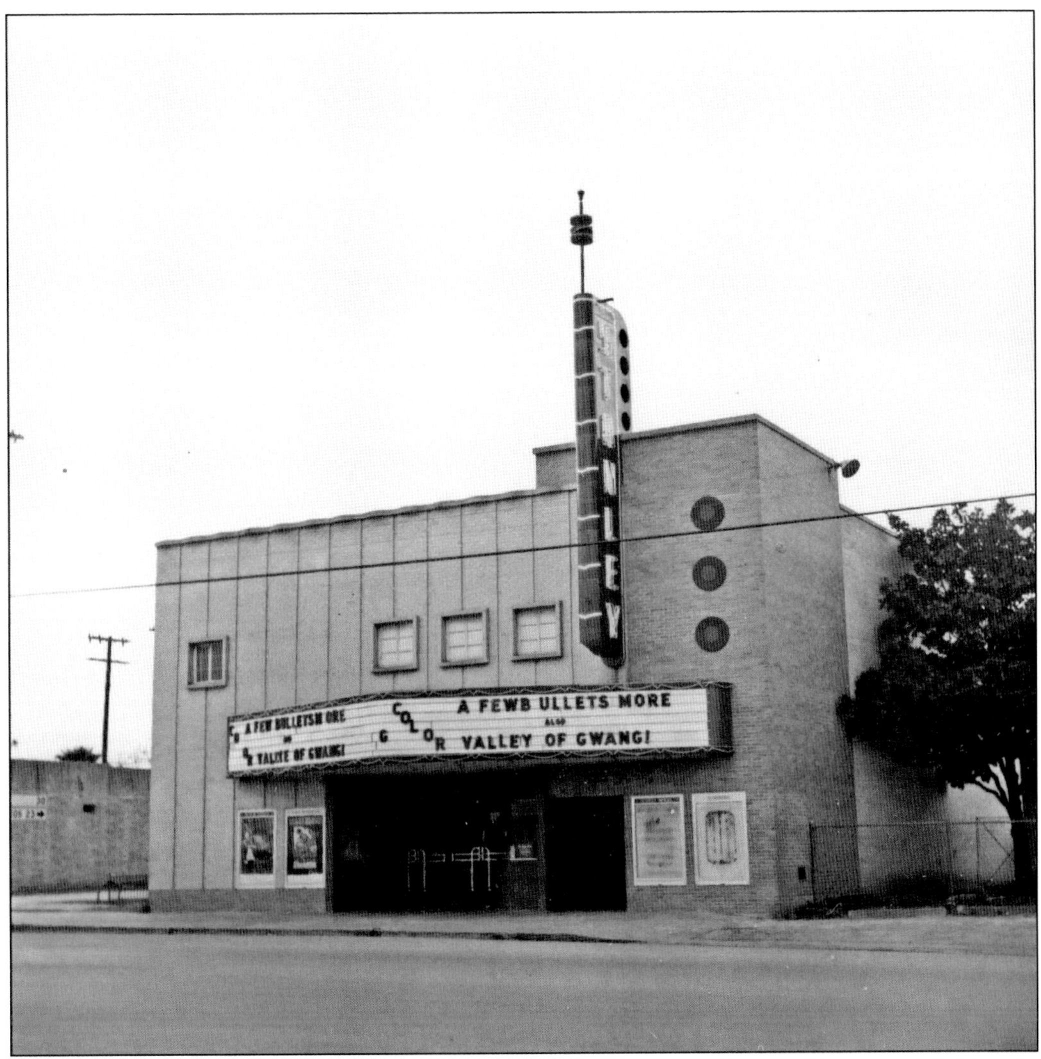

The Stanley Theater is now an antique store operated by Linda and Charles Wright with Jeff Davis, located at 710 East Davis Street. This image is perhaps from 1970, as the top-billed movie, *A Few Bullets More*, was produced in 1968 and filmed in Spain and Italy, while *The Valley of Gwangi*, filmed in Germany, was a 1969 production. When the motion picture theater was forced to discontinue showing motion pictures, it became the antique store it is today and houses a huge collection of virtually every kind of collectible. (Courtesy Linda Wright Photograph Collection.)

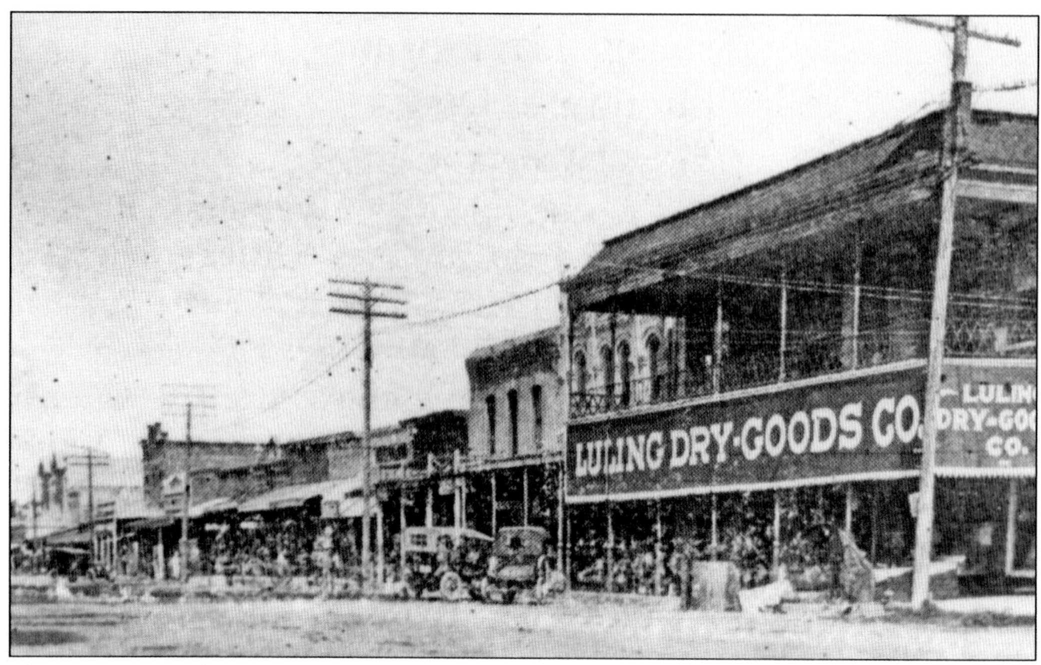

This is an unusual view of Luling's main street, as most photographs show Davis Street looking east. This view is looking west and was made at the intersection of Davis and North Laurel Streets. The imposing building on the corner, the Luling Dry Goods Company, still stands, although today it is Suzanne's Design on the immediate corner, and next is the Aptiva Interior Floor Store. (Courtesy G&H Society.)

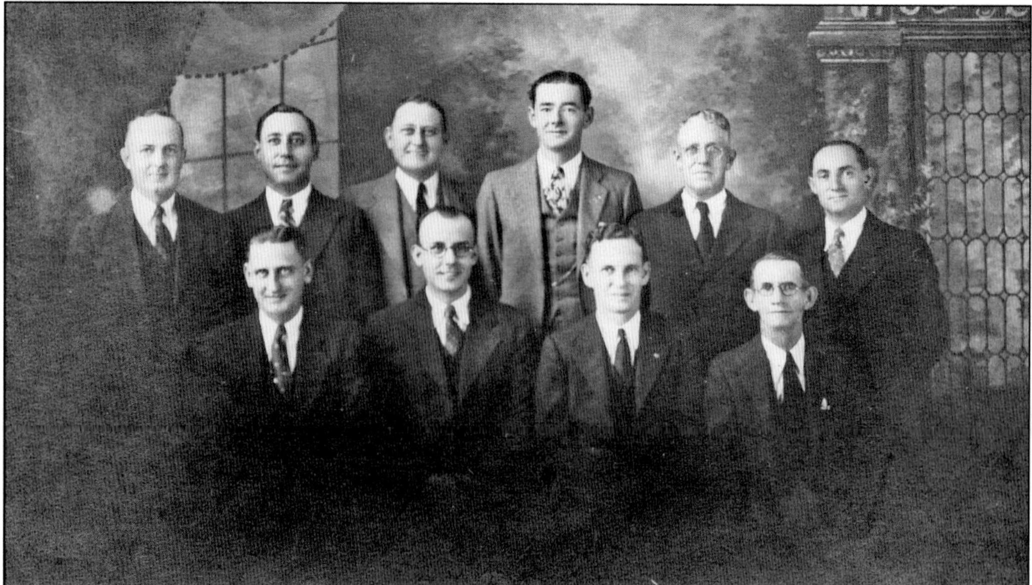

These well-dressed Luling businessmen perhaps considered themselves the heart and soul of the business fraternity. From all outward appearances, they are successful in their respective business endeavors. From left to right are (first row) Joseph Smith, Dr. H. B. Henry, Clifton Mackey, and Clyde George; (second row) George Walker Jr., H. Miller Ainsworth, Henry Stevi, ? Stair, Will Gregg, and Max Finkel. (Courtesy G&H Society.)

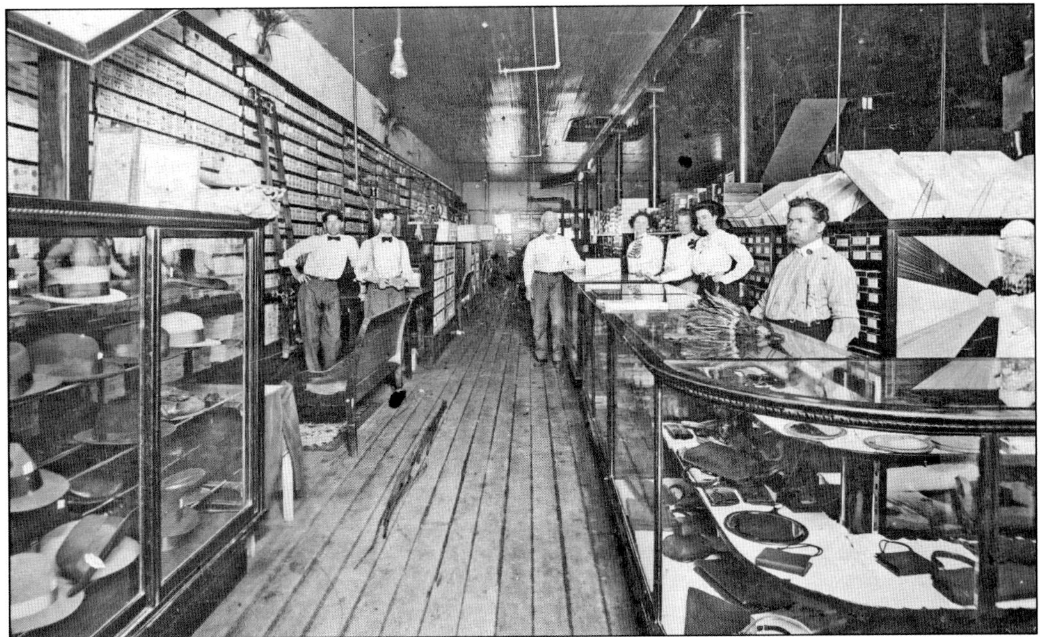

The interior of the historic Walker Brothers building is seen here early in the 20th century. None of the clerks are identified, but note how well dressed they are. The women and men wear neckties, and although not visible, the ladies no doubt are wearing long skirts. On the left are a great variety of men's hats, also an indicator of how times have changed. (Courtesy G&H Society.)

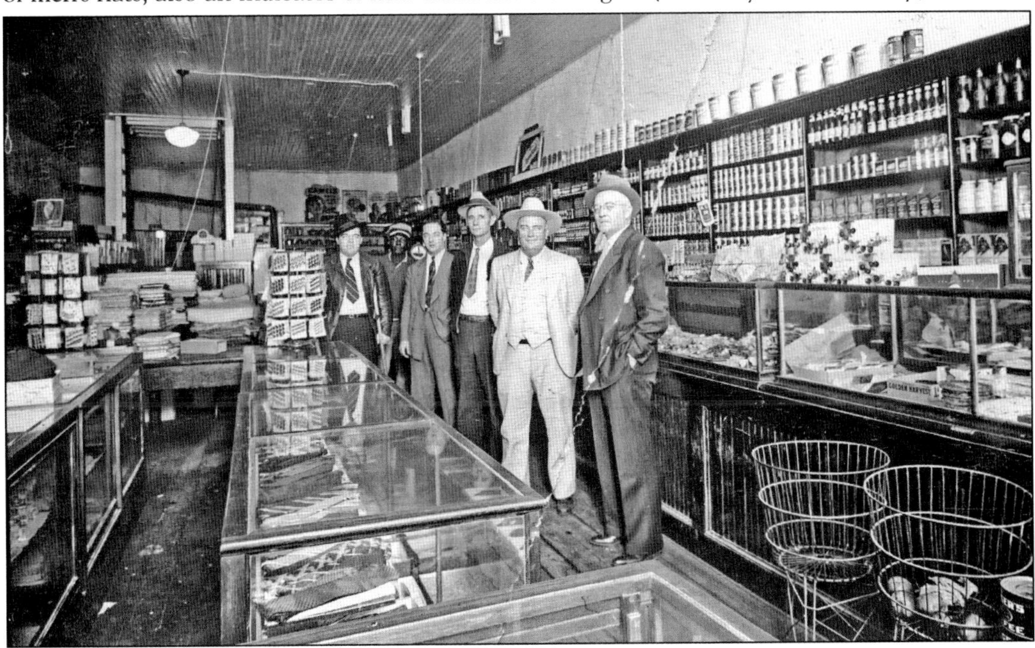

Another view is of the interior of the Walker Brothers store as it appeared during the 1920s. From left to right are Jack Brown, unidentified, Joe W. Brown, Joe Blackwell, Earl Bridges, and Gus T. Brown. Foodstuffs are placed along the wall at right. Note several wastepaper baskets in the right corner. The middle display cases reveal a wide variety of men's neckties. (Courtesy G&H Society.)

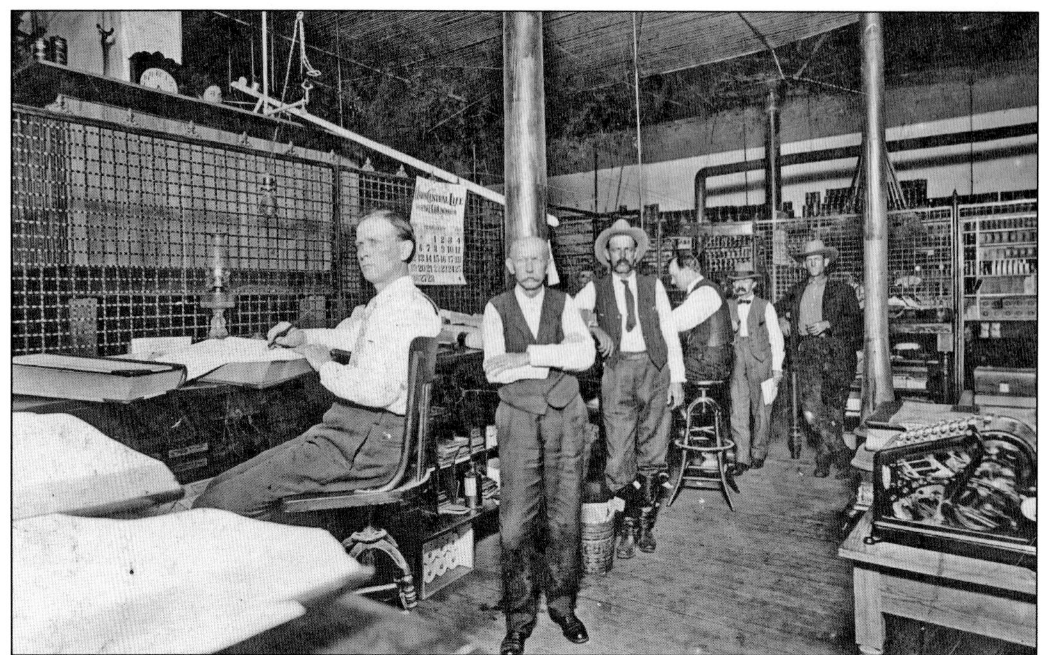

In this view of the interior of the Walker Brothers and Company rear office, seated at left is James Ervin Taylor, who attended a San Antonio business school before becoming partner and bookkeeper. Taylor, born November 9, 1871, retired in 1930 after being a member of the firm for 37 years. After retirement, he farmed on his land near Luling. Taylor died on October 18, 1955. (Courtesy G&H Society.)

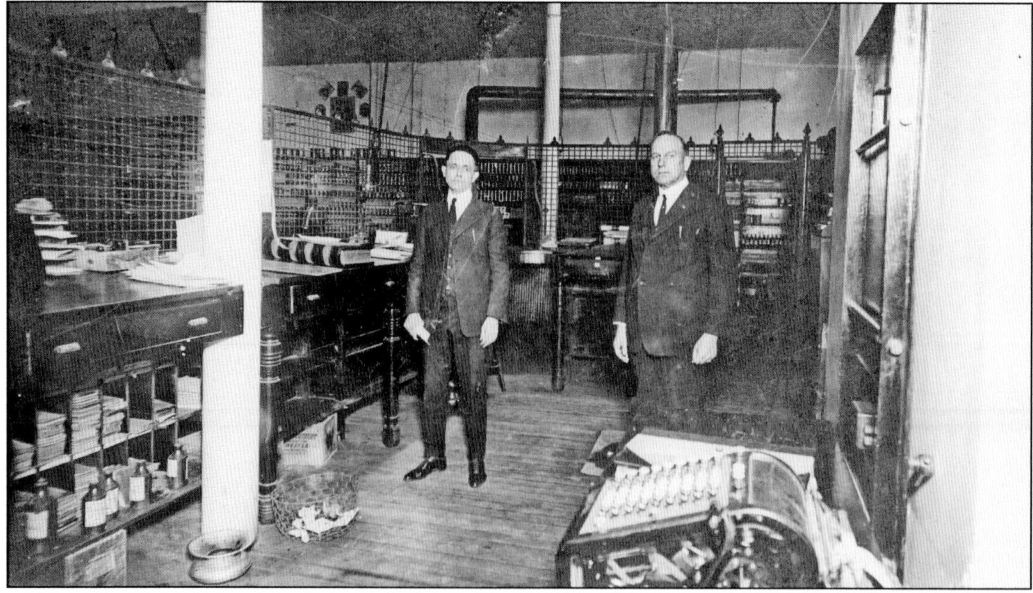

H. J. Mayton is shown standing at left with James Ervin Taylor (right) in this *c.* 1920 interior view of the Walker Brothers and Company store. The photograph reveals succinctly how society has changed: note the spittoon at center left. Also note the large ledger on the desk holding accounts. The details of the building have hardly changed since this photograph was made. (Courtesy G&H Society.)

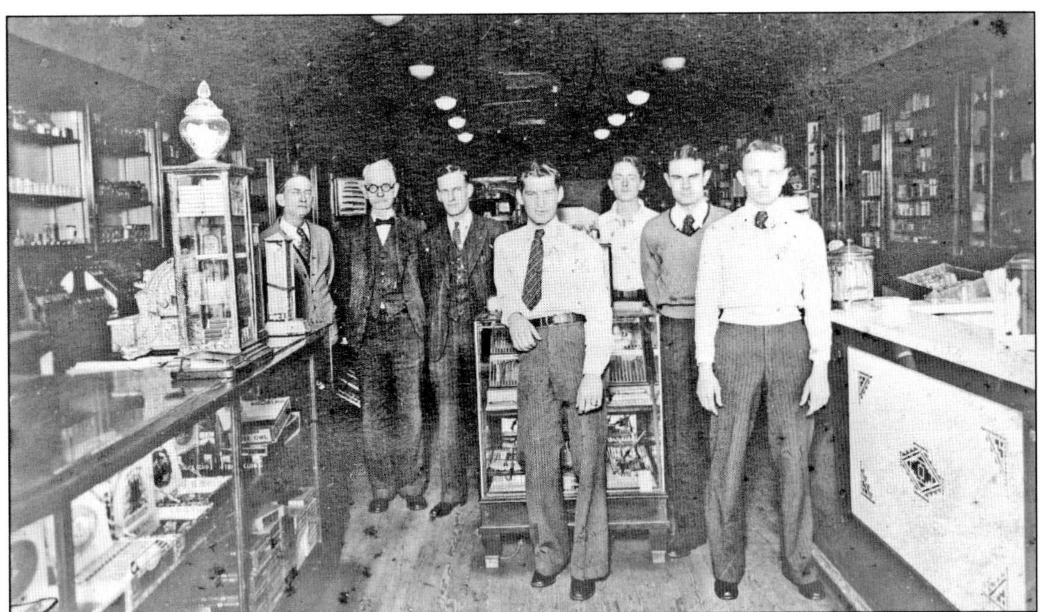

These individuals, all serious-minded, are employees of the J. R. Mackey Drug Store, then located at 419 East Davis Street. From left to right are unidentified, J. R. Mackey, Clinton Mackey, Walter Langston, and three unidentified individuals. Note in the display case at left what appears to be a great variety of fine cigars, another indicator of how times have changed. (Courtesy G&H Society.)

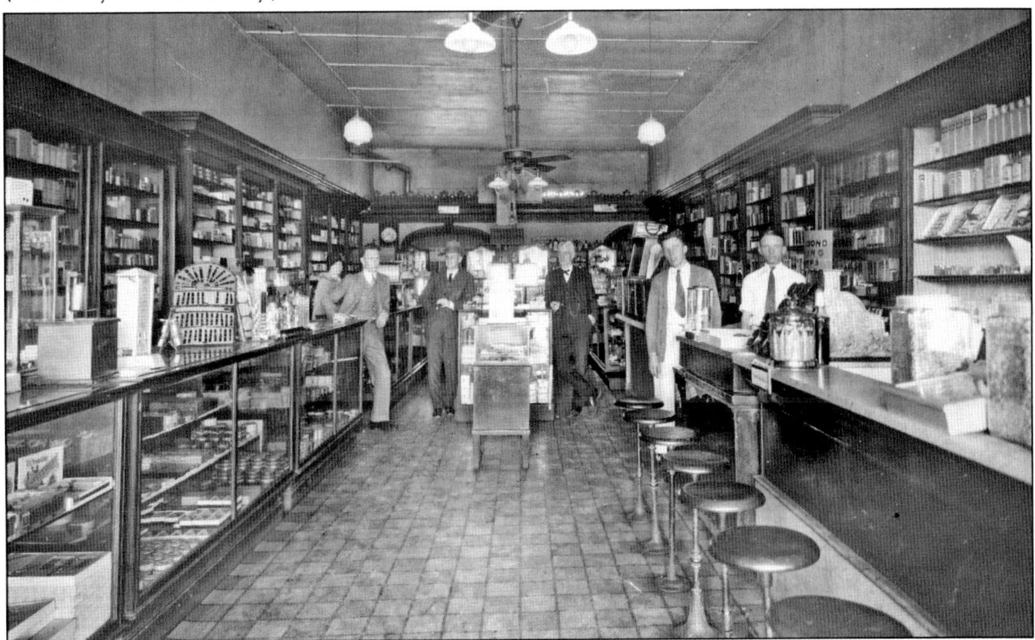

Mackey was in business in Luling for 40 years. This interior view of the J. R. Mackey Drug Store reminds one of the small mom-and-pop stores, where virtually everything was available. While the prescription was being filled, patrons could browse among the various products on display or simply sit on a counter stool and wait. Note the "antique" cash register on the counter at right. (Courtesy G&H Society.)

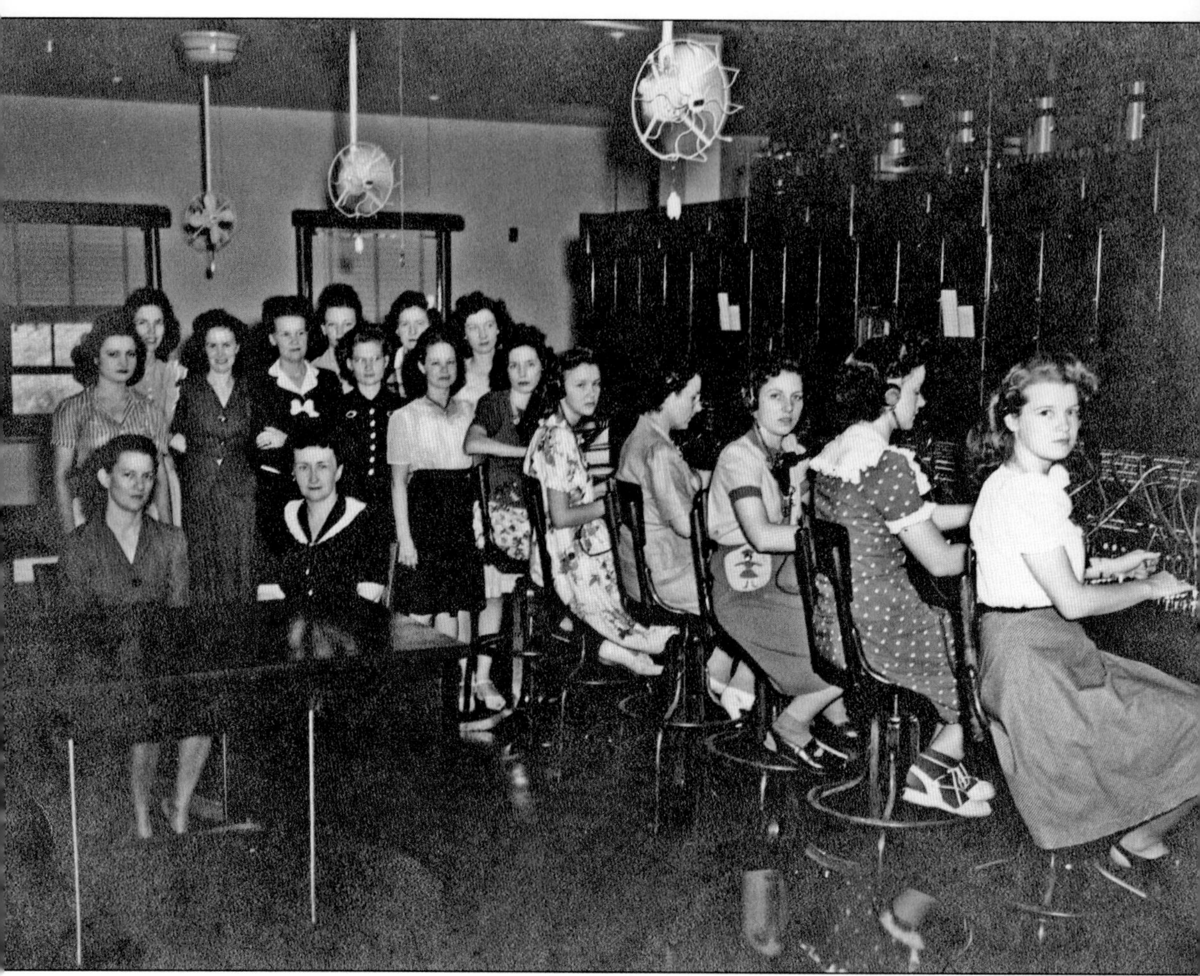

Long before touch tones and speed dial, these ladies were trained to answer as "Central." Although it is undated, the style of dress worn by these operators suggests the photograph was made in the 1950s. Identification is not complete, but from left to right are (first row, seated on stools) Gloria Cardary Turner, Edna Frances Holcomb, Myrtle Fuqua, Johnnie Wilkins, Lillian Fuqua Clary, and Billie Jay Hendricks; (second row, seated) Elizabeth Manning and Fern Fuqua; (third row) Georgia Mae, ? Benner, Daphane Holcomb Lebow, Winna Margaret Holcomb, Virginia Fletcher, Opal Reedy, Florine Williams, Florence Toungate, and Florence Williams. (Courtesy Carol Voigt and the Central Texas Oil Patch Museum.)

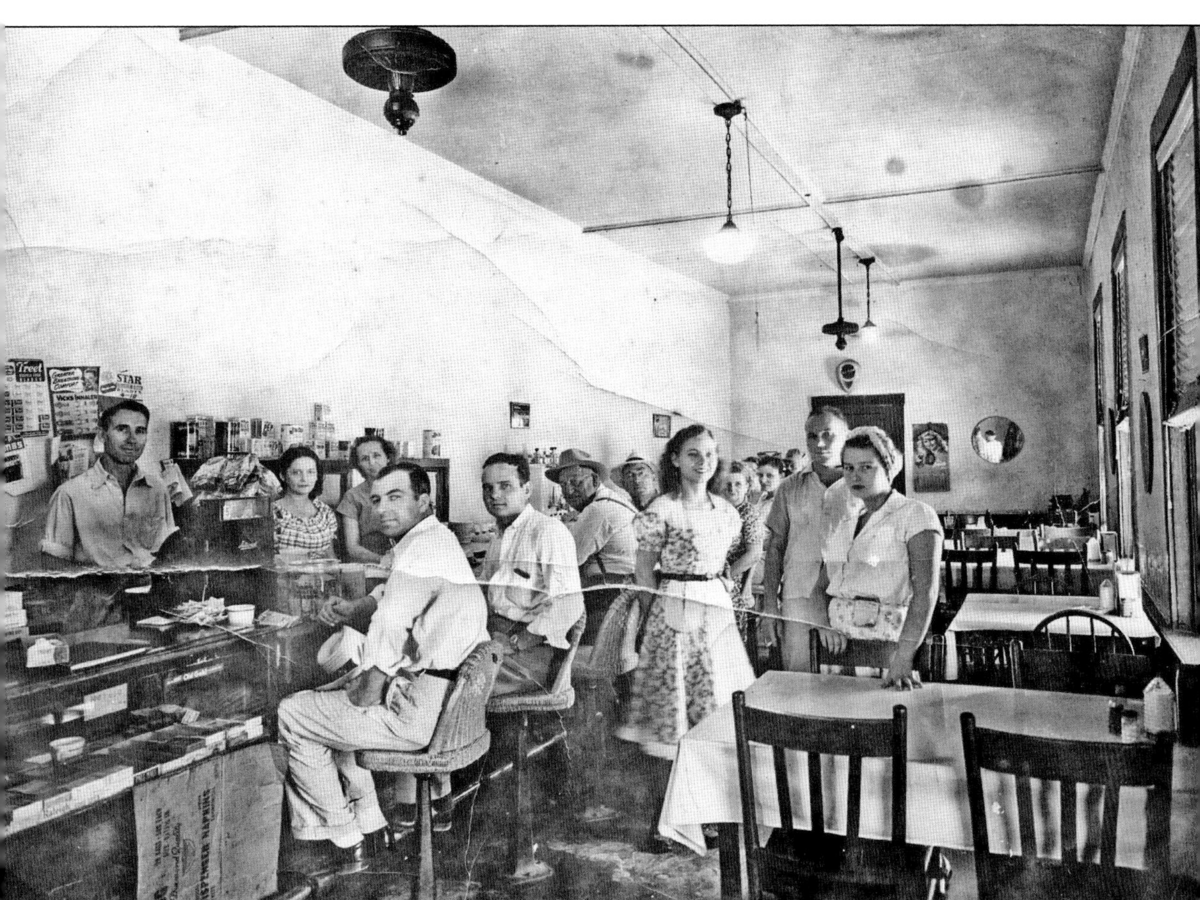

In this interior view of the Wilson Hotel on Luling's Davis Street, only three individuals are identified. At left behind the counter is A. O. "Frenchy" Broussard. The other two, Corlie Martin and Alonzo Biggs, are perhaps the gentlemen at the counter. Frenchy Broussard wrote, "I am a Cajun that migrated to Caldwell County in 1929, and stayed. I had sold my café in Navasota, and was job hunting when I heard a friend, Stanley Gillette, had purchased Wells' Restaurant in Luling and was needing a chef to manage the kitchen. [Luling] was very busy—going day and night. I started work not too long before Stanley died suddenly. His widow asked me to manage the place for her, so I stayed." Frenchy worked other places along Davis Street until 1963, when he sold out and retired. During the 1950s, the Wilson Hotel and Coffee Shop was also a bus stop for Greyhound lines. (Courtesy G&H Society.)

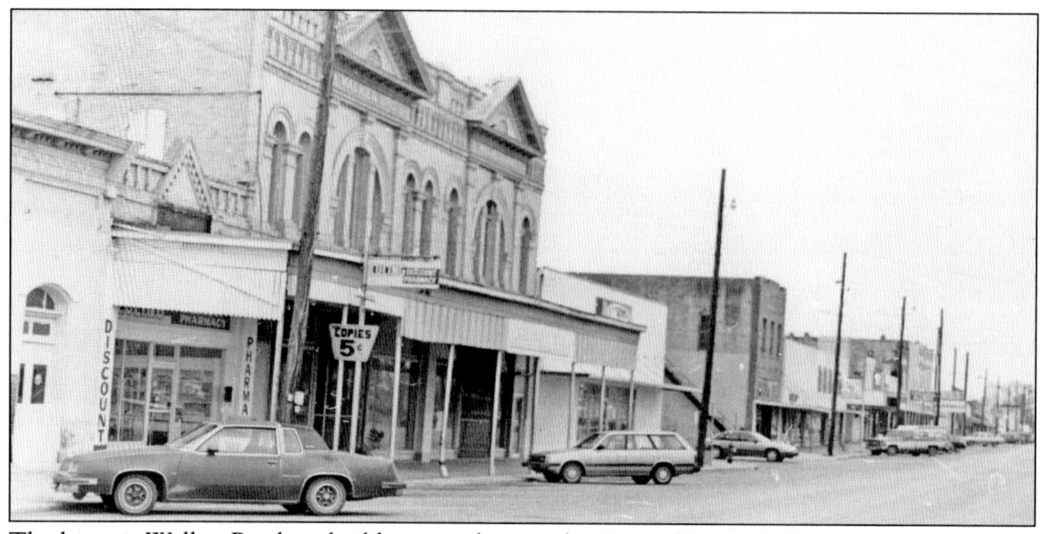

The historic Walker Brothers building now houses the Central Texas Oil Patch Museum as well as the Luling Chamber of Commerce and headquarters for the annual Watermelon Thump. Founded in 1990 as a nonprofit educational foundation, the museum was established to preserve the history of the life and time of the Central Texas "oil boom in the oil patch." The museum hosts numerous cultural events throughout the year. (Courtesy G&H Society.)

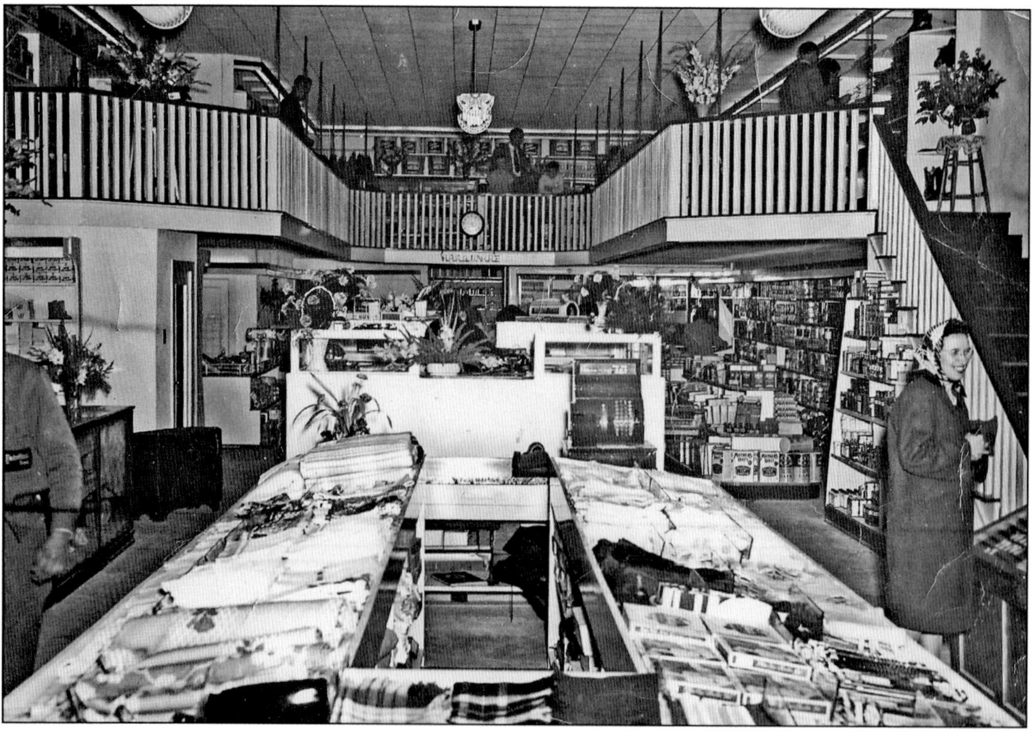

This is opening day at the Tom Brown Webb Department Store. Webb was a Luling native who not only spent 27 years owning and operating the store but was also active in various civic organizations. He was a member in the Lions Club and the chamber of commerce. He was on the Luling School Board for 13 years, serving as president for all of them. He served on the ASCS (Agricultural Stabilization Conservation Service) Board for Caldwell County. (Courtesy Jessica Knotts.)

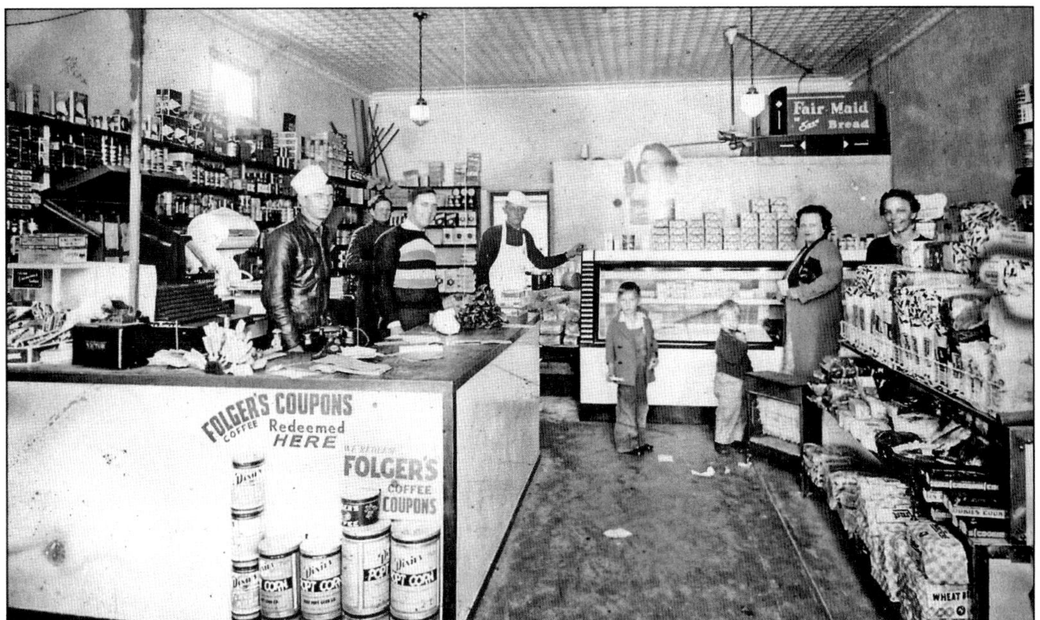

At what is known as the "Post Office Grocery and Market," this late-1930s view shows clerks and customers. From left to right behind the counter are Bob Allen Jr., Vivian Mooney (striped shirt), and R. E. Allen (wearing apron). The owner was R. E. "Bob" Allen Sr. Note it was here one could redeem their Folger's coupons. (Courtesy Randy Engelke.)

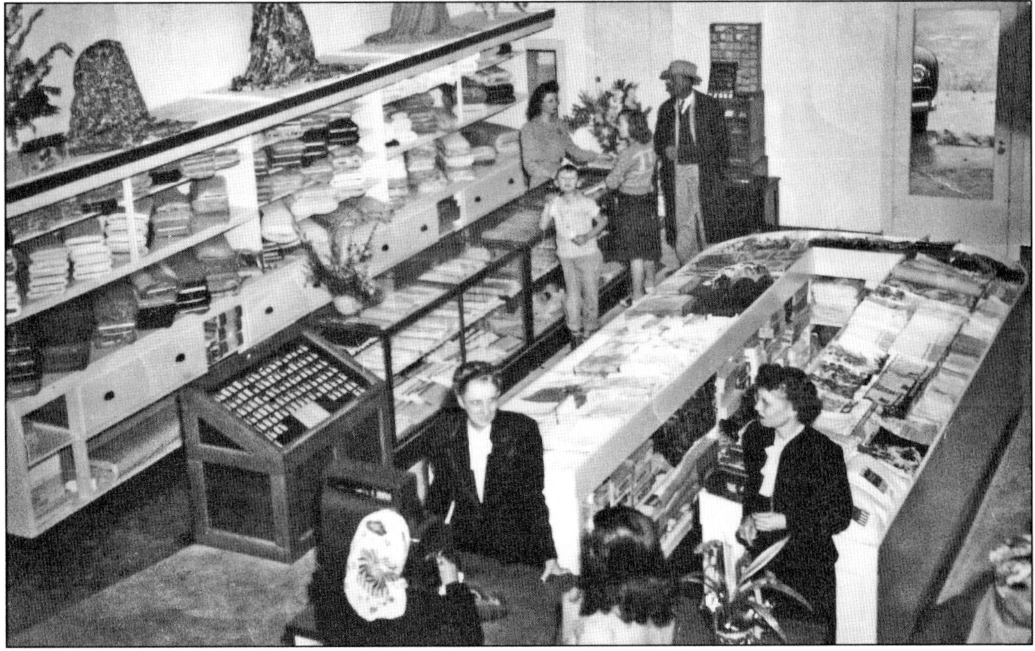

This view of the Webb General Merchandise Store is seen from the second floor. (There were very few two-story buildings then.) The photograph was made in 1947 and shows, from left to right, (foreground) Linne Roberts and Ima Allen Johnson; (background) Edna Ethridge Shotwell, Thomas Brown "Brownie" Webb, Sadye Jean Webb Ethridge, and J. F. Webb. (Courtesy Jessica Knotts.)

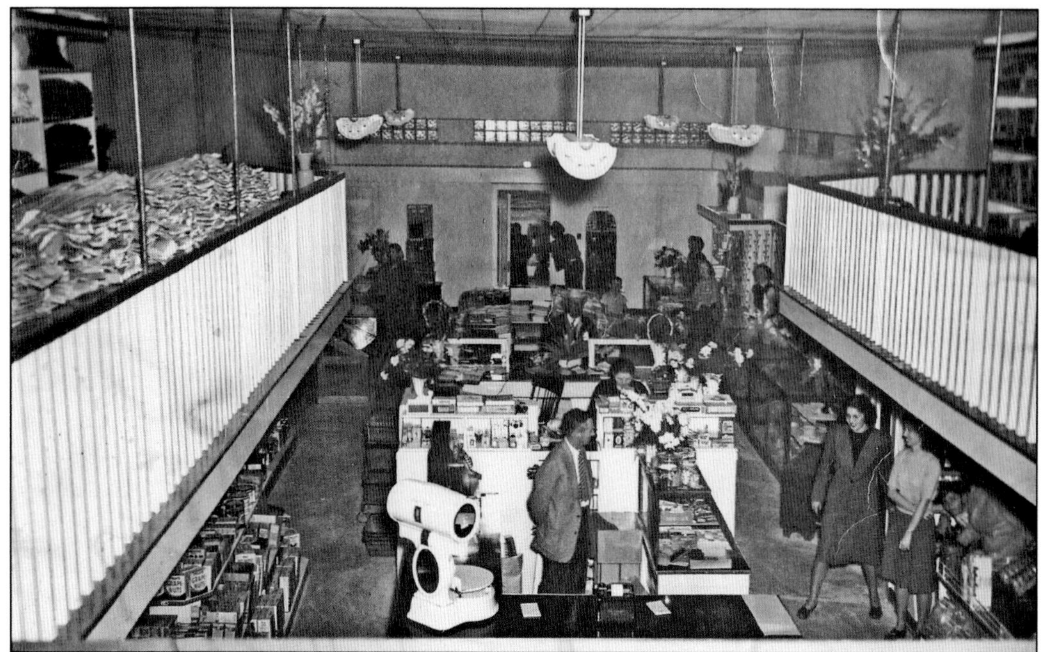

Another view of the Webb Department Store was taken from the second floor. Manager Tom Brown Webb is seen standing in foreground, to the right of the white scale. Clerks Ruth Allen Poe and Dodie Ellison Ethridge are seen under the balcony at right. This image was made on the store's grand opening day. Webb's was the place where virtually anything for the home, ranch, or farm could be obtained. (Courtesy Randy Engelke.)

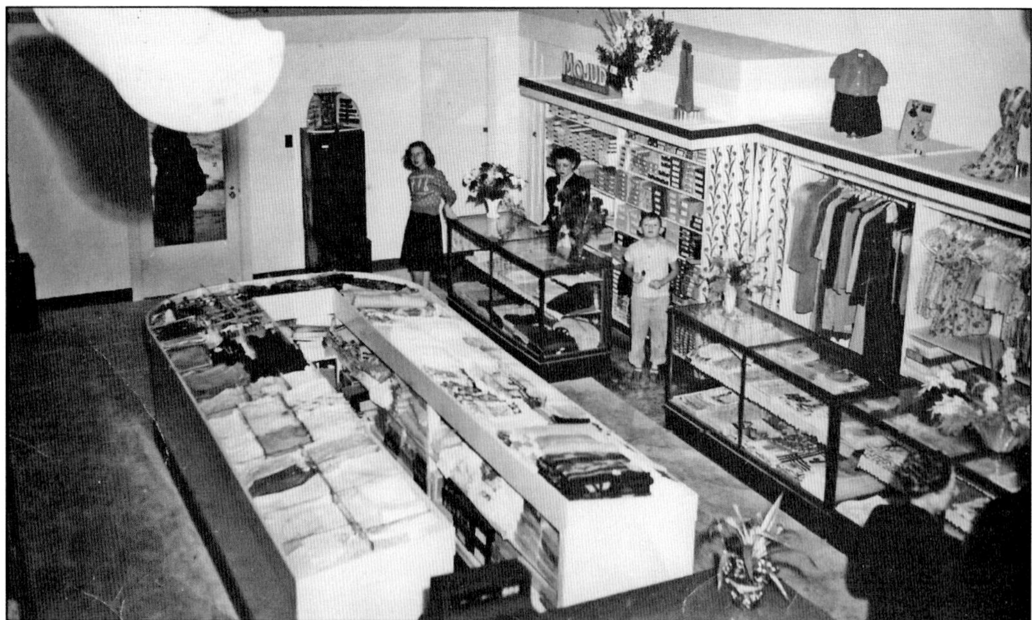

From a different angle, three key workers for the Webb Department Store look up to the unidentified photographer on opening day. From left to right are Sadye Jean Webb Ethridge, Ima Allen Johnson, and Tom "Brownie" Webb Jr. As this shows on opening day, everything is in its proper place, stacked neatly and hanging straight. (Courtesy Randy Engelke.)

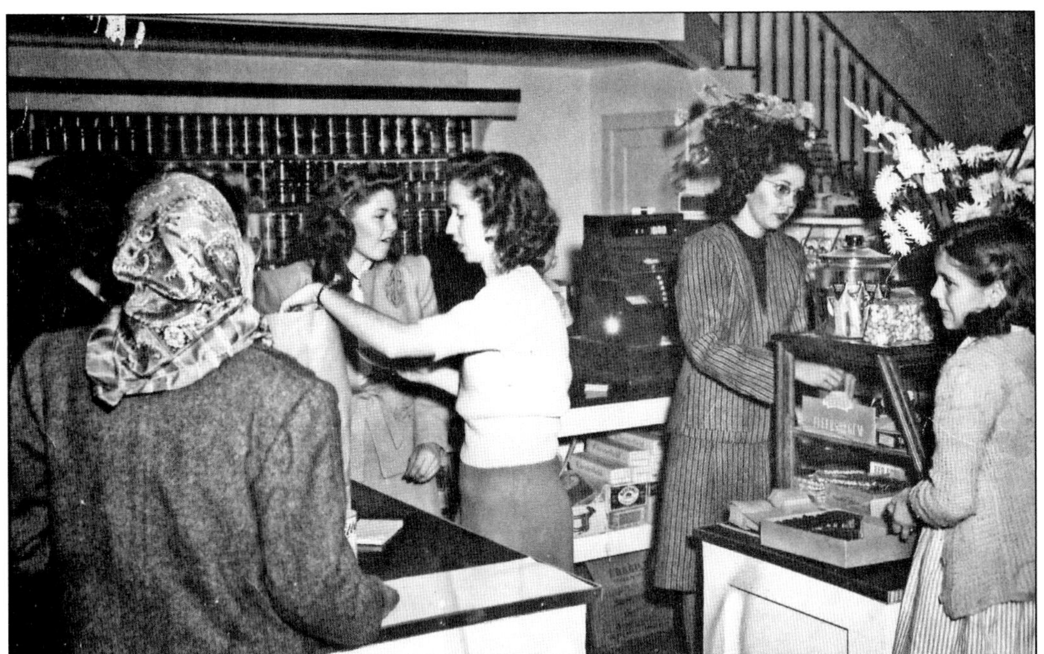

Clerks Dodie Ellison Ethridge (left) and Ruth Allen Poe (right) are busy at work in the Webb Department Store in 1947. Webb's two-story department store was located at 601 East Davis Street, located on the corner of present-day State Highway 183 and Davis Street. The building was razed; today Gary Collins's Home Grown business is successfully operated. (Courtesy Randy Engelke.)

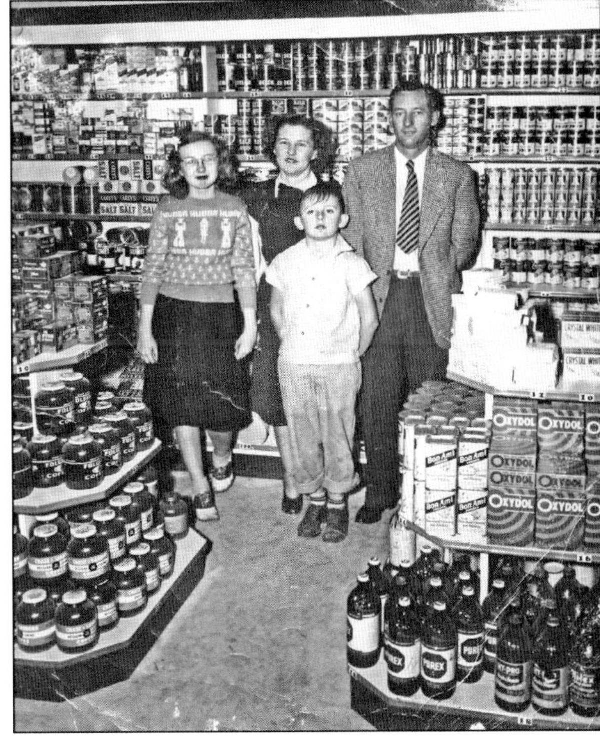

A family is ready to work on the day of the grand opening of Webb's General Merchandise store. From left to right are Sadye Jean Webb Ethridge, Naomi Allen Webb, Tom Brown Webb Sr., and (standing in front) Tom Brown "Brownie" Webb Jr. Webb, born in Luling on December 16, 1912, married Naomi Allen in 1932 and successfully operated the store and a ranch. The store was under his guidance for 27 years. (Courtesy Randy Engelke.)

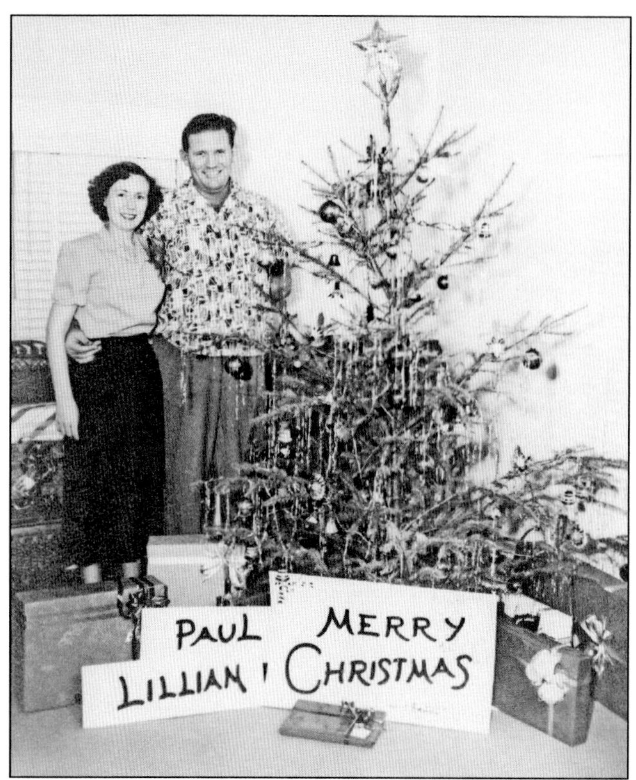

We are fortunate that Paul B. Conley was a photographer, as many of his photographs have been preserved. Here he and his wife, Lillian, show their Christmas spirit with their own seasonal card. Paul's studio was at 619 East Davis Street. Lillian worked in the same office selling "General Insurance." They shared the same phone number. From 1940 to 1957, Paul was Luling's fire chief. (Courtesy Linda Wright Photograph Collection.)

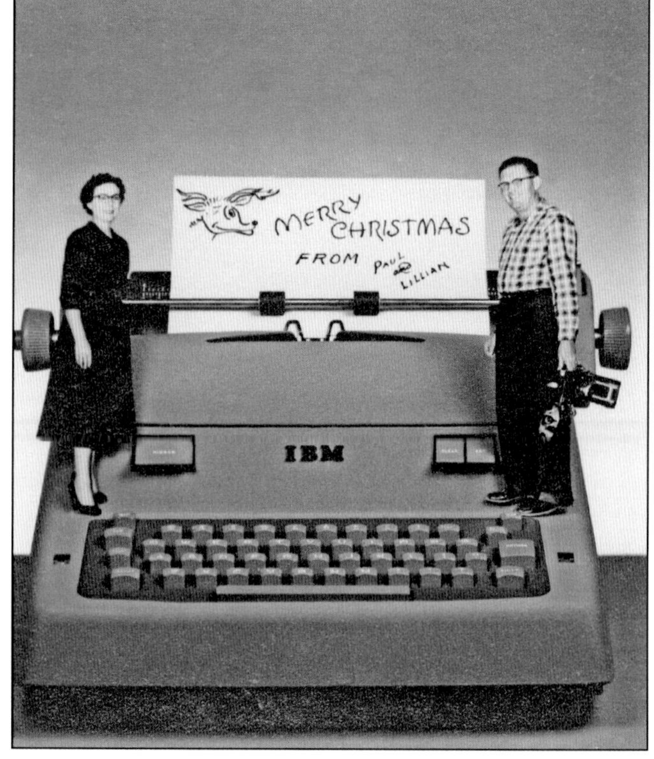

The Conleys reveal here their sense of humor, not only creating their own Christmas cards but "cutting and pasting" their images standing on an IBM typewriter. It is a manual, not yet an IBM Selectric. Wonder how they would create a Christmas card with today's computer technology? What would their Web site be? (Courtesy Linda Wright Photograph Collection.)

Is this the world's largest Santa Claus? It first appeared in 1931 on Davis Street, the brainchild of city commissioner Herman Howerts. An article in the December 2, 1955, issue of the *Luling Signal* announced the giant Santa Claus was celebrating its 25th birthday. The first Santa was destroyed by fire in 1947 but was rebuilt on a grander and larger scale. (Courtesy G&H Society.)

The Lehmann's Store is viewed from the intersection of Davis and Laurel Streets. It had earlier been a large dry goods store and shows little change in this photograph made during the early 1950s. It appears that the crowd is waiting for a parade to pass. At least, it is obvious the majority of the ladies are dressed up for a special occasion. (Courtesy G&H Society.)

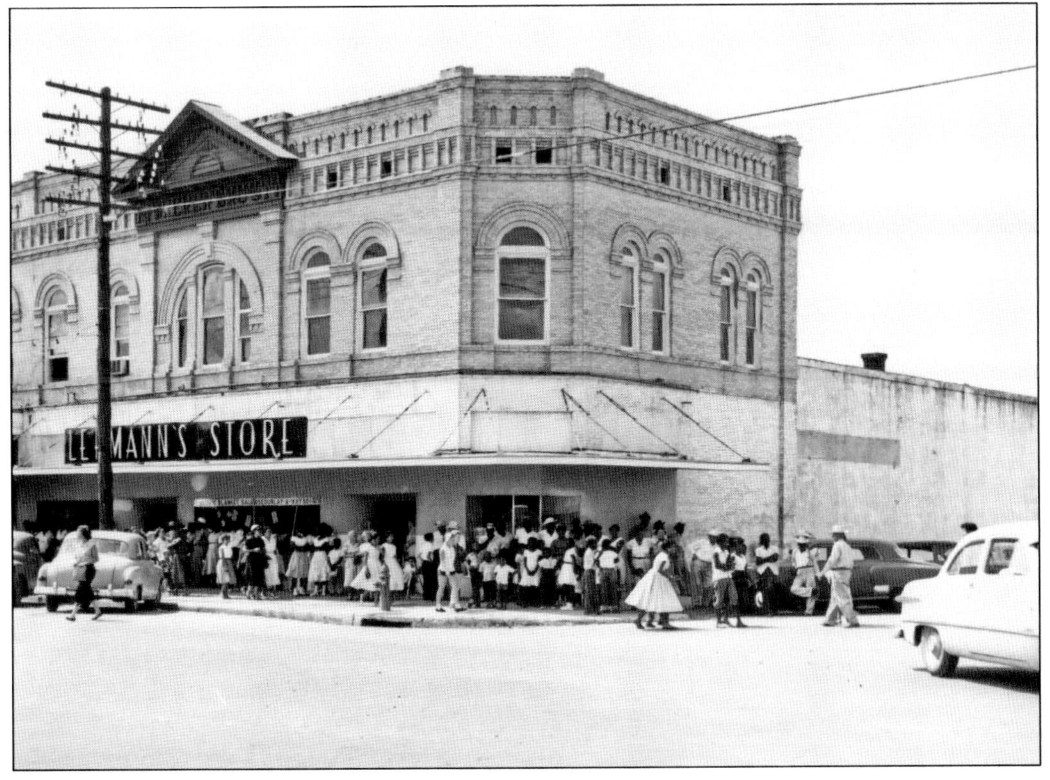

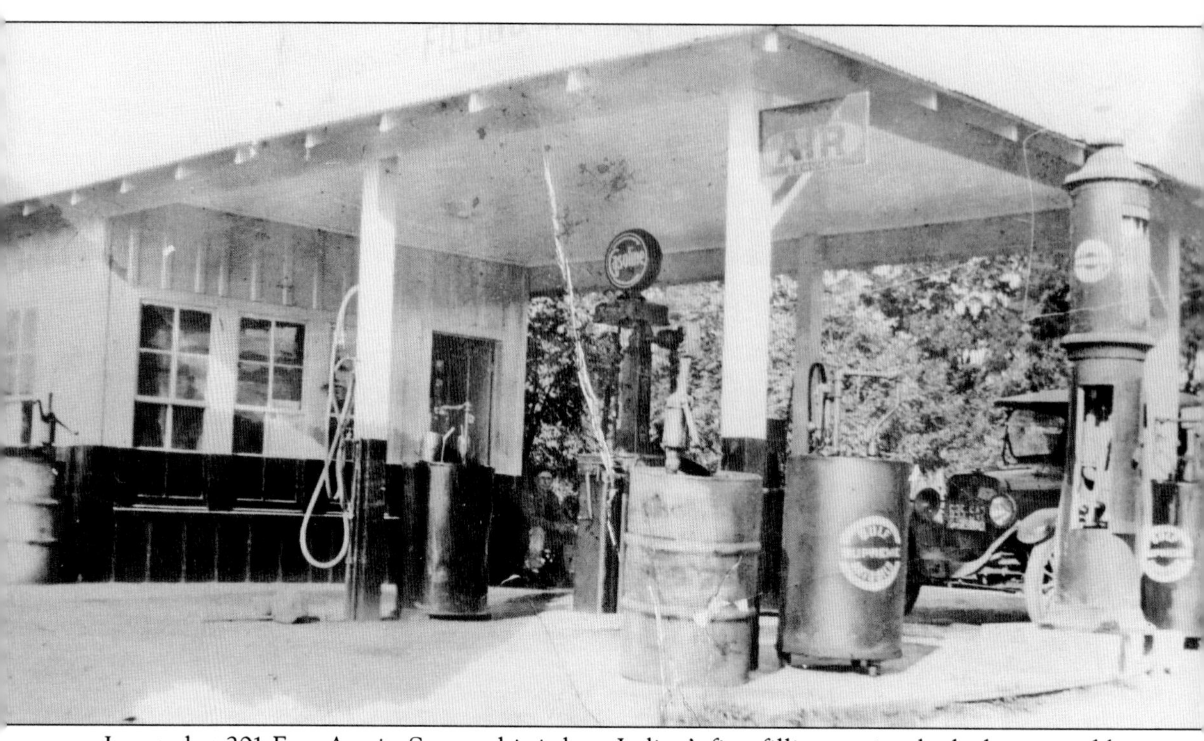

Located at 201 East Austin Street, this is how Luling's first filling station looked, operated by Henry J. Beversdorff. The term "filling station" is rarely heard today, but until a few decades ago, the filling station was what is now the convenience store, or simply the "C-store." It was a place where virtually anything could be purchased, competing with grocery stores. H. J. Beversdorff was born in Luling on July 31, 1880, and married Martha Huff of Flatonia, Texas. Beversdorff was a pioneer citizen of Luling, his obituary stating that he "took an active part in all community interests, having been a member of the Luling Band, a member of Mrs. Miles' Choral Club and also an active member of the Firemen . . . a member of the First Baptist Church for many years, and was also a member of the W.O.W. [Woodmen of the World] organization at the time of his passing," which occurred on May 6, 1941. (Courtesy G&H Society.)

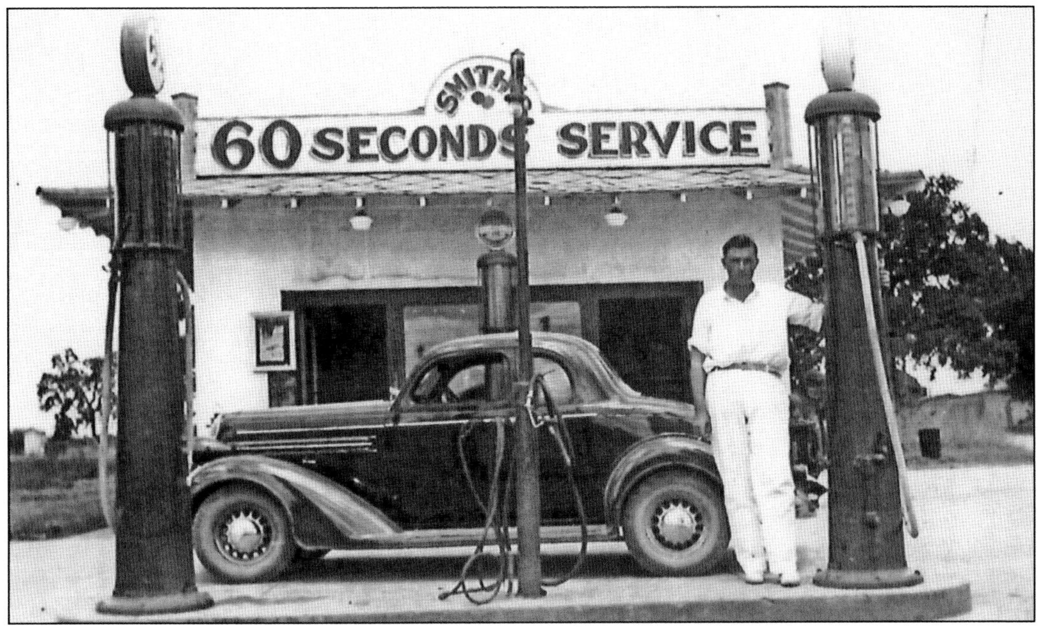

Edward "Ed" Ira Moses stands proudly in front of his 60 Seconds Service station on East Davis Street. Note the antique gas pumps and antique automobile with running boards. Luling native Moses was born on March 25, 1914, and worked for the Rainbo Company for 32 years. Active in civic affairs, he organized the local Little League and served as coach for the American Legion baseball program. (Courtesy Barbara Clark.)

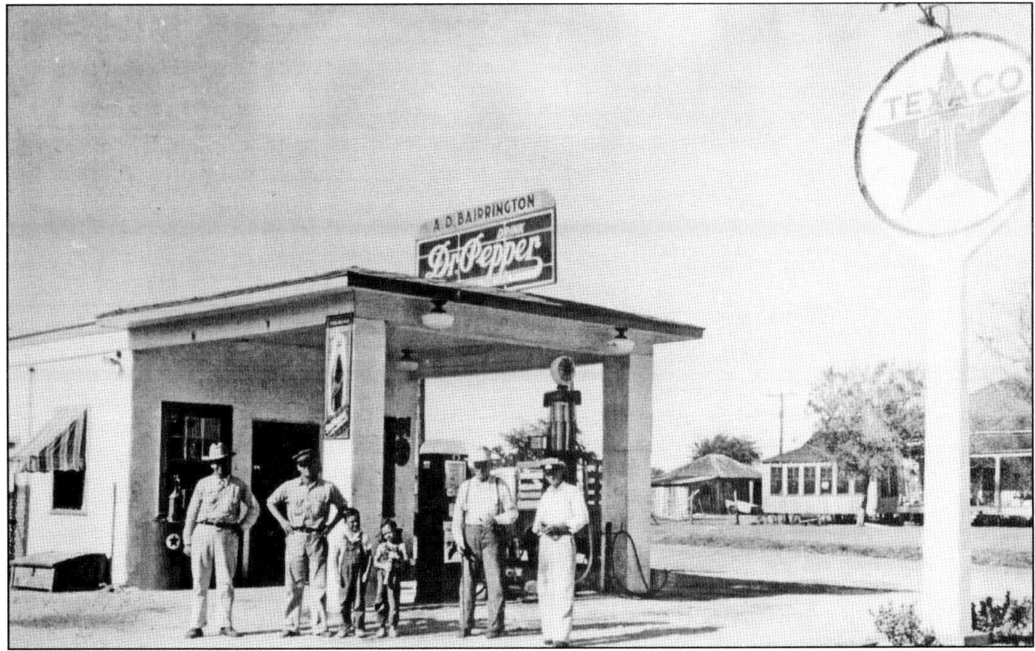

A. D. Bairrington's Texaco Filling Station stood on the corner of Pierce Street and Pine Street. From left to right are Enoch Horn, Alva Bairrington, children Johnny and Ira Bairrington, William D. Bairrington, and Dewey Bairrington, son of John and Lillian Frances (Pearson) Bairrington. Today the Smiley Tire Shop is at this location. (Courtesy Linda Wright Photograph Collection.)

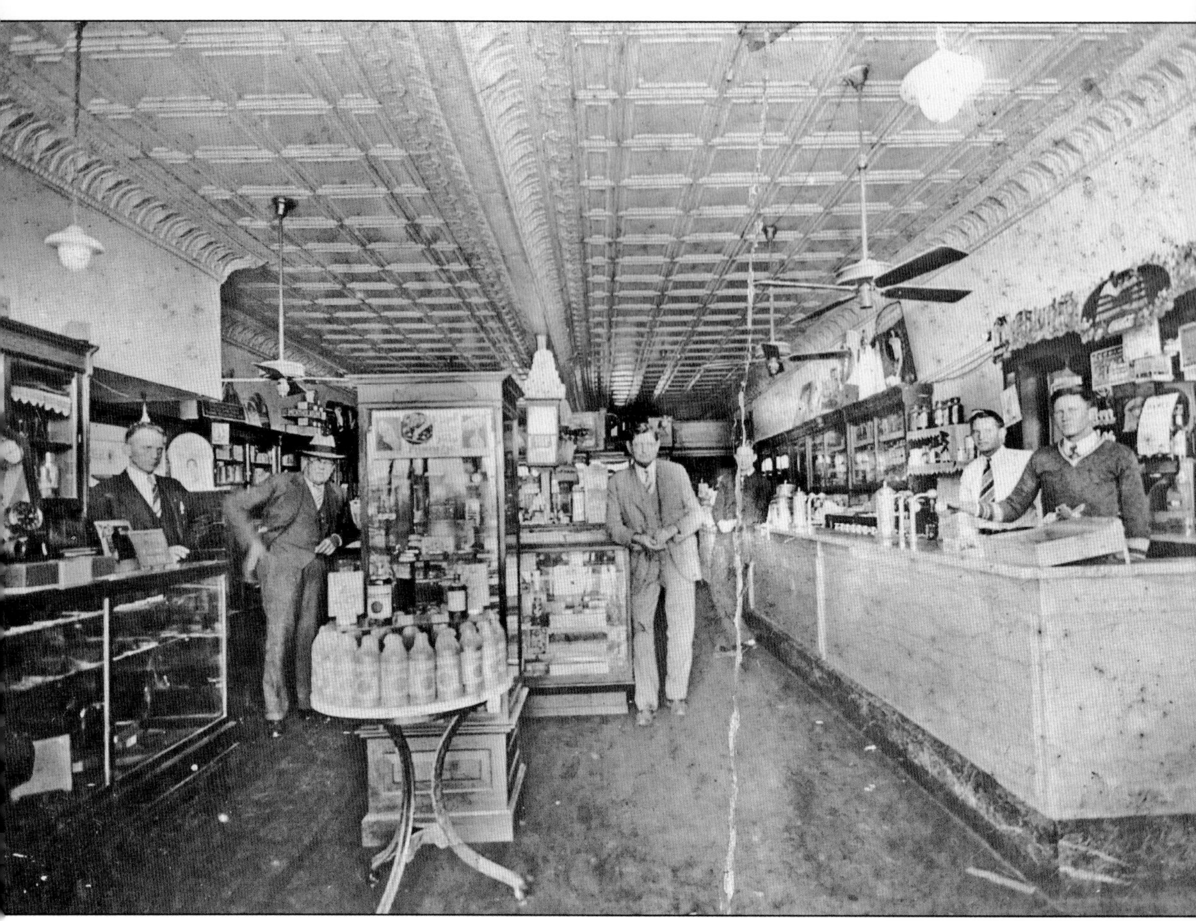

Serving Luling from 1900 to 1983, Dr. John McKenree Watkins and his family touched the lives of nearly everyone. Dr. Watkins made house calls in a horse-drawn carriage or on horseback, healing the sick and delivering babies. His work made him a valuable asset to the community. In 1925, he purchased what became known as the Watkins Drug Store. He is shown here (second from left) in a 1928 photograph with his sons John and Bill; the others are unidentified. Watkins died March 14, 1939. He and his sons John and Bill managed it until it was dissolved. John ran the pharmacy while younger brother Bill ran all other operations: the Western Union, sundry items, and the soda fountain. The eldest Watkins daughter taught in Luling throughout her life. She died having never married on June 4, 1981. (Courtesy G&H Society.)

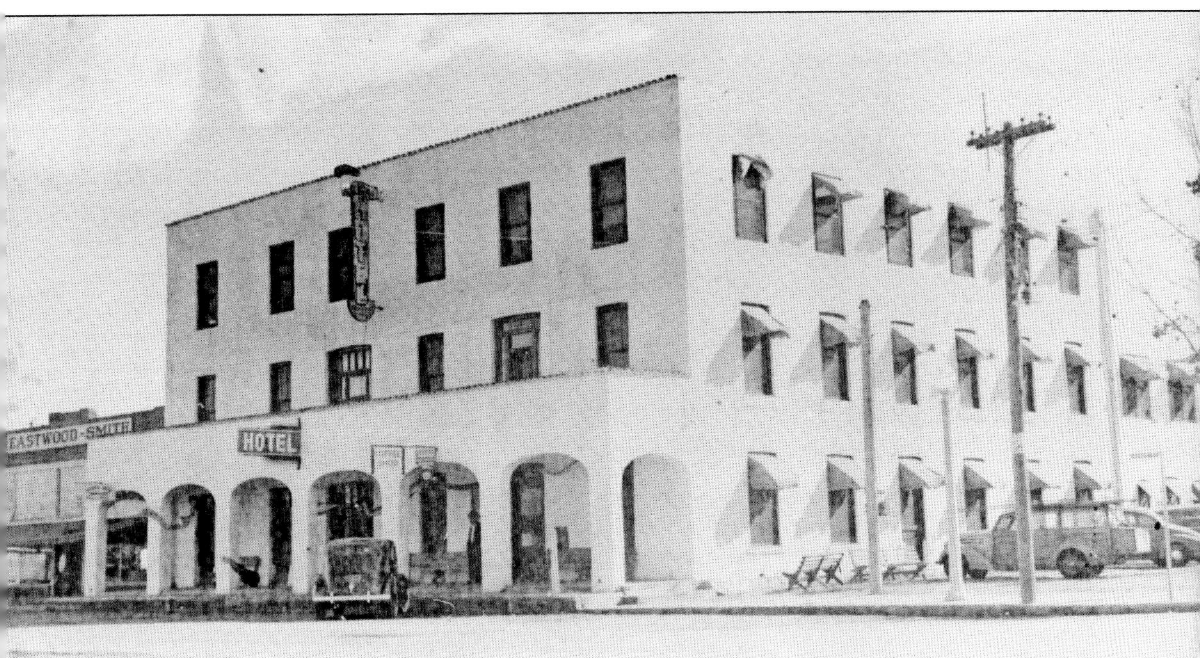

Luling's leading hotel, the Wilson House, was built by English-born Thomas Wilson. Wilson was responsible to a great degree for the success of Luling's growth during the late 19th century. He came to Texas in 1877 as an immigration agent for the Galveston, Harrisburg, and San Antonio Railroad. His assignment: bring people to lands along the railroad. In 1883, he built his home, the White Lily. In 1887, he built the Wilson Hotel, which stood until 1979 when it was demolished. Wilson's writings, in English, French, and German, extolled the virtues of Texas and Luling. According to the late local historian Eva Wilson, he was "a self-educated near genius because of his many talents and unbelievable capabilities. He was a man whose vision placed him well ahead of his generation." (Courtesy Don and Judy Lightsey.)

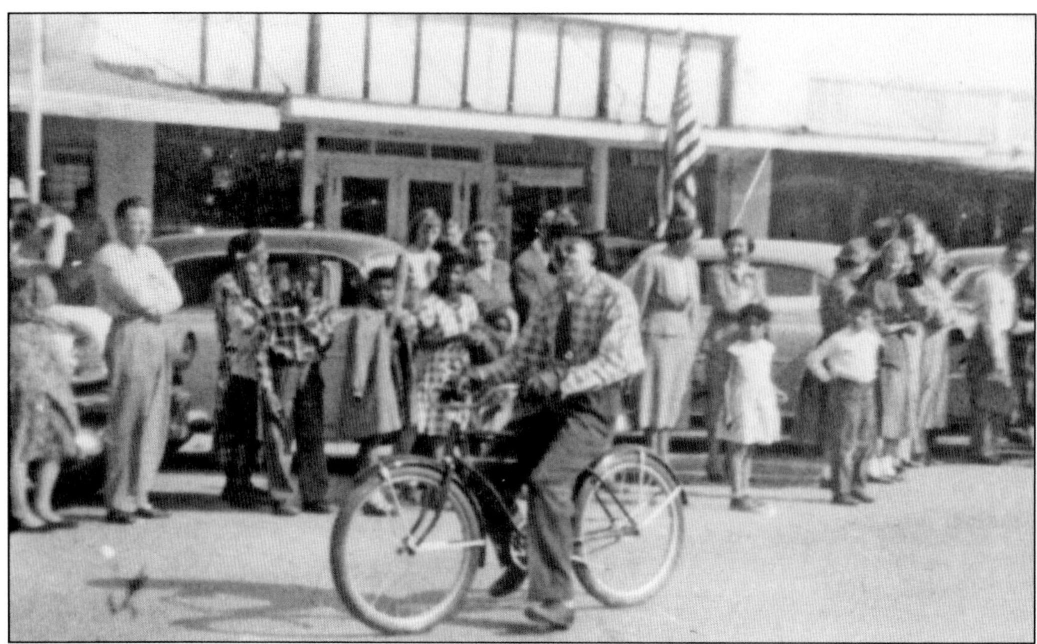

Not all was serious among the business houses of Davis Street, as proven in these two photographs. Above is an unidentified clown bicycling. It appears to be an image from the 1950s, judging from the size of the bike tires. And below is an unusual view of a parade marching eastward along Davis Street. Usually photographs show the beginning of a parade rather than the "tail-end." Again this photograph is undated but is perhaps from the 1950s. Note the children seated on the rooftop of the Wilson meat market at left, next door to the Citizens State Bank. Farther down is the historic Walker Building, now the Central Texas Oil Patch Museum. (Both courtesy G&H Society.)

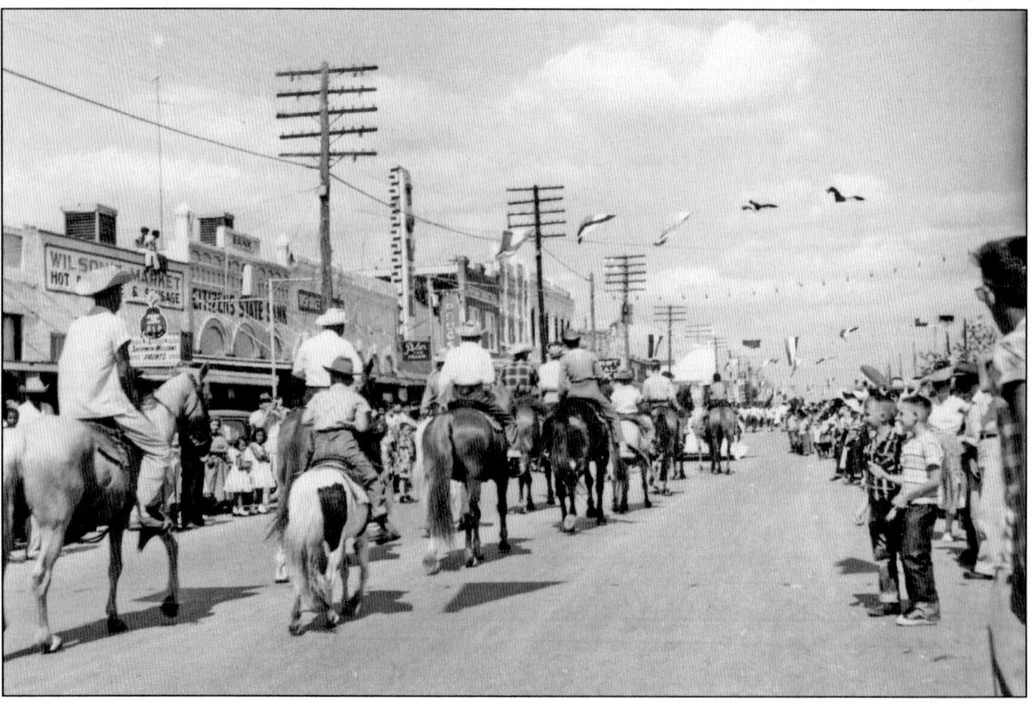

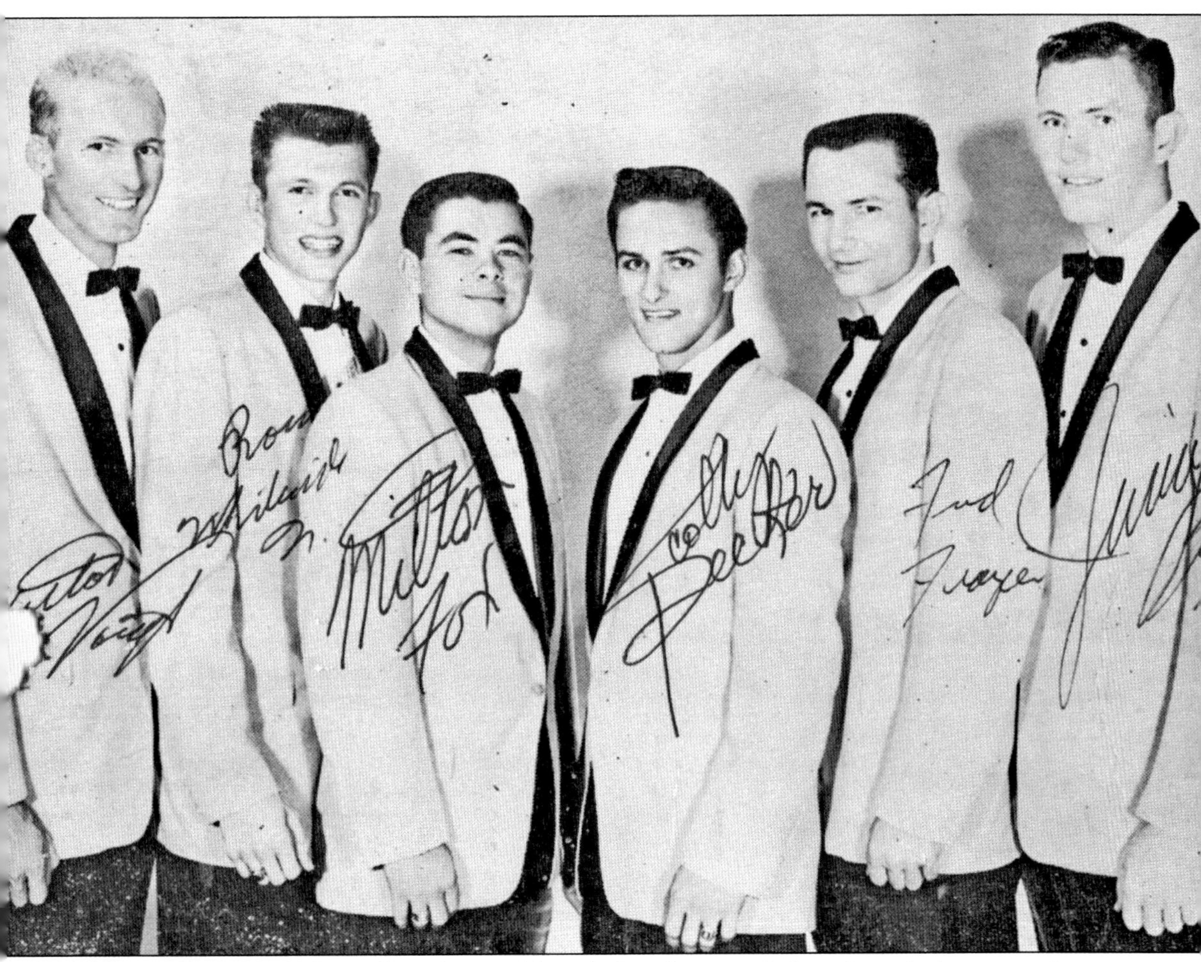

The Moods is a sextet that still performs, although this photograph dates from their younger days. From left to right are Cotton Voigt, Ross Whiteside Jr., Milton Fox, Scotty Decker, Fred Frazier, and Jimmy Bazar. Their sport coats remind the viewer of a song from the 1950s, "A White Sport Coat and a Pink Carnation," and rightly so as the band found its successful beginnings during that decade of rock 'n' roll, but they continue performing these good old songs as well as country and western hits. The Moods entertain young and old in communities such as Hallettsville, Shiner, Moulton, Luling, Lockhart, Beeville, and many others. (Courtesy Carol Voigt.)

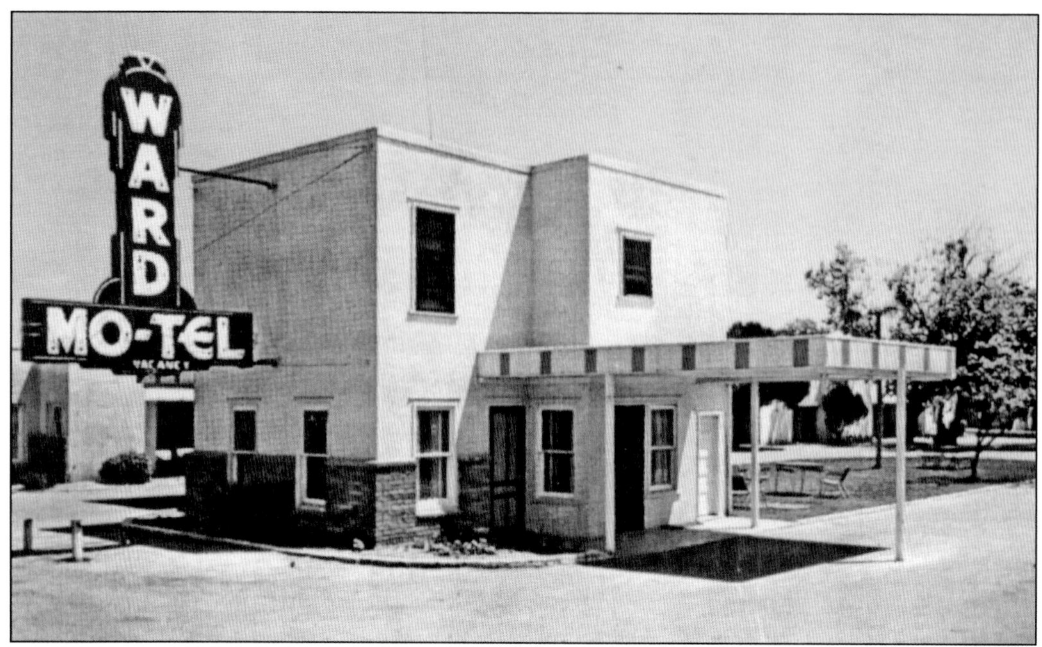

The Ward Motel on the west side of Luling on Highway 90 was, in its heyday, able to boast that every room was "air cooled" with carpeted floors, running ice water, and "everything furnished for your comfort and convenience." The owner was D. H. Ward. Today it is an abandoned eyesore on the western outskirts of Luling. (Courtesy Linda Wright Photograph Collection.)

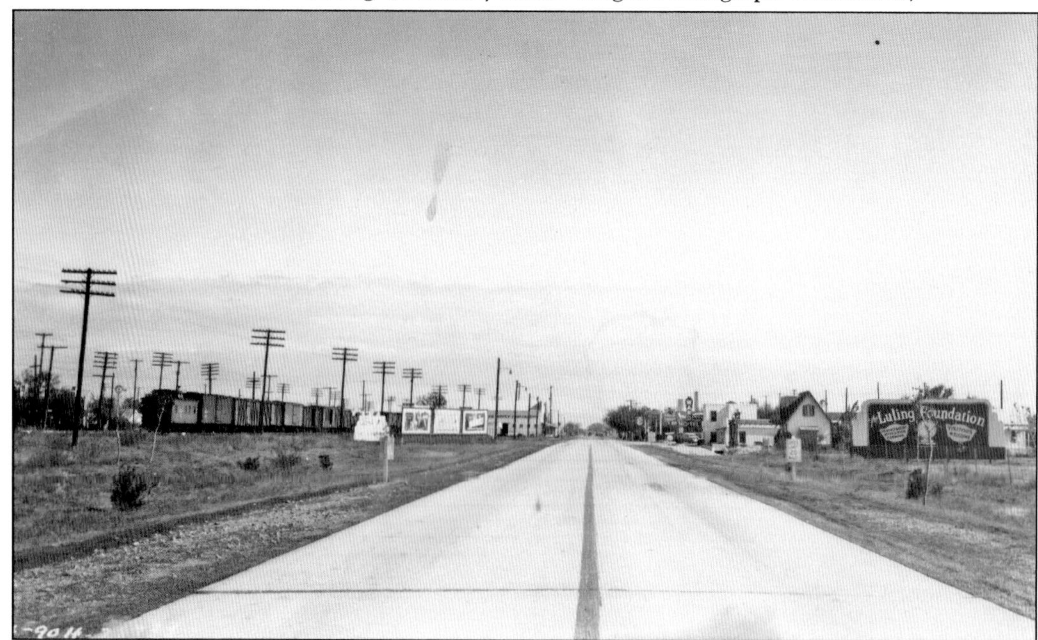

A rare view of early Luling is seen on Highway 90, facing east. The traveler who goes on this stretch of 90 today may have left Seguin, then gone west through Kingsbury, then what was once Sullivan, and then into Luling. The highway becomes Pierce Street, past the Ward Motel, H. E. B., and other businesses and continues on to Gonzales in the adjacent county. (Courtesy G&H Society.)

Three

Schools and Churches

Luling had no church building in 1874. Bishop Robert W. B. Elliott, 34 years old, was on his way to Seguin in Guadalupe County, but because of the high waters of the San Marcos River, he was forced to stop at Luling, the terminus of the Galveston, Harrisburg, and San Antonio Railroad. It was December 20, and he was determined to hold services. He arranged to hold worship services in a passenger coach. That inspired Luling residents to organize a facility for worship. Thanks to the generosity of T. W. Pierce, property was deeded for a church. Rev. Nelson Ayres began constructing a church with his own hands in early 1876. The first service in a building for that purpose was held on April 15, 1877: it was the Episcopal Church of the Annunciation. Today's church stands on the same site, only greatly modified. A Texas State Historical Marker stands on the corner of Bowie and Walnut Streets in front of the church.

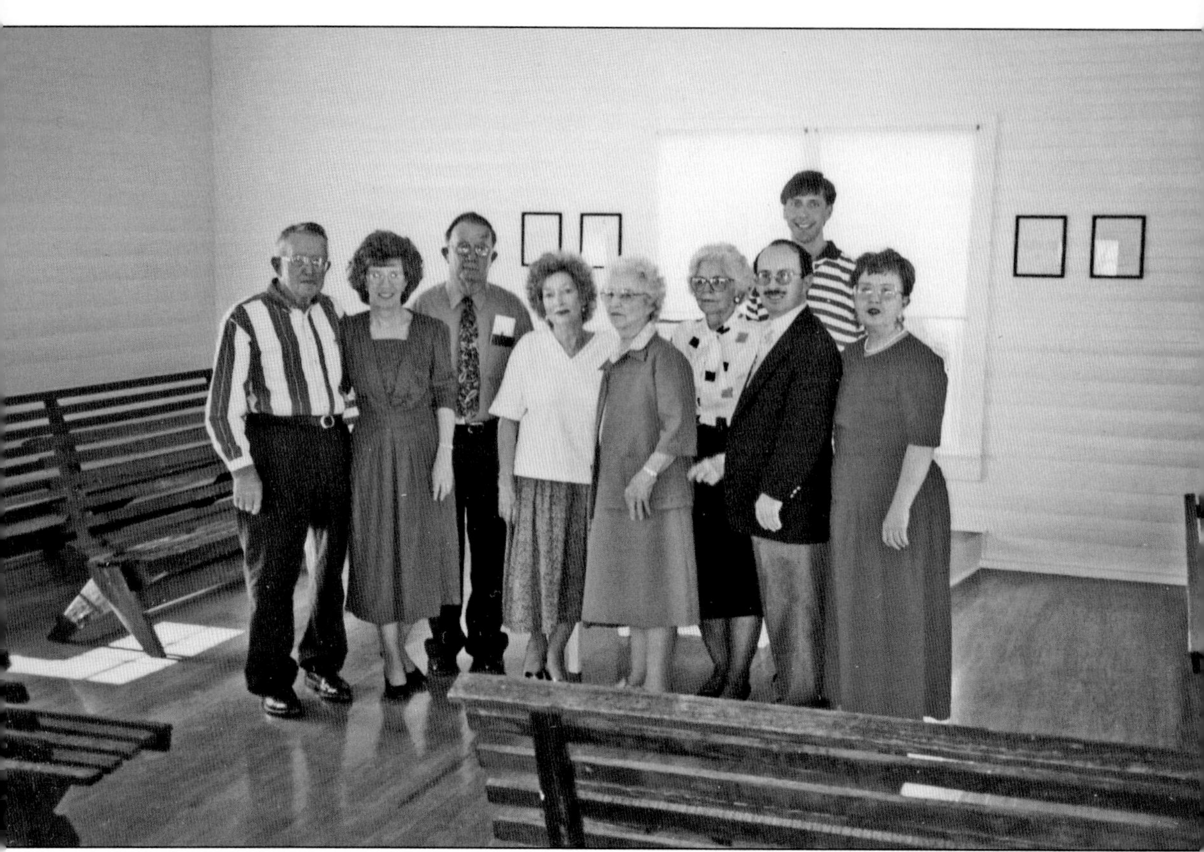

The San Marcos Primitive Baptist Church, now located on Blanco Street, is considered by some to be the earliest of Luling's churches. The church itself began in 1853 when Elder George Daniels and Elder R. W. Ellis constituted it. Charter members were William Baker and his wife, Vashti White Baker; Hannah Daniels; I. D. Owen; and Sylvanna Daniels. Elder J. M. Baker served the church from 1862 until his death in 1910, never collecting a fee for his services. The first church building is believed to have been located southwest of where William Baker's home was. In 1886, the present building was constructed and has remained virtually unchanged ever since. The adjacent cemetery contains over 500 graves. In 1930, the church congregation moved to Blanco Street but continued services in the original building every fourth Sunday until the mid-1960s. In 1970, all services were discontinued there and are now held at the Blanco Street location. Elder T. H. Brown of Luling began conducting services in 1980 and remains the current pastor. The photograph shows descendants of William and Vashti Baker. From left to right are Saint Armo Baker, Martha Baker Aiken, Weldon Marshall "Pete" Baker, Patricia Baker Perryman, Linne Sobotik, Ada Ruth Poe, John Marshall Baker, Billy Perryman, and Pat Baker Parsons. (Courtesy Elder T. H. Brown.)

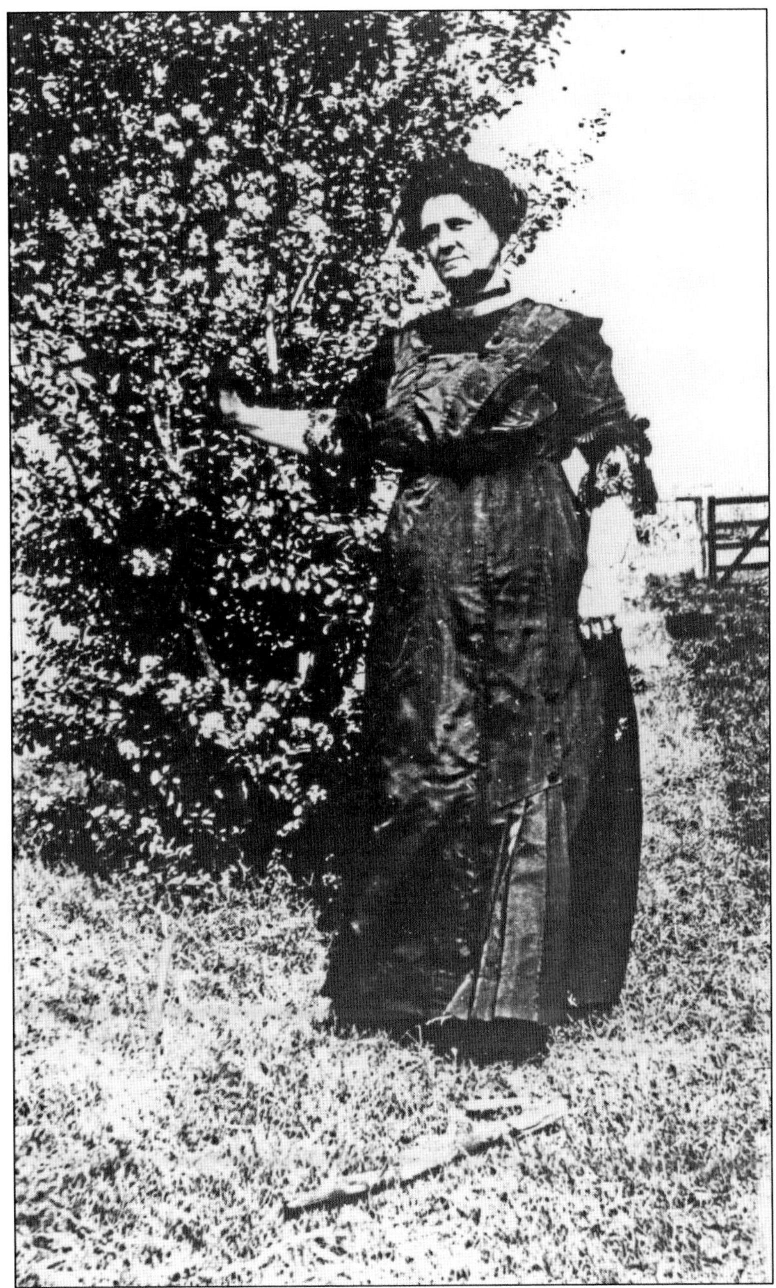

Jennie Clarke is remembered as the founder of the Belle Haven Orphanage in Luling. She saw the need to alleviate the plight of homeless and orphaned children. She was born Jennie Everton in Indiana on July 29, 1862, the youngest of six children. After she earned a college degree in Illinois, the family moved to Texas, where Jennie taught school in Caldwell County. She first married widower Lee Echols, who brought two children into the marriage. The Echolses had one daughter, Nora, before Lee died in 1894. In 1896, Jennie married Alan G. Clarke of New York. A son died in infancy; the Clarkes were divorced in 1898. In 1899, Jennie opened her home to 12 homeless children. From the auspicious beginning, the home grew significantly. (Courtesy G&H Society.)

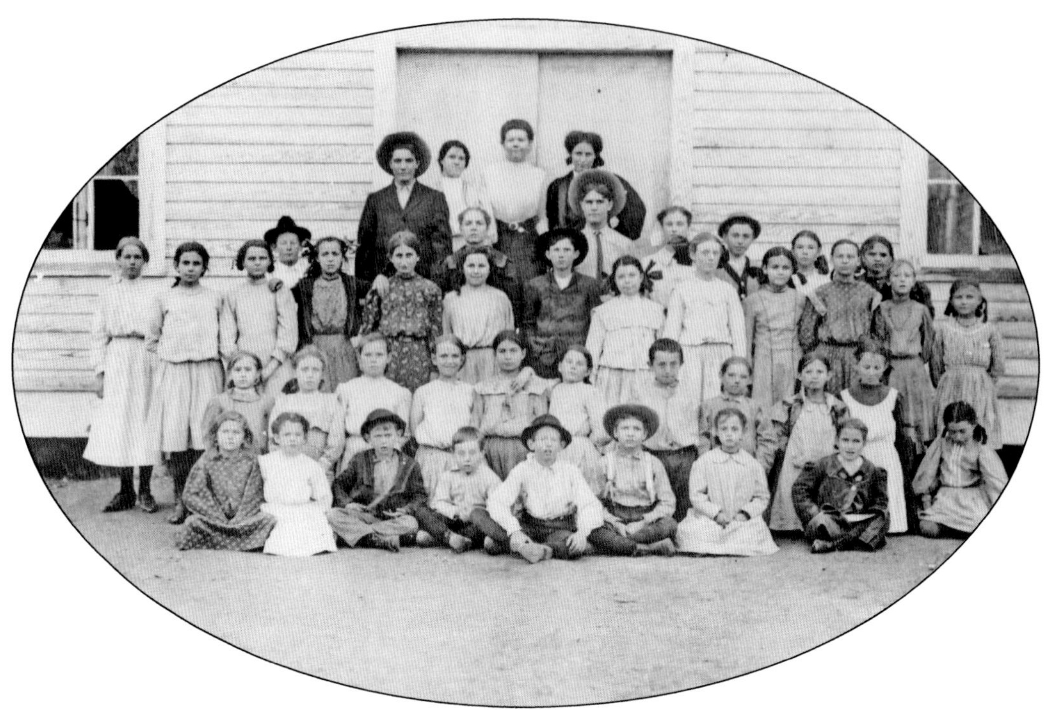

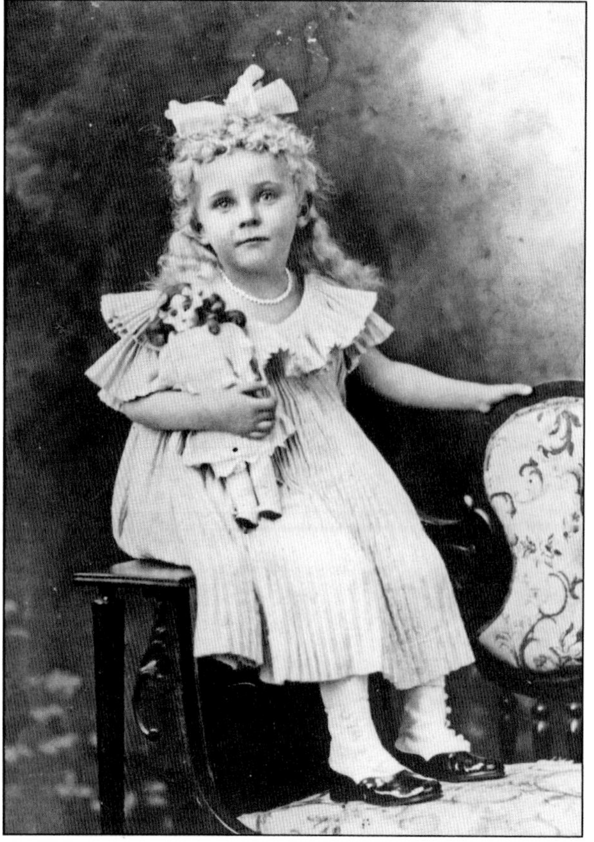

Occasionally Jennie Clarke brought a photographer onto the grounds, thus providing images, fortunately preserved for posterity, of the wards. The photograph above is dated 1907–1908. By this time, the Church of Christ was built and Jennie was able to provide religious instruction as well as a traditional education to the children. None of these children are identified. All appear to be well disciplined and secure in their surroundings. (Courtesy G&H Society.)

This angelic-looking child is identified as Alice Cooper, but little else is known for sure. The 1910 Caldwell County census shows her as a three-year-old white girl, born in Texas, and nothing else. The 1920 census records her only as 14 years of age. How long she had been a ward is unknown. She obviously has been well dressed for the photographer. (Courtesy G&H Society.)

Annie Peters, shown here exhibiting quite an air of confidence, remains mysterious. When she came to Belle Haven is unknown, but in 1929, she was listed as a ward born in Texas, could read and write English, and was 18 years old. No other information is available. Note the orphanage residence building at left and the Church of Christ at right in the background. (Courtesy G&H Society.)

This group photograph of the residents of Belle Haven reflects Jennie Clarke's great success in bringing to children not only a physical shelter but a caring upbringing as well. Without her, what upbringing would they have received? None are positively identified, but it is believed Jennie Clarke is the seated figure at the right with the teacher standing behind her. Older children of course are standing in the back row. (Courtesy G&H Society.)

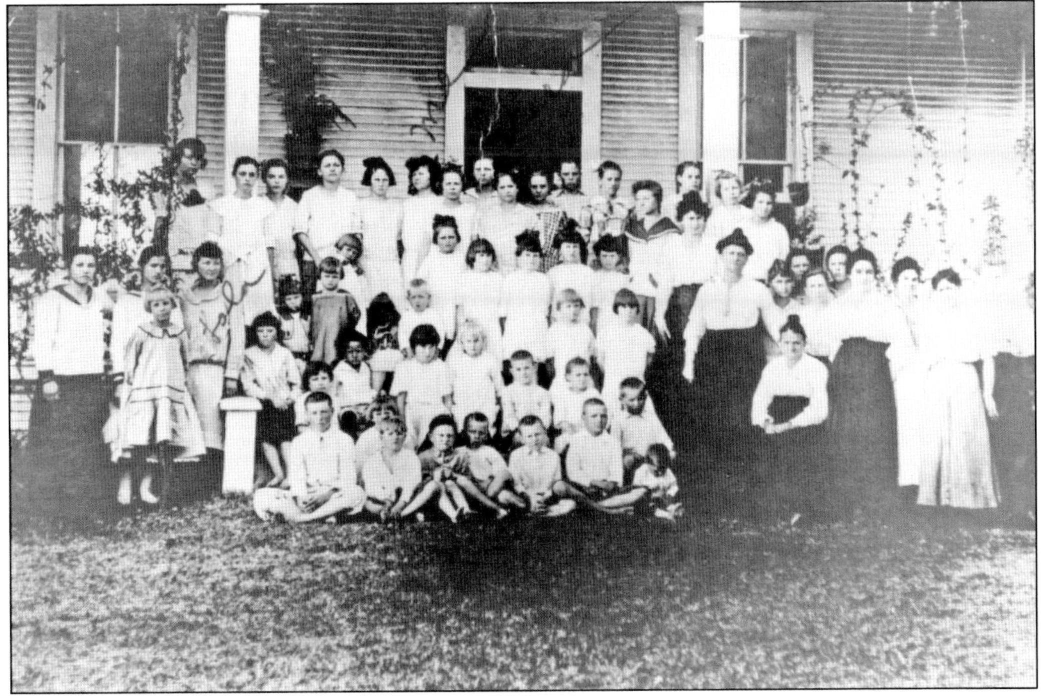

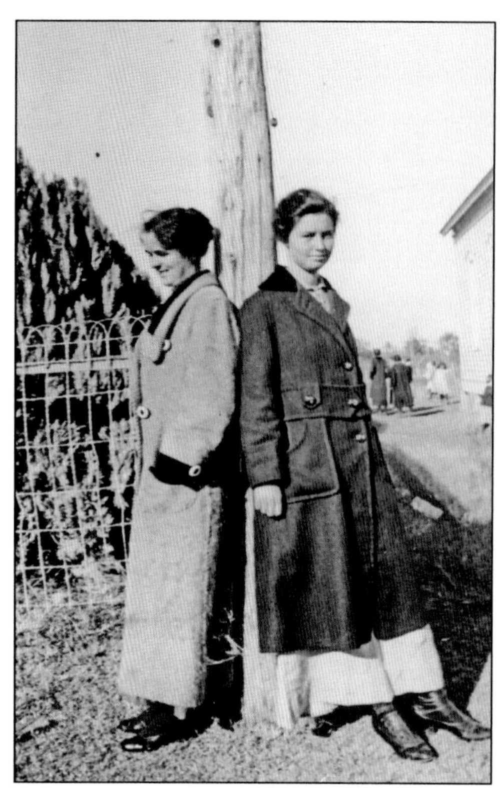

Information about the wards of Belle Haven is rare indeed. What is known is usually not more than names on a census page. A few photographs provide material, but unfortunately these also are few in number. Shown at left are Lillie Newton (left) and Ola Johnson, identified as teachers, around 1915 or 1916. They both appear to be in their early 20s or late teens. Note in the background the young children, perhaps at recess, around the edge of the church building. Below is a photograph of two wards identified as Beulah (left) and Hettie Green. Nothing further is known of the two teachers or the two Green children. (Both courtesy G&H Society.)

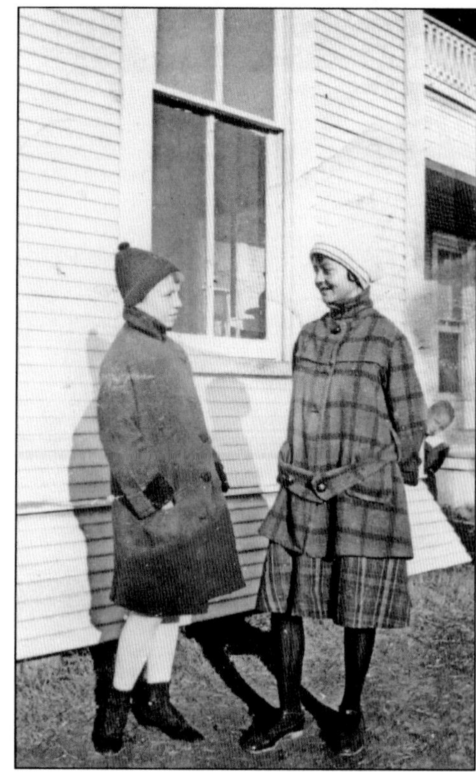

Jennie Everton lost her first husband in 1894, leaving her with their daughter, Nora, as well as his two children from a previous marriage. In 1896, she married Alan G. Clarke. The Clarkes were divorced in 1898. Jennie and her mother, Martha Everton, were both devout members of the Church of Christ. Shown here is the church erected on the orphanage grounds. (Courtesy G&H Society.)

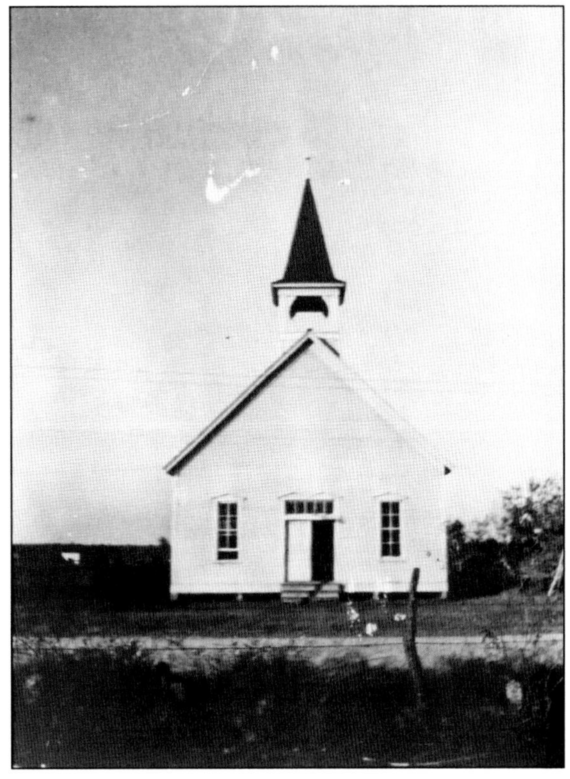

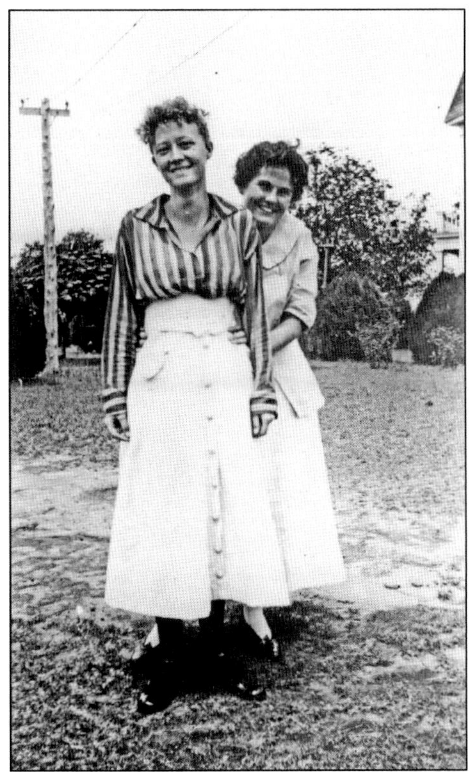

Annie Peters (foreground) and Onita Breedlove were two wards of Jennie Clarke's Belle Haven Orphanage. No date is on this photograph, but both are in their late teens or early 20s. Onita Breedlove was born about 1899, while Annie was born about 1902. By this time, they were perhaps considered trusted assistants to Jennie Clarke, trusted to work with all the younger children. (Courtesy G&H Society.)

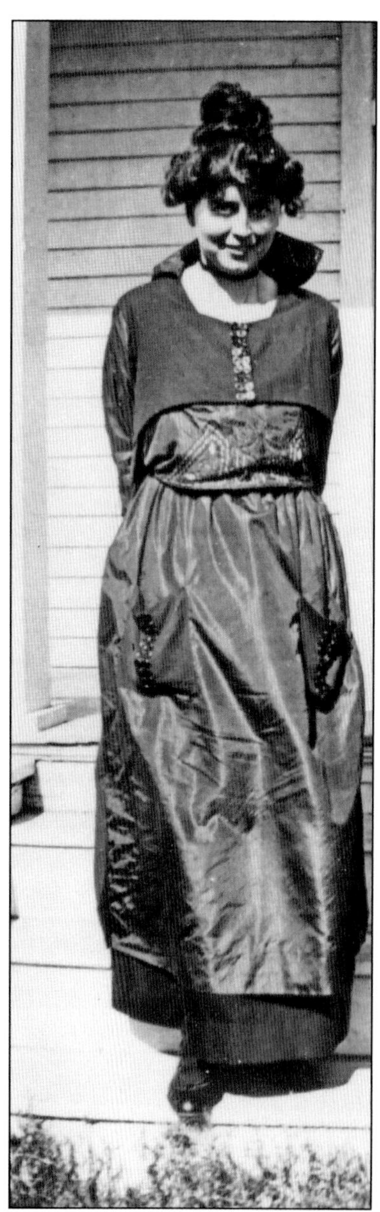

Nora Echols was the only daughter of Jennie and widower Lee Echols. After Lee Echols died in 1894, after only four brief years of marriage to Jennie, Nora grew up hardly ever knowing her father. Jennie stipulated in her will that upon her death, Nora would have control of the facilities as long as they were used for the orphanage. (Courtesy G&H Society.)

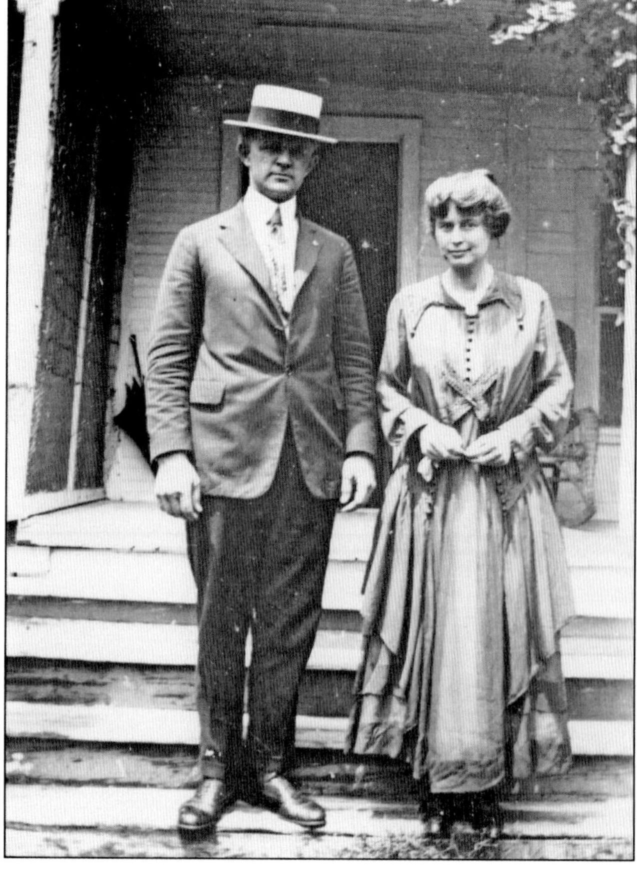

Jennie's daughter Nora Echols, born in 1892, grew up and remained with the orphanage. With a good education, she became office secretary to Jennie. Here she is shown with her husband, a Mr. Levy, about whom little else is known. Here he is shown as the well-dressed gentleman of the early 20th century. (Courtesy G&H Society.)

The entrance to Belle Haven Orphanage is pictured here. Was it merely an oversight that the painter spelled the name "Bell" instead of the generally accepted spelling of "Belle"? Or was it a matter of indecision as to the proper spelling? From the letterhead, it is obvious that "Belle" was the name decided upon. (Courtesy G&H Society.)

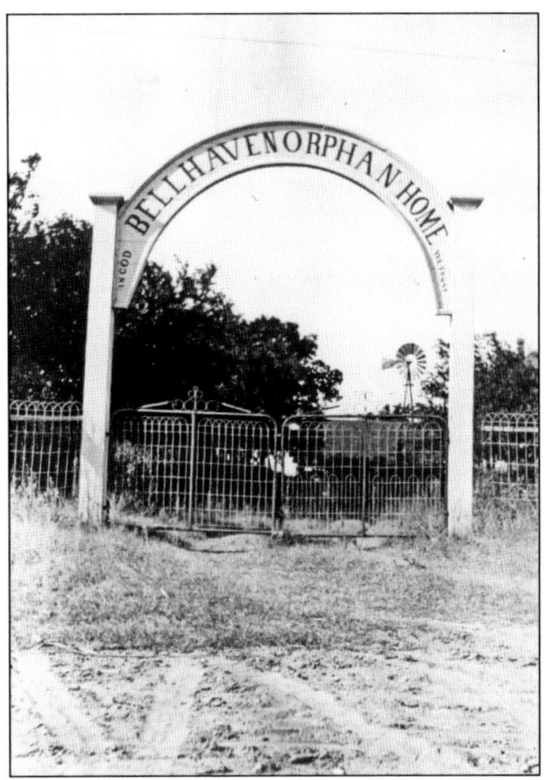

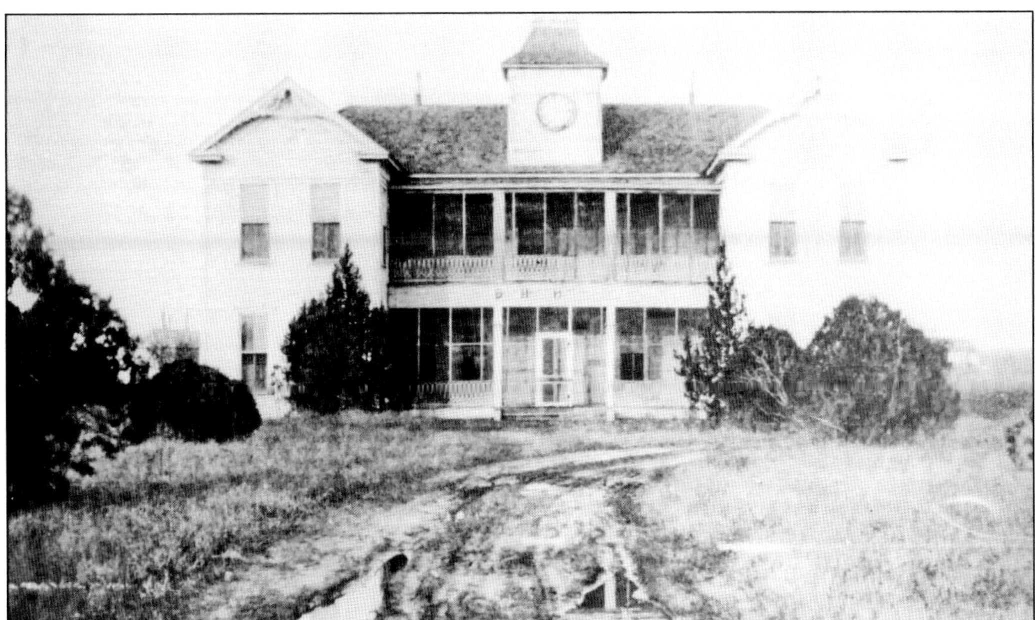

Here is an excellent view of the Belle Haven Orphanage on the San Marcos highway. The remnants of the structure are barely visible today, but the general outline of the entire facility can be visited. With a little imagination, one can "hear and see" the laughter and gaiety of the children whose life was made much more meaningful thanks to Jennie Clarke and her compassion for the young. (Courtesy G&H Society.)

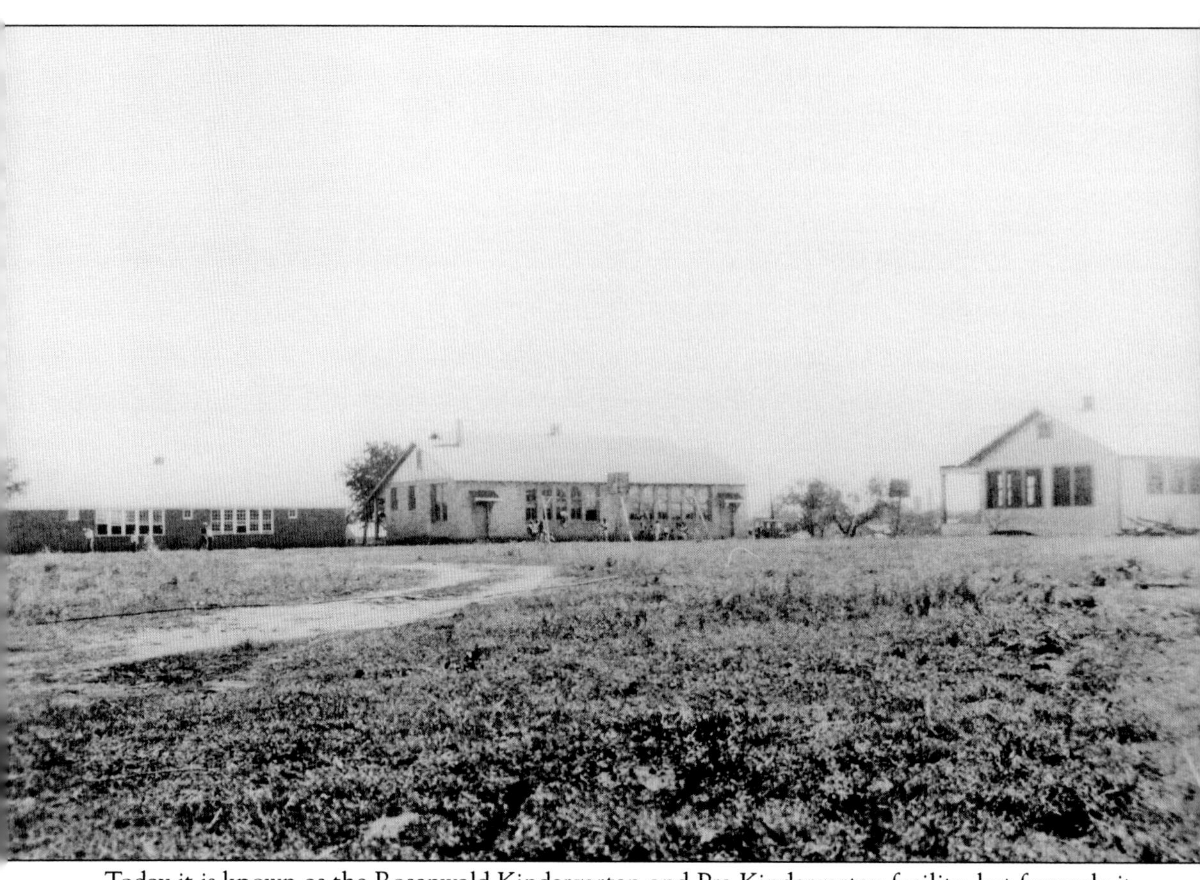

Today it is known as the Rosenwald Kindergarten and Pre-Kindergarten facility, but formerly it was simply the Rosenwald Schools, for black children only. The Rosenwald rural school program was a major effort to improve the quality of public education for African Americans in the early 20th century. In 1912, Julius Rosenwald gave Booker T. Washington permission to use some of his donated money for the construction of six small schools in rural Alabama. These were opened in 1913 and 1914. Rosenwald was so pleased with the results, he gave even more money. In 1928, one in every five rural schools for black children in the South was a product of Rosenwald. The program concluded in 1932, having produced 4,977 new schools and provided homes for 217 teachers and 163 shop buildings. It served students in 15 states. The Luling Rosenwald was built on 2.5 acres at a total cost of $10,000. Included were a shop and a library. (Courtesy G&H Society.)

Ray A. Harrison, born in Gonzales County, Texas, spent 40 years teaching youth of all ages. He taught agriculture, math, and history at high schools in Luling, Lockhart, and Seguin. His later years were spent as principal of an elementary school in Goliad, Goliad County. He was principal of the Luling Rosenwald School. Harrison, active in the chamber of commerce and the American Heart Association, died December 18, 1985. (Courtesy Meatra D. Harrison.)

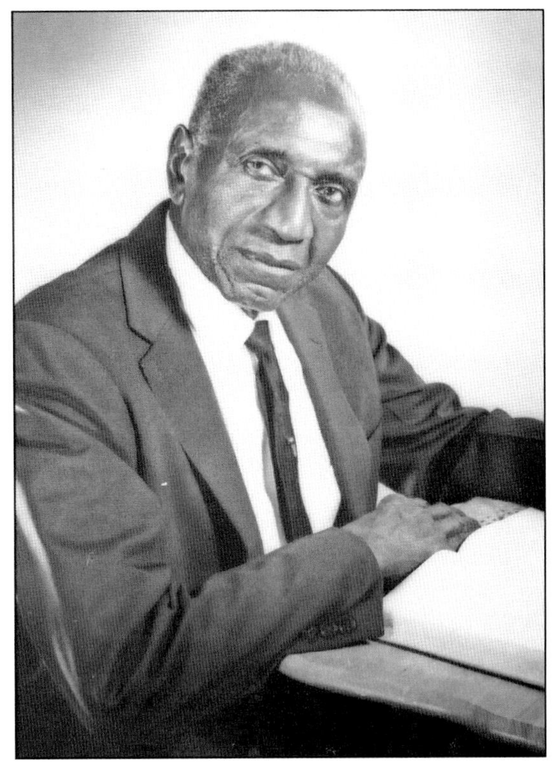

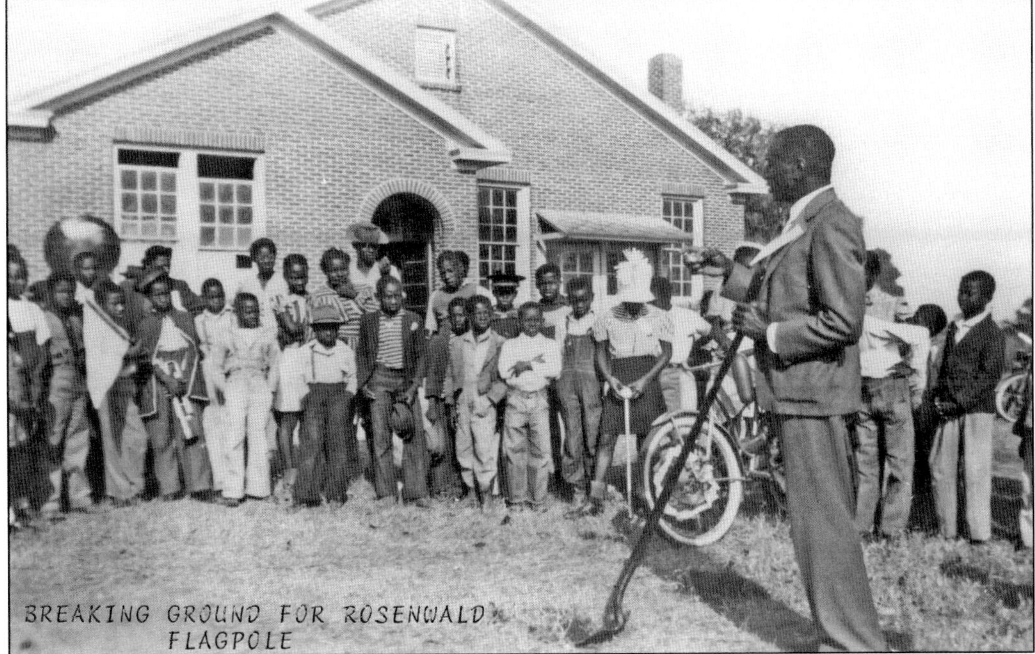

This rare photograph shows the ground-breaking ceremony at Luling's Rosenwald School, today Rosenwald Pre-Kindergarten and Kindergarten. The flagpole still stands at 102 West Newton Street. Unfortunately the individual with the spade is not identified but may be R. A. Harrison himself. Note the bicycles visible in the photograph. (Courtesy Meatra D. Harrison.)

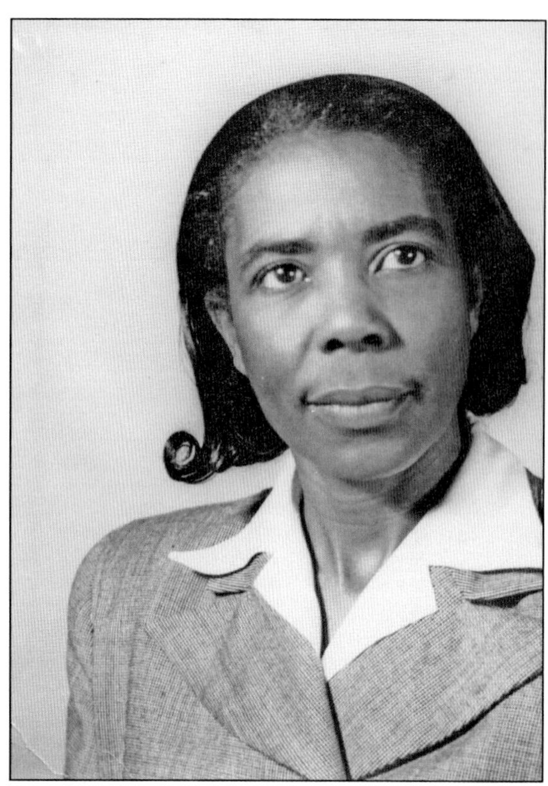

Meatra Lawson Harrison, wife of R. A. Harrison, taught first grade at the Rosenwald Elementary School for many years. Her influence, along with that of her husband, provided a solid beginning for many of Luling's children. The school today provides educational facilities for pre-kindergarten and kindergarten for all children, regardless of race. (Courtesy Meatra D. Harrison.)

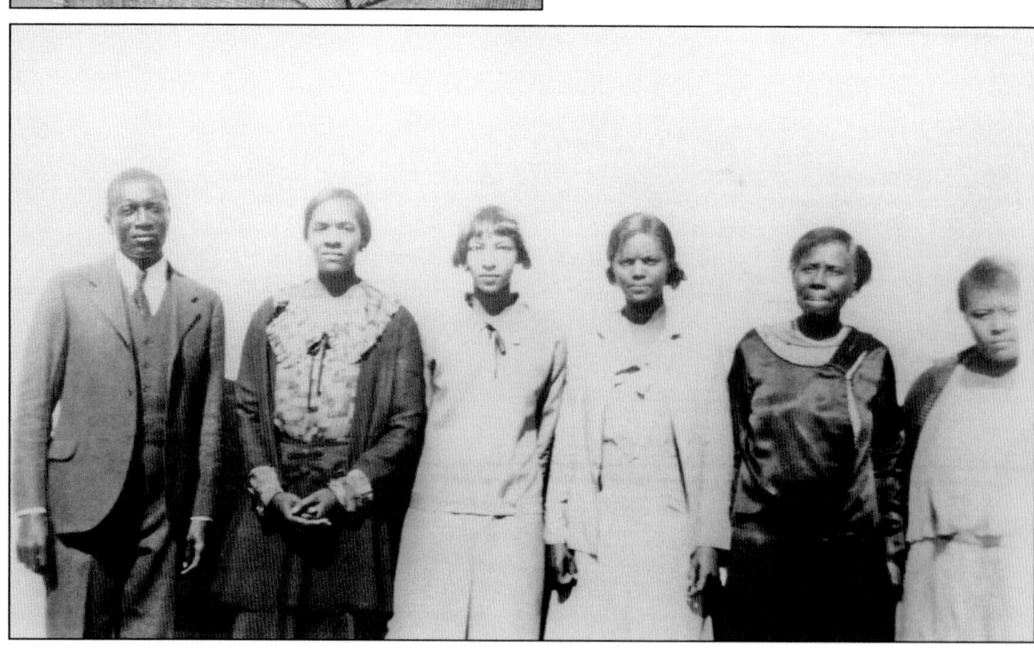

Educational leaders of the Rosenwald School are shown in this image by an unidentified photographer. In 1930, these leaders are, from left to right, Principal Ray A. Harrison, Hallie Merriweather, Hattie Marie Jenkins, Minnie Lomax, Ella Mae Ratcliff, and Goldie Mae Bell. From the small number of teachers, the teacher-student ratio could not have been high. (Courtesy Meatra D. Harrison.)

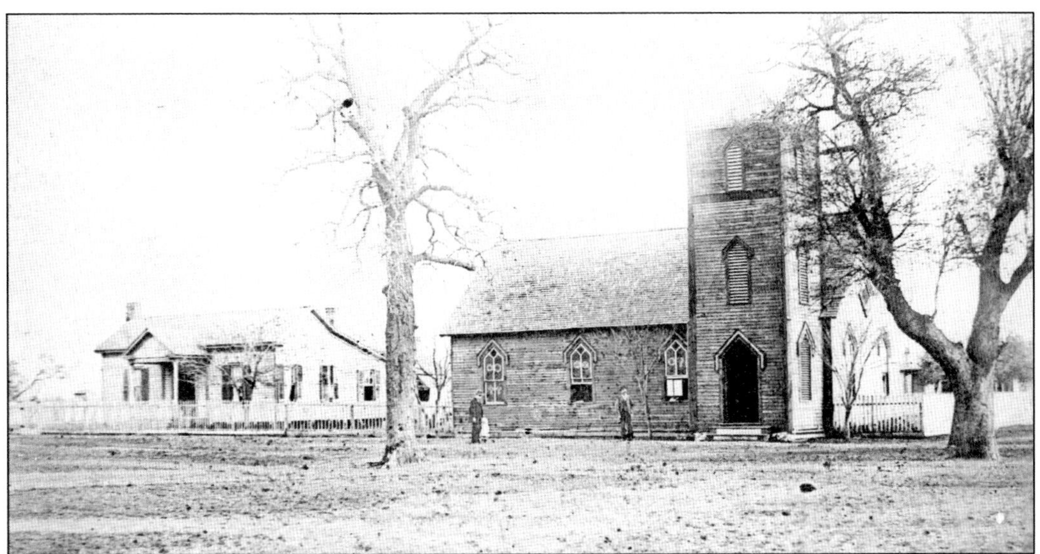

With no church building in the early 1870s, it remained for Thomas W. Pierce to show his generosity. Thanks to Pierce, property was deeded for a church with a rectory. Construction began in 1876, and the first services were held here on April 15, 1877, in the Episcopal Church of the Annunciation. It remains on the same grounds, on the corner of Bowie and Walnut Streets, although the building has been greatly modified. (Courtesy Russel Matthews.)

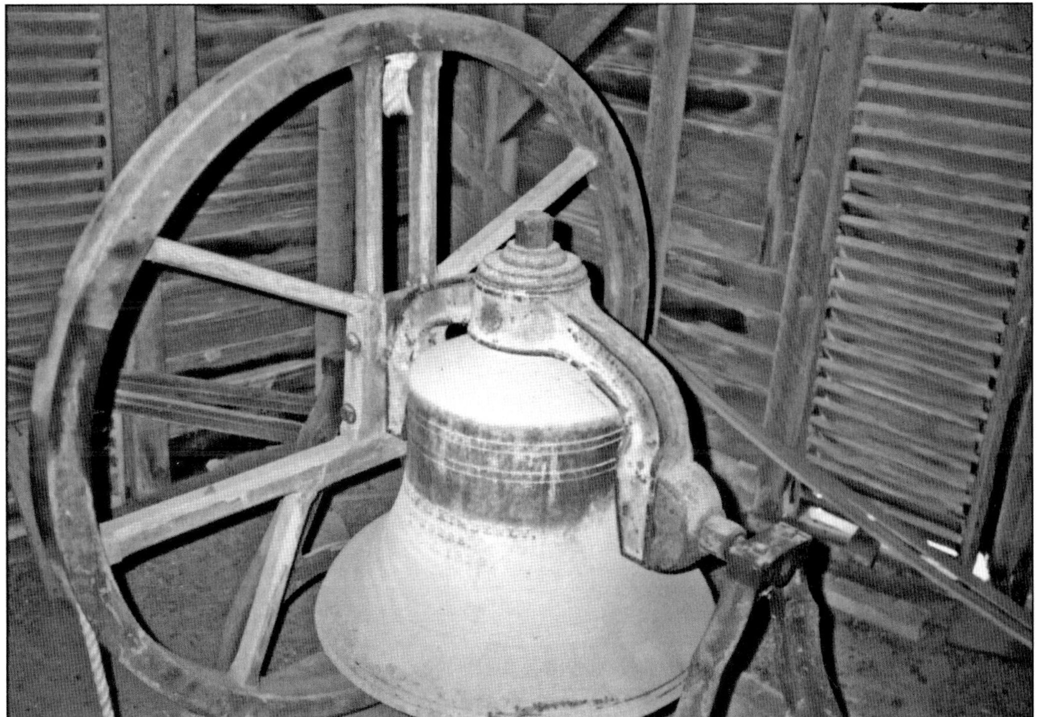

One rarely hears today the church bells that were once so common on a Sunday morning, ringing to call worshippers together. This is the original bell in the belfry of the Episcopal Church of the Annunciation. On close examination, one can observe the wooden pegs used in the construction of the bell holder. (Courtesy Russel Matthews.)

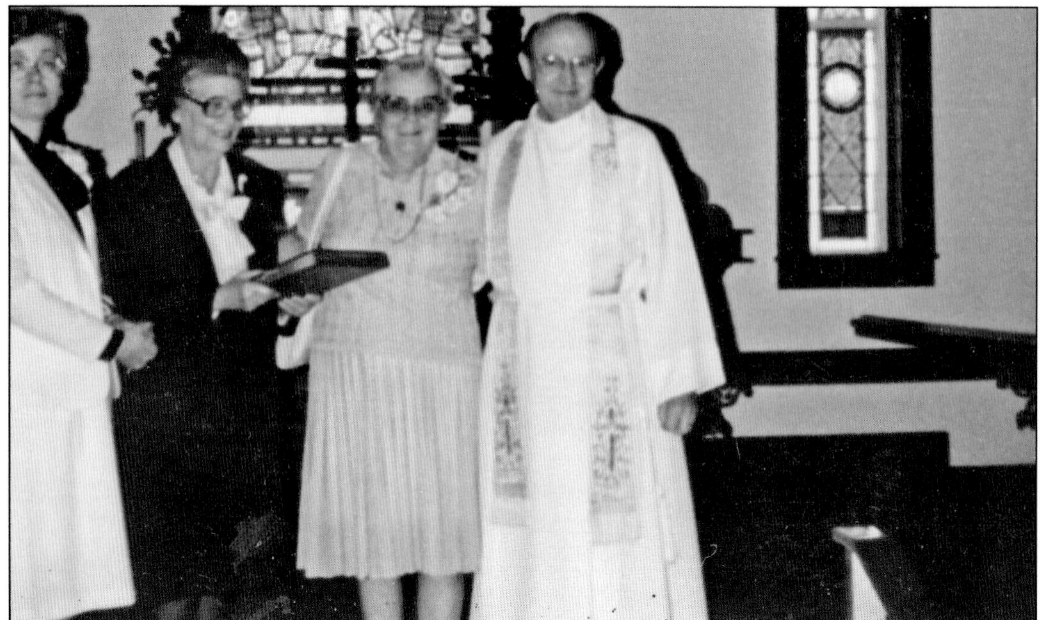

When the Magna Carta toured America in 1984, Luling was one of five Texas cities it visited. It remains one of the priceless documents of world history, providing such legal guarantees as the right of habeas corpus. The Texas cities were Luling, Austin, San Antonio, Houston, and Dallas. Shown here are several individuals who were responsible for getting Luling as one of the "Magna Carta" cities. (Courtesy Wanda Carter.)

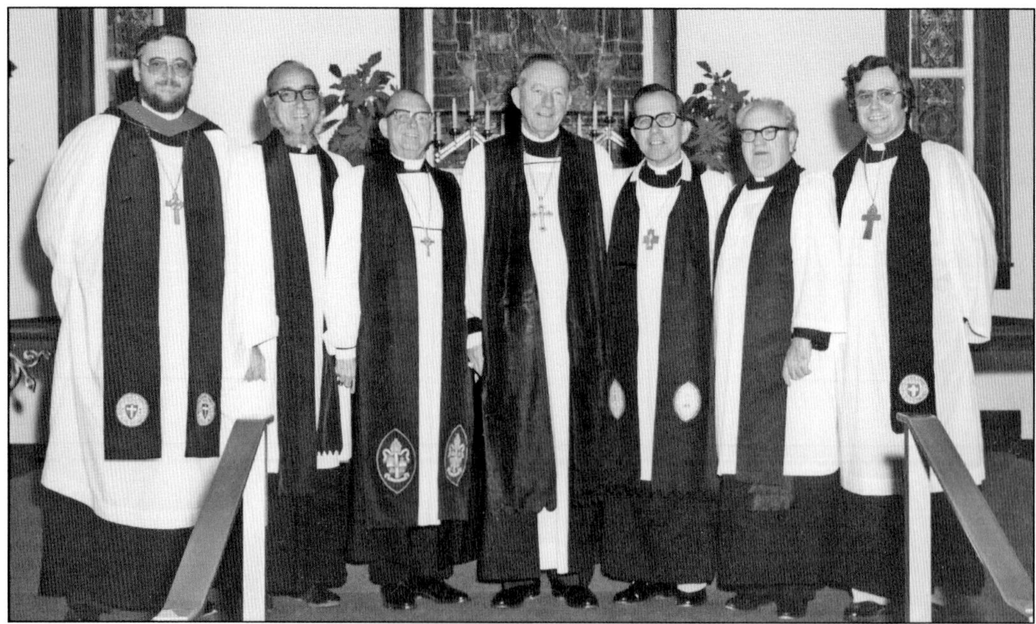

Seven church leaders gathered to participate in the centennial celebration of the Church of the Annunciation on December 20, 1974. From left to right are the Reverend Ray Powell, the Reverend John Thompson, the Right Reverend Bishop Harold C. Gosnell, the Right Reverend R. Earl Dicus, the Reverend (later Bishop) Earl McArthur, the Reverend Harold Nickells, and the Reverend Douglas Thomas. (Courtesy Wanda Carter.)

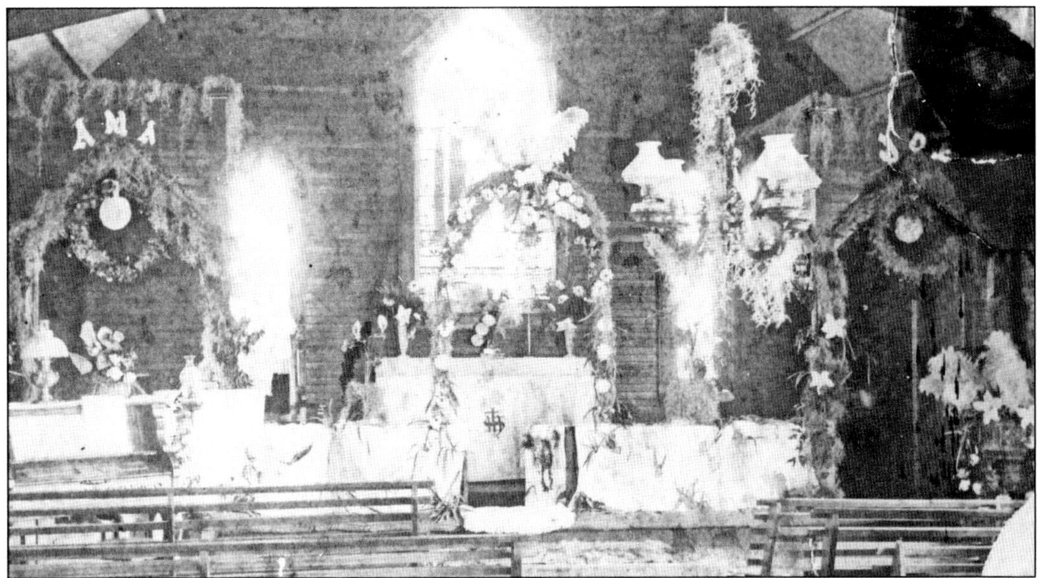

The Episcopal Church of the Annunciation, whose interior is shown here, was Luling's first church building. Rt. Rev. Robert Elliott held his original service in the Missionary District of Western Texas in a railroad car on December 20, 1874. In 1876, construction began, started by Rev. Nelson Ayres with his own hands. The first service was held on April 15, 1877. The church was remodeled in 1938 and 1965. (Courtesy Russel Matthews.)

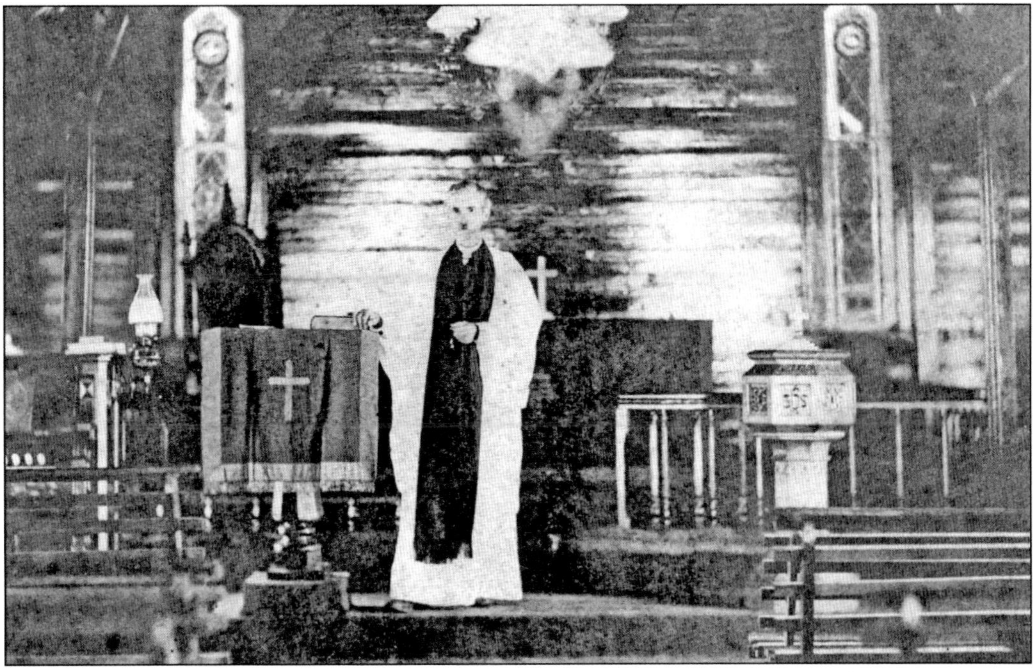

This photograph of the Reverend W. B. Fuller at the altar of the Church of the Annunciation was presented as a birthday gift to Bishop David Gregg. On the reverse of the original is written, "Commemorative of his new birth unto righteousness, into which he was begotten by baptism, whereby he was made a member of Christ' Body, the Church. Luling, April 27th, 1884. From his friend and pastor." (Courtesy Russel Matthews.)

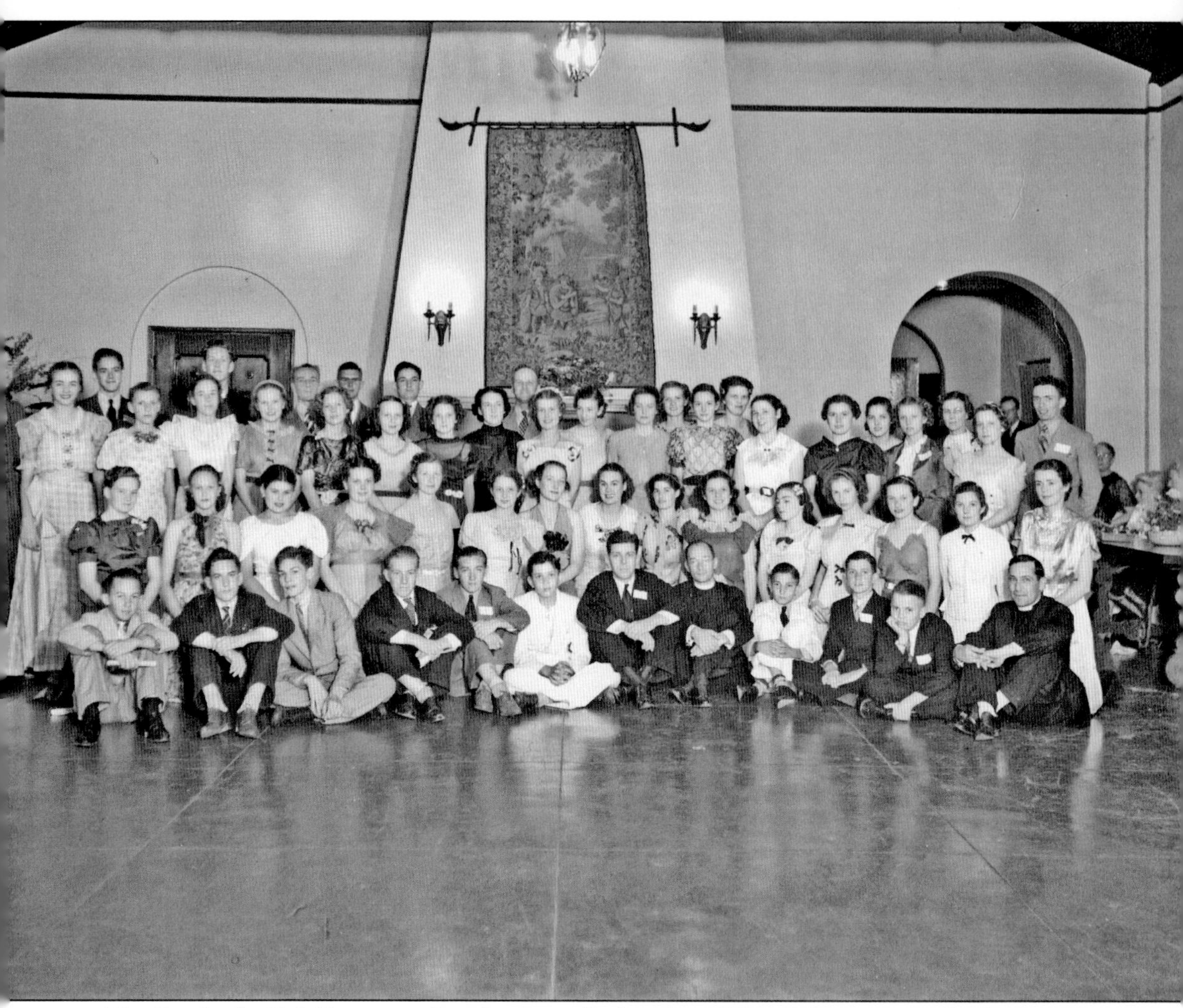

The Southside Club House, a gift to the City of Luling from Edgar B. Davis, proved to be a meeting place for a great variety of groups and organizations. This group shows a Young People's Fellowship gathering, sponsored by the Luling Church of the Annunciation. The fellowship event took place on April 17–18, 1937. Among other rules for the young people was the following: "Please don't go off in cars without permission of a Chaperon." Only a few have been identified. The young lad in the first row center whose reflection is visible on the floor is Robert J. Carter. To the right of him is Rev. W. H. Manning. To his left is Rev. A. R. DeMaris. Then continuing in the first row from left to right are H. B. Henry, Walter Wilcox Cardwell, William Walter Cardwell, and Rev. Herber W. Weller. (Courtesy G&H Society.)

The First United Methodist Church is pictured as it appeared around 1935. Located at 221 South Magnolia Street, the church had as its first pastor, Reverend Jilled. The church laid its foundation in 1876, a physical foundation of cedar blocks, plank walls, a roof, and window openings, which were boarded up at night. Improvements were made through the years; in October 1880, the building was dedicated. The Reverend Buckner Harris was the first resident minister. Early pastors included such notables as Rev. Homer S. Thrall, H. G. Horton, and W. H. H. Biggs. Below is a group photograph of a gathering of Methodist church members appearing on the front steps of the modern Methodist church. (Right courtesy Don and Judy Lightsey; below courtesy G&H Society.)

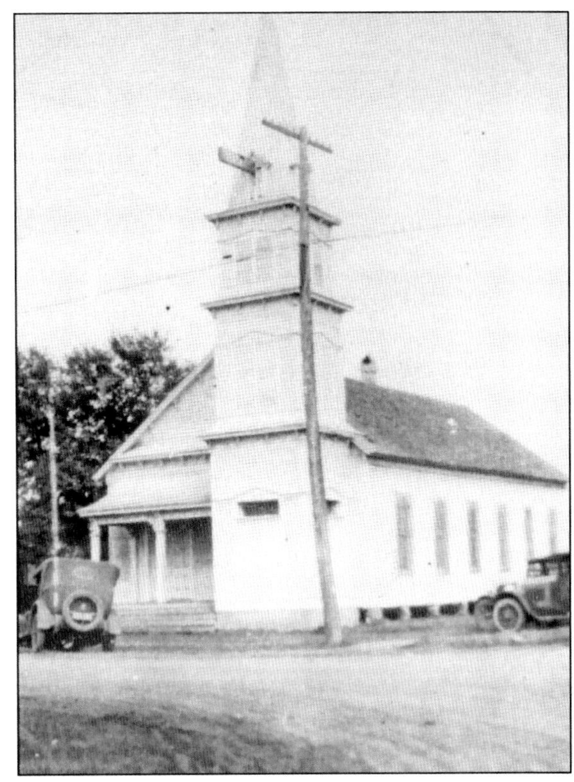

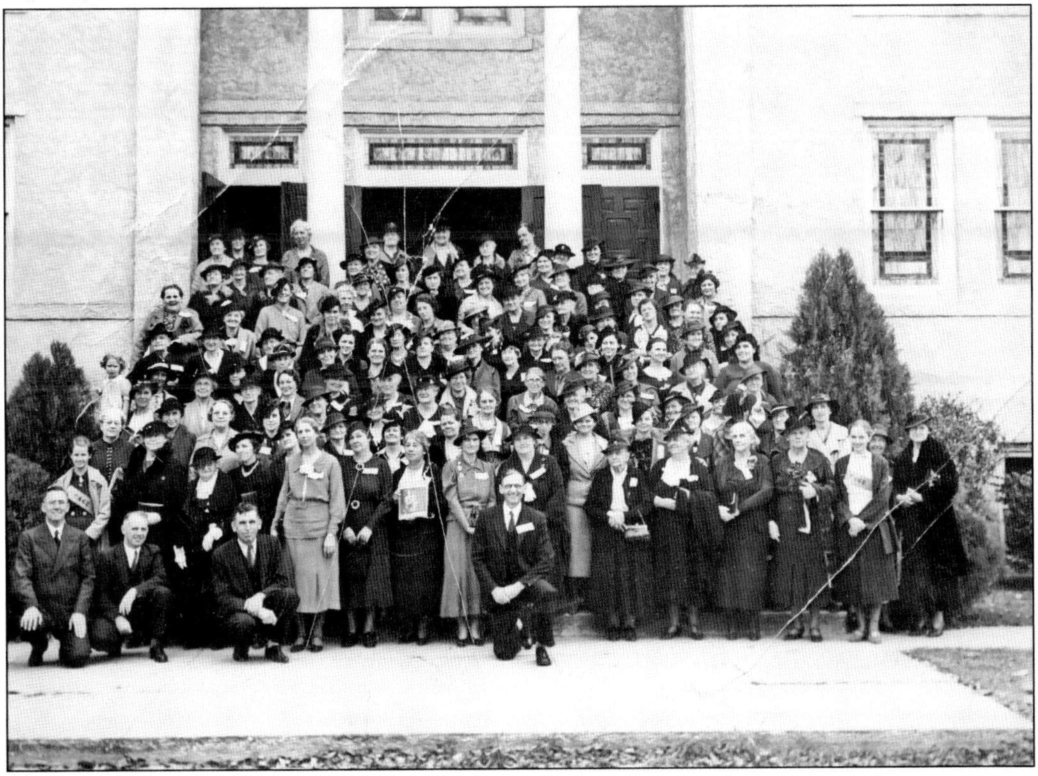

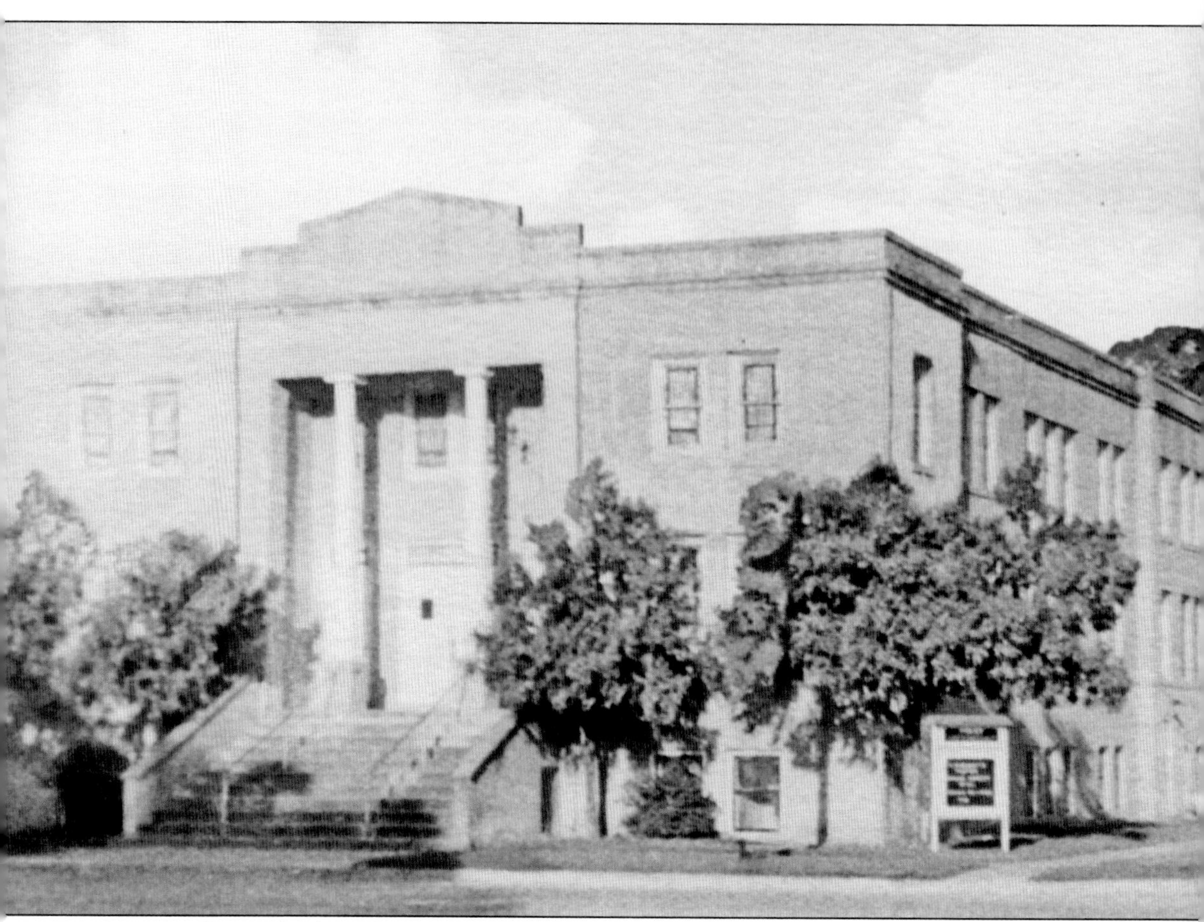

In 1876, the Methodist Church of Luling laid its foundation. All of Luling cooperated in raising funds and donating labor. Through the years, many improvements were made. By 1880, the building was considered ready for dedication. In 1927, a move was made into a second building, a two-story structure with beautiful stained-glass windows. On September 28, 1980, Luling's Methodist Church celebrated its centennial. During the century between 1880 and 1980, there were 45 pastors. (Courtesy G&H Society.)

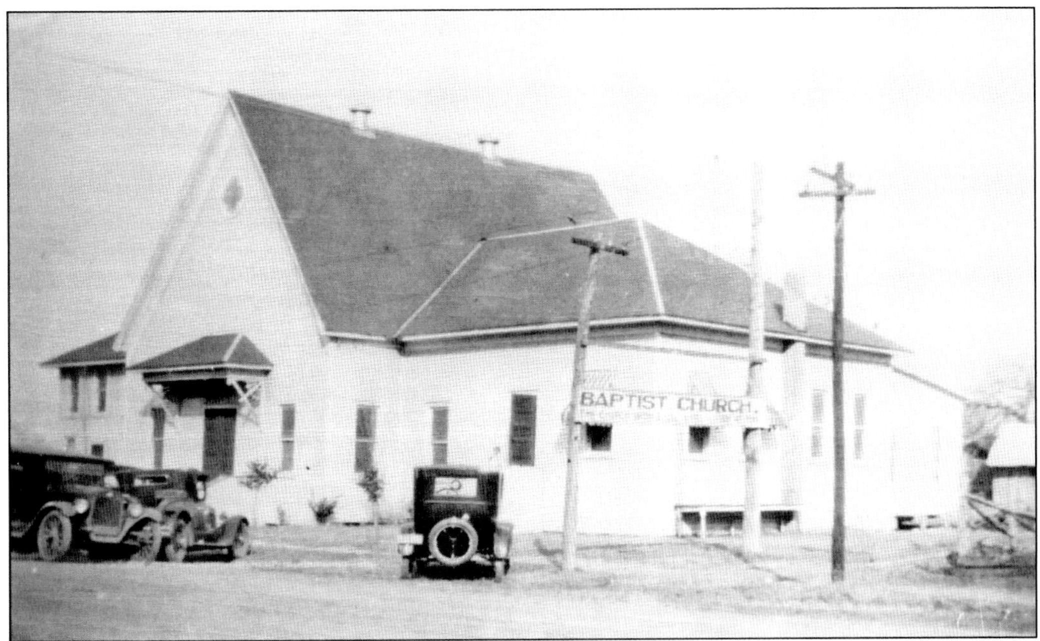

A magnificent view is shown of the First Baptist Church of Luling, then located at 218 North Magnolia Street, then on the very edge of the city limits. This photograph was made around 1926. This is the edifice that burned in April 1939. The church today bears the same address, served by Pastor Jimmy Lammers. (Courtesy Don and Judy Lightsey.)

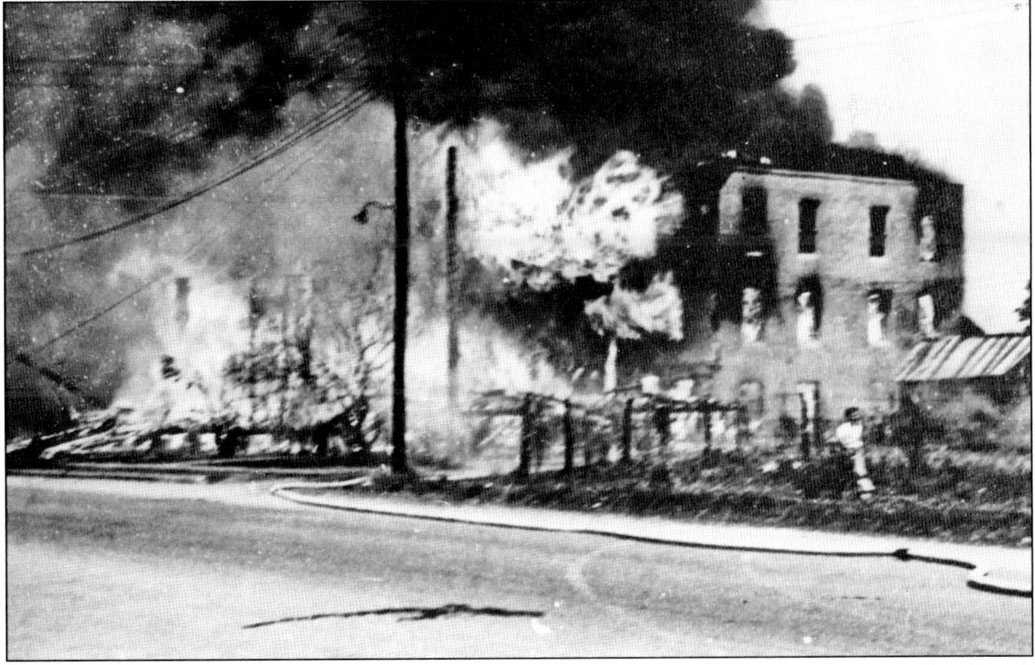

The cornerstone of the First Baptist Church was laid in 1876. On Easter Sunday 1939, the church burned to the ground. Supposedly the fire originated in the gas water heater and destroyed the entire church. It was rebuilt the same year with a large dedication ceremony with Texas governor W. Lee O'Daniel participating. (Courtesy Don and Judy Lightsey.)

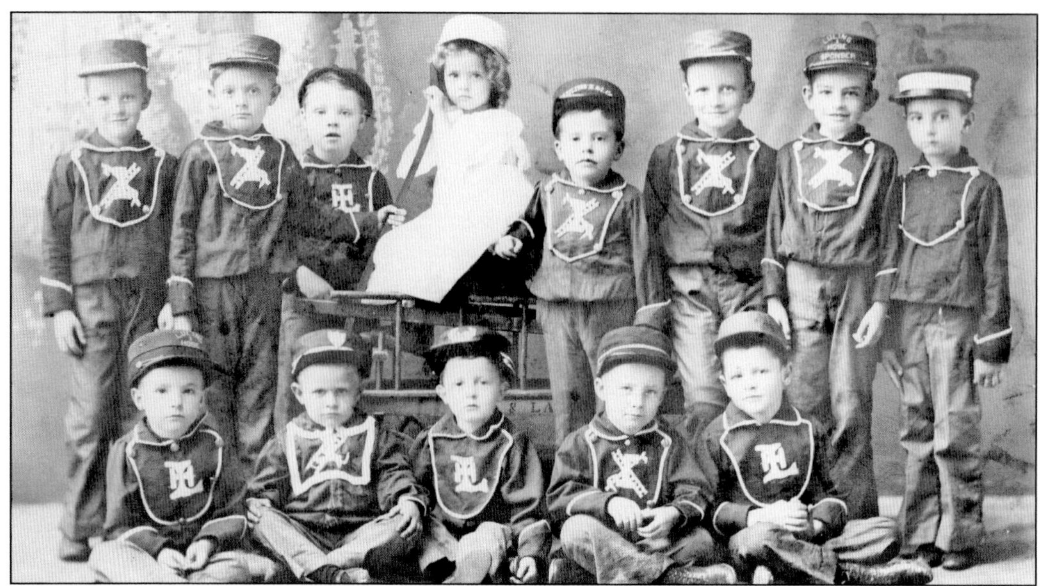

This 1905 photograph proves the importance of learning fire safety at an early age. Luling's (Junior) Hook and Ladder group was composed of Queen Glenn Miles and a dozen fire fighters. From left to right are (seated) Gregg Francis, Lyle Griffin, George Walker, Guy Cocreham, and Clyde Glithers; (standing) Robert Carter, John Bishop, Will Thompson, Miles, Maston Nixon, Sidney Carter, Otis Muenster, and Lester August. (Courtesy G&H Society.)

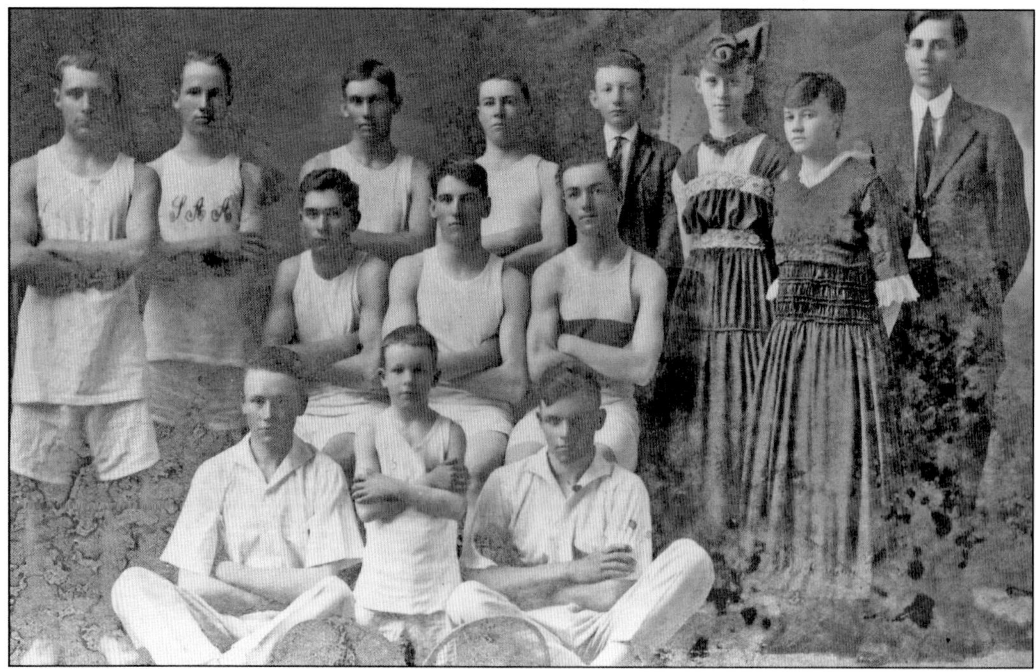

The identification is incomplete but this image shows members of the Luling Athletic Association, perhaps a tennis club, from around 1925. From left to right are (first row) Martin Davenport, Creston Taylor, and George Wilson; (second row) unidentified, Abner Ussery, and ? Topham; (third row) two unidentified, Baker Davis, Bill Stagner, Harold Hyman, Glenn Miles, Alta King, and Philip Schackel. (Courtesy G&H Society.)

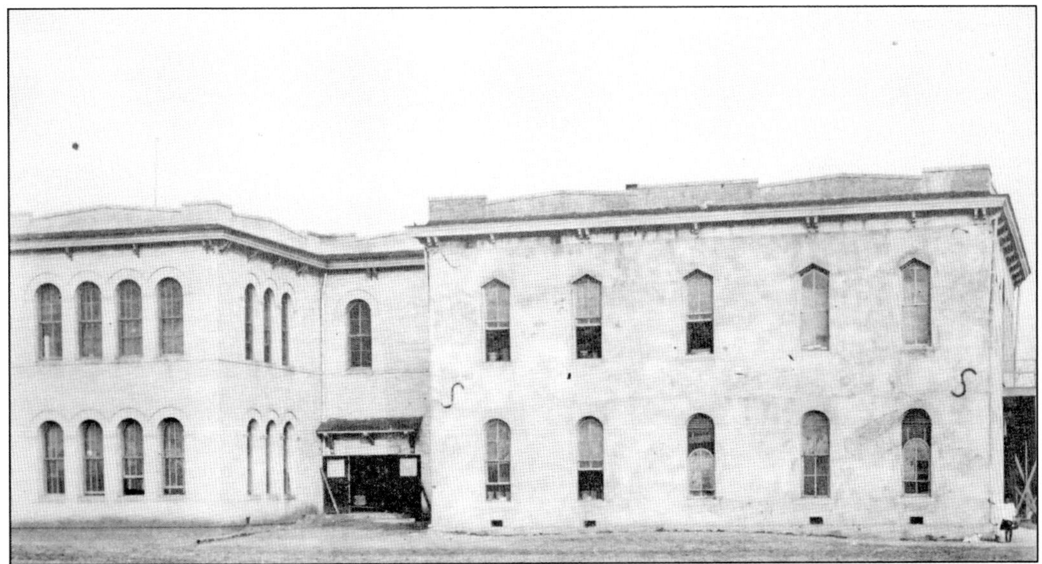

In 1922, this two-story structure was the Luling High School. One of the teachers, John H. Vordenbaum, served as transitional superintendent while the new high school was being constructed. The new facility, a three-story work built adjacent to the old, was finished in 1925. Neither facility remains in use today. (Courtesy Don and Judy Lightsey.)

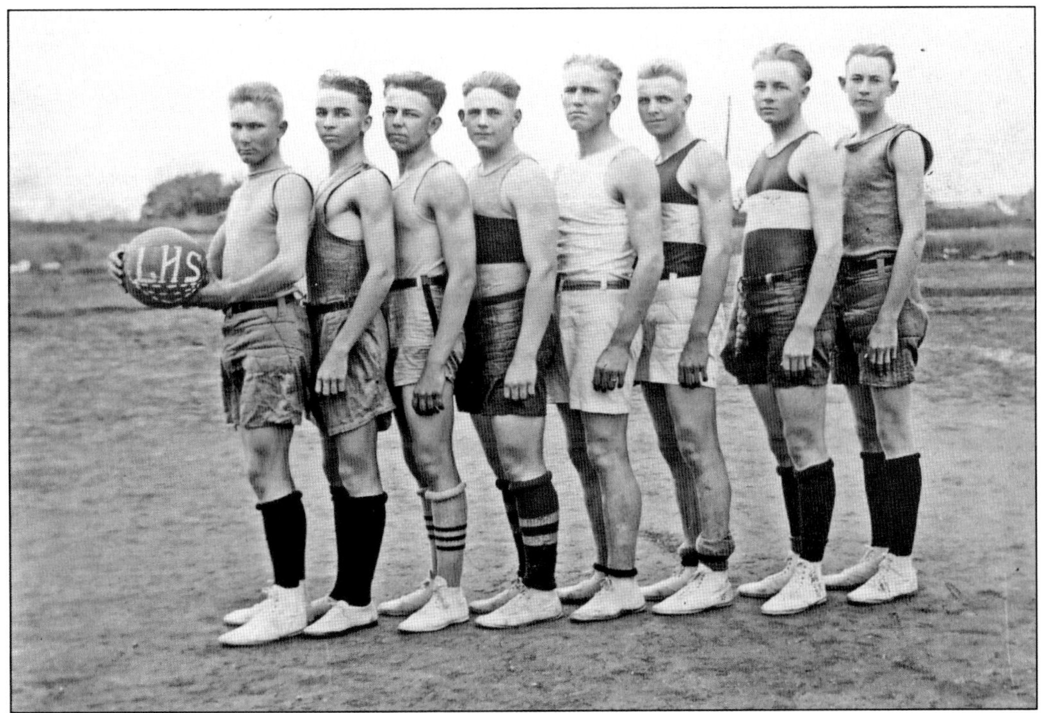

The Luling Eagles high school basketball team in 1922 included, from left to right, Houston Carter, Roscoe Carter, Knox Clark, Raymond Allen, Loys Carter, Edward Wilson, Carlton Smith, and Murray Chipman. Judging from what the boys are wearing for this school picture, school regulations did not require all to wear a uniform. (Courtesy Donald Henslee and the G&H Society.)

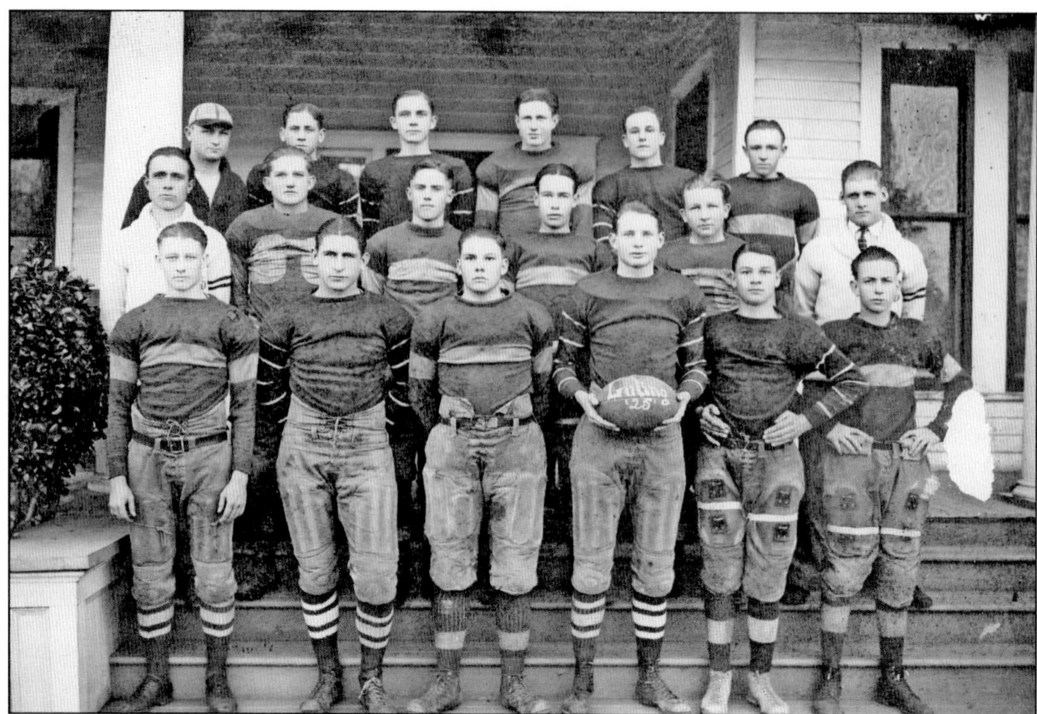

The Luling Eagles football team of 1925 included, from left to right, (first row) Willie Watson, J. T. Cagle, "Polly" Fuglar, John Watkins, Carlton Weaver, and Joe Humphrey; (second row) Ellis Crabb, "Whitey" Benbow, Hugo Allen, Foy Pierce, Miles Robinett, and Clyde McDonald; (third row) coach Albert Leissner, Walter Allen, Ben Acord, Bill Watkins, Creston Taylor, and Max Chipman. (Courtesy G&H Society.)

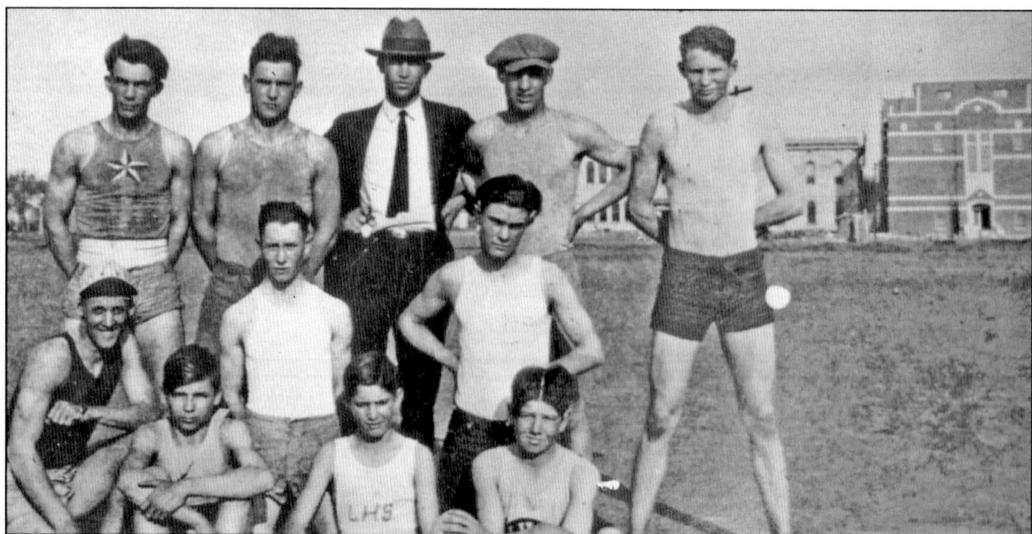

This unusual image is in the Lightsey collection of historic photographs from the early 20th century. This is the 1928 Eagles track team, which appears to consist of both high school and middle school boys. The only one identified in this image is the tall figure standing at right: John Watkins. What is unique is that in the background appear the old and the new high school buildings. (Courtesy Don and Judy Lightsey.)

Texas native John H. Vordenbaum was superintendent of Luling schools during the transition of the old high school to the new in the 1920s. Little else is known of Vordenbaum, but in 1920, he was a teacher in the Luling High School; a decade later, he was a student at the University of Texas, now with a wife, Oma E. The photograph was made in 1927. (Courtesy Don and Judy Lightsey.)

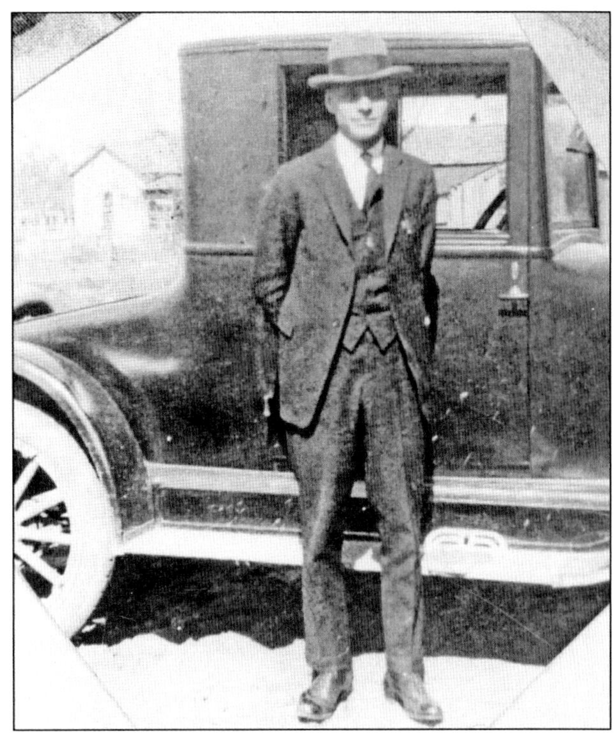

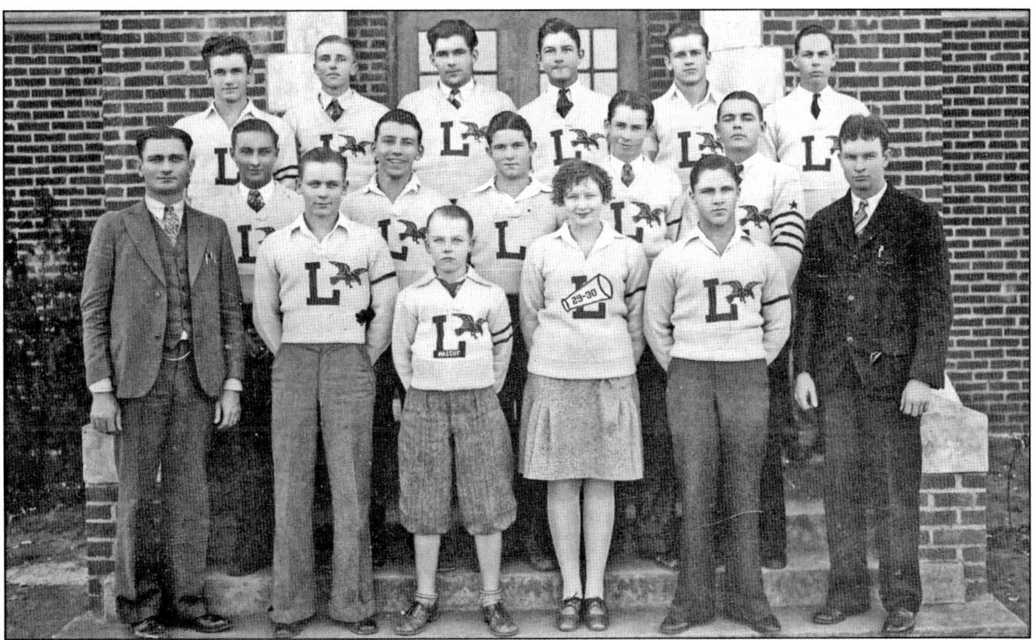

The Luling Eagles are pictured in 1929. The group of well-dressed student-athletes poses proudly on the high school steps. From left to right are (first row) coach C. C. Pluennecke, Meredith Payne, team mascot Joe Wilson, cheerleader Jacqueline Greenwood, Norman Bellard, and coach ? Ferguson; (second row) Carlton Bell, Fancher Hammontree, Houston Haves, Francis Wilson, and Wilson Bell; (third row) Henry Freeman, John Wilson, Leon Seay, Charles Ward, Bob Baker, and Phelan Dunlap. (Courtesy G&H Society.)

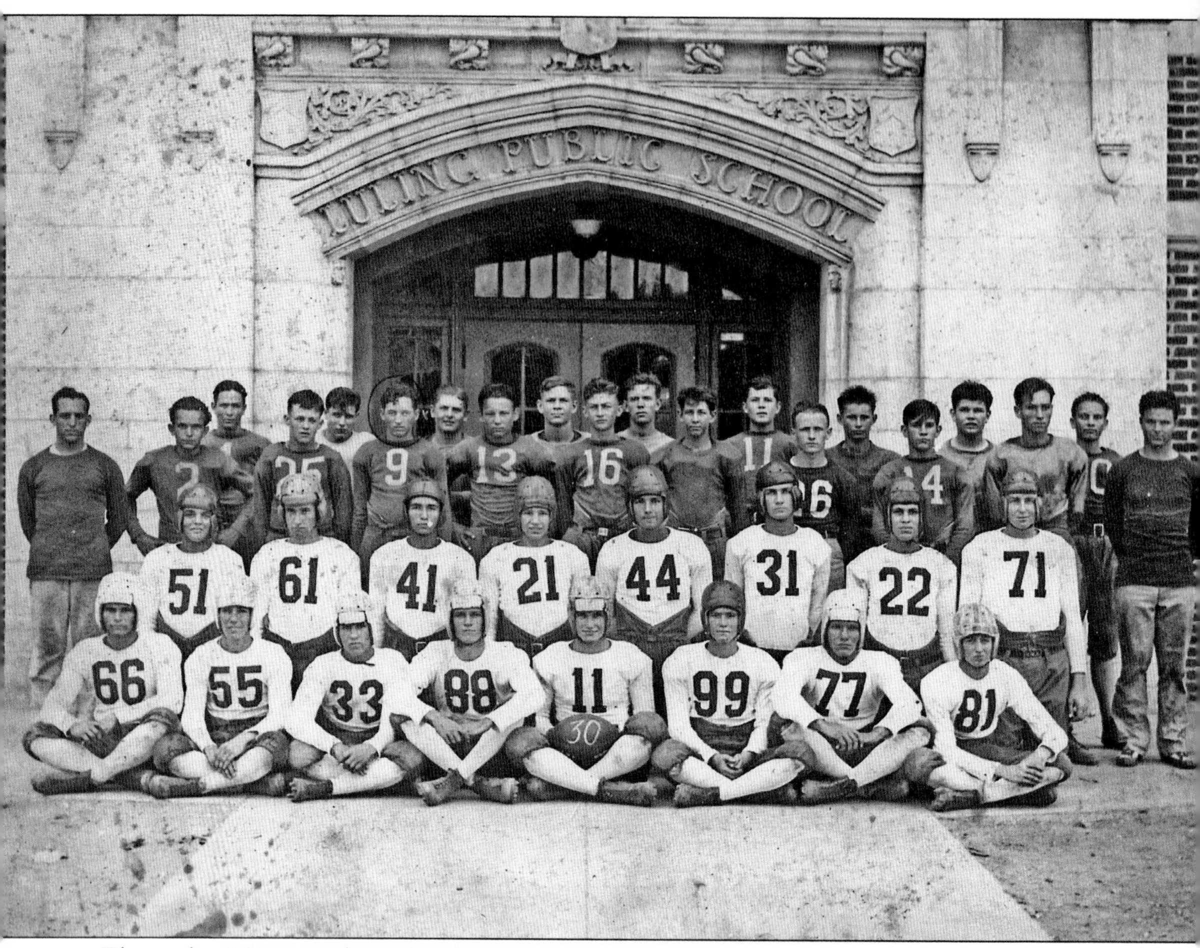

This is the 1930 equivalent of *Friday Night Lights* in Luling. High school football was and remains the most popular sport in Texas and with few exceptions the most popular sport at the college level as well. This group photograph of the Luling Eagles football team was made in 1930 on the front steps of the high school building, since razed. From left to right are (first row) T. J. Poe, James Burris, Bill Holland, Addison Brigham, Ray Smith, Henry Freeman, James Carter, and Fancher Hammontree; (second row) Jack Brown, John Pierce, Waymond Tiller, Jim Davis, Norman Ballard, Walker Davis, Wray White, and Ed Moses; (third row) coach L. J. Smelley, Keith Stuart, Jack Cantrell, unidentified, H. Havis, Tom Brown Webb, Ray Burgin, James Schuhart, Byron White, Richard Callihan, Nixon Holcomb, Joe Brown, Tom Baker, Milton Landry, "Bud" Nobles, James Leslie Dilworth, Ernest Seay, Allison Payne, Claude Walker, and A. A. Browning. The identification is courtesy of James Leslie Dilworth, No. 14 in the third row. (Courtesy Barbara Moses Clark.)

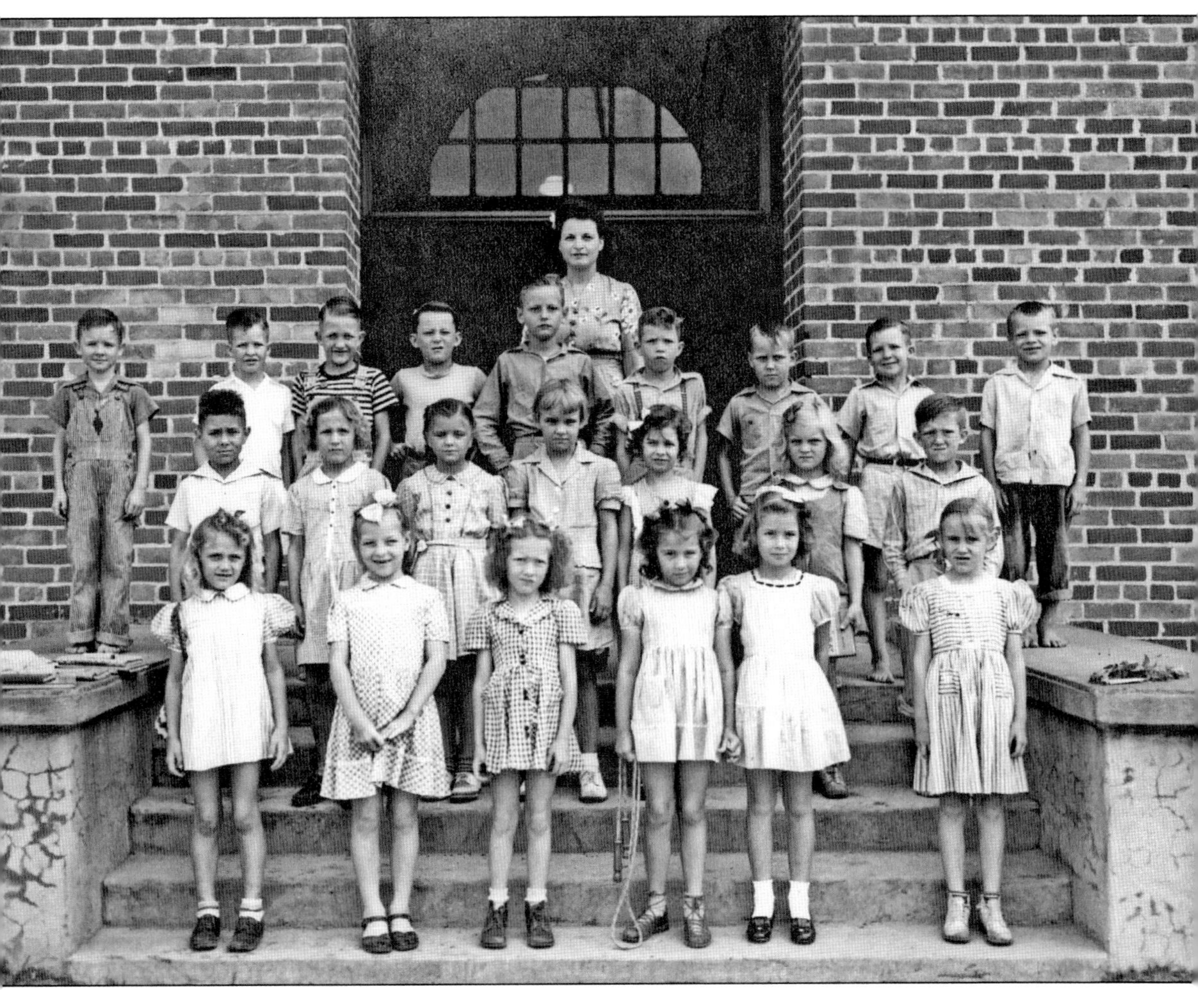

An elementary class of Luling poses in 1943 or 1944, with teacher Cora Clark Withers standing back and center. Note the little girls wear shoes with anklets, while the little boys are barefoot. From left to right are (first row) Anna Joy Wells, Mary E. Goates, Ima Sue Troell, Billie Jeanette Schomerus with the jump rope, Carol Wimberly, and Dal Holcomb; (second row) Harry Whitaker, Shirley Ann Davis, Floylene Davis, Dinah Eklund, Barbara Thomas, Maxine Scroggins, and Lamar Chuter; (third row) Havord Hyde, Jimmie Barnett, James Otis Smith, Robert Biggs, Wilson Alexander, Bob Malser, Wesley Glover, Ray Willis, and Ben Fletcher. Note also to the left on the steps are several books and notebooks tossed rather carelessly, rather than carefully placed. Apparently the idea of having the school picture taken was not a pleasing one, as the smiles are hardly noticeable on these faces. Note also that these children are years away from even thinking of tattoos or body piercing. (Courtesy G&H Society.)

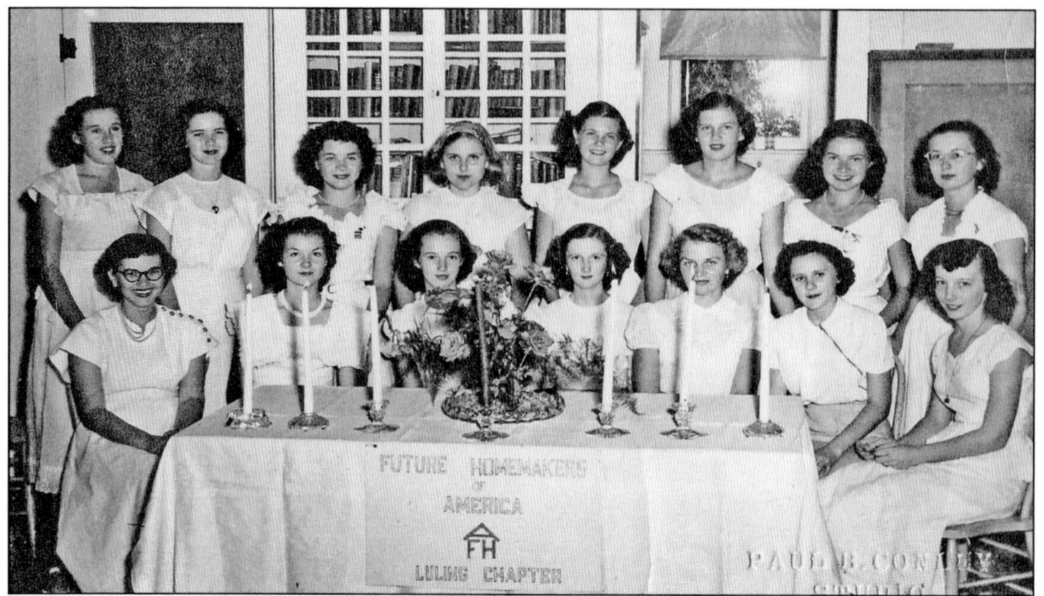

Luling's chapter of the Future Homemakers of America (FHA) in 1948 are, from left to right, (seated) Carmen Kinney, Mary Lou Field, Madeline Watkins, Bobbi Jo King, Mary Agnes Gunkel, Peggy Nelson, and Jo Nell Reed; (standing) Sara Beth Merritt, Janell King, Shirley Crowder, Shirley Elam, Elizabeth Ward, Pat Graham, Sally Nichols, and Sadie Jean Webb. (Courtesy G&H Society.)

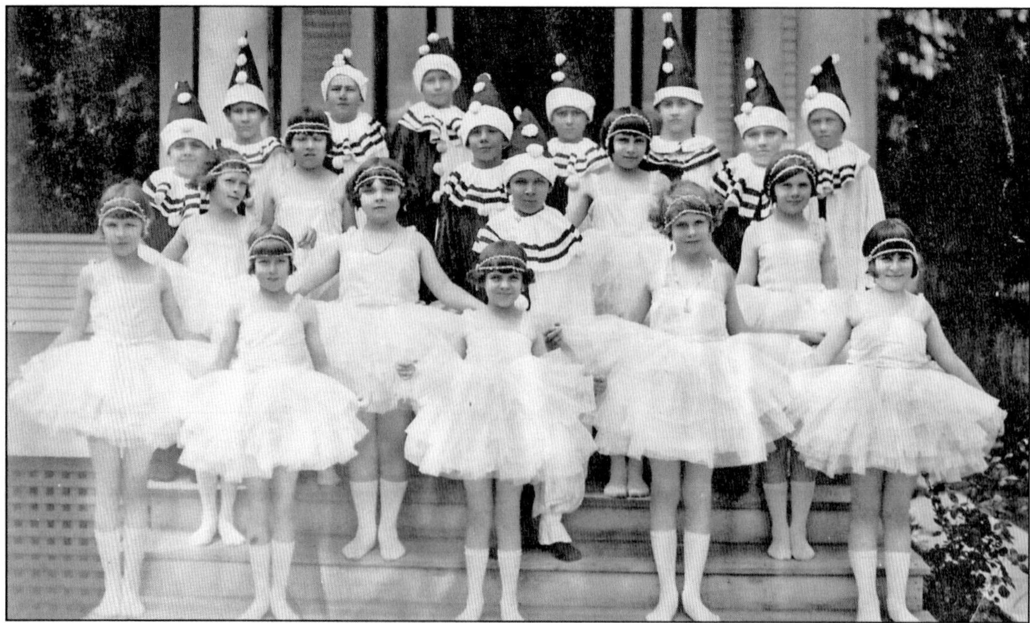

This is an unusual photograph from the early 20th century, but unfortunately the only ballerina identified is the little girl standing at left, Tori Webb. What the photograph does indicate, however, is that there was considerable interest in many of the parents of Luling that their children receive more than just the "bare bones education" that some families were satisfied with. Beyond reading, writing, and arithmetic, there were the "finer things in life" such as art and dancing and music. (Courtesy Jessica Knotts.)

Four

Meriwether Lewis, Zedler, and Creating the Mill

Fritz Zedler, born in Friedberg, Prussia, on March 23, 1840, came early to Texas, arriving at Indianola in 1852 with his family. He was then 12 years old, but he left a legacy still remembered in the history of Luling. The family settled in Yorktown, DeWitt County, and on February 22, 1862, he married Louise Fechner of Yorktown. But Fritz Zedler is remembered best in Luling's history as a mill builder and operator. After a few years in adjacent Gonzales County, he came to Caldwell County in 1880 where he took over a failing mill. He developed a thriving business with a sawmill, gristmill, and cotton gin. During the next two decades, he and his boys built four more mills, three at the same site after disasters destroyed two structures.

The site for the mill was on the San Marcos River. In 1885, he, John Orchard, J. K. Walker, and Bob Innis organized the Luling Water Power Company. Power was generated for sawing timber, grinding corn, and ginning cotton. He ultimately became sole owner. In 1890, water pumping equipment was added, with water mains extending into Luling and a standpipe erected. In 1894, electrical generating equipment was installed, providing Luling with electricity. In 1914, the timber dam on the river was replaced with a concrete structure, which still stands today and is functional.

Fritz and his wife, Louise Fechner Zedler, had 11 children. To prove the claim that hard work enables one to live long, Fritz lived to the age of 93, dying on September 16, 1932. His wife, Louise, lived to the age of 99. The Zedler home was restored in 1972. The home and mill received Texas State Historical Markers in 1974.

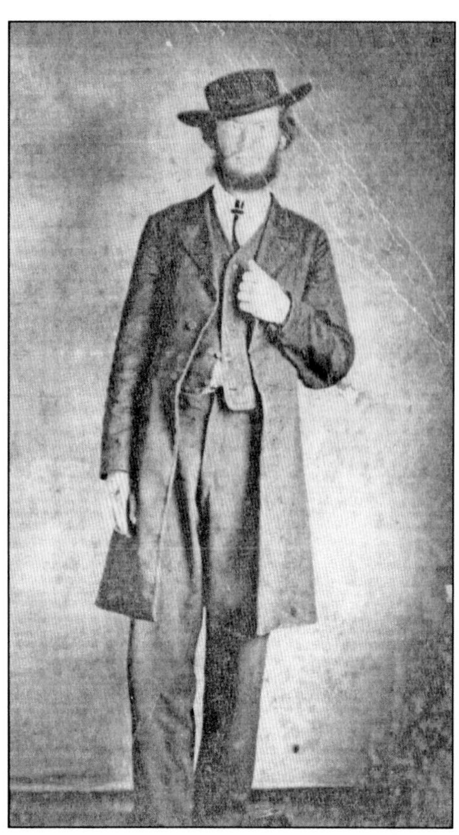

James Meriwether was the builder of the original gin and mill that became Zedler's Mill. James and his brother John W. built the original gin and mill, but after several years of operating at a loss, they surrendered it to J. K. and J. P. Walker. The Walker brothers later sold it to Fritz Zedler, who made a commercial success of the entire operation. (Courtesy Randy Engelke.)

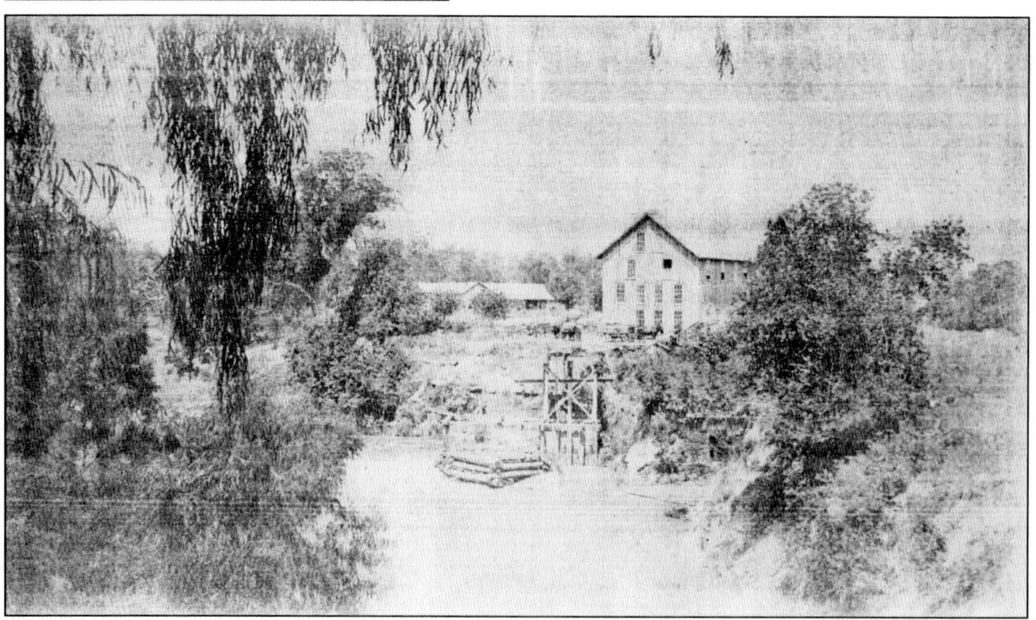

This early view of the Zedler Mill is certainly among the earliest existing photographs of the historic county site. The gin burned to the ground on October 15, 1888, but was rebuilt by Zedler. It was back in operation within seven weeks. For some years, the site was allowed to fall into disrepair but is currently being restored. (Courtesy Randy Engelke.)

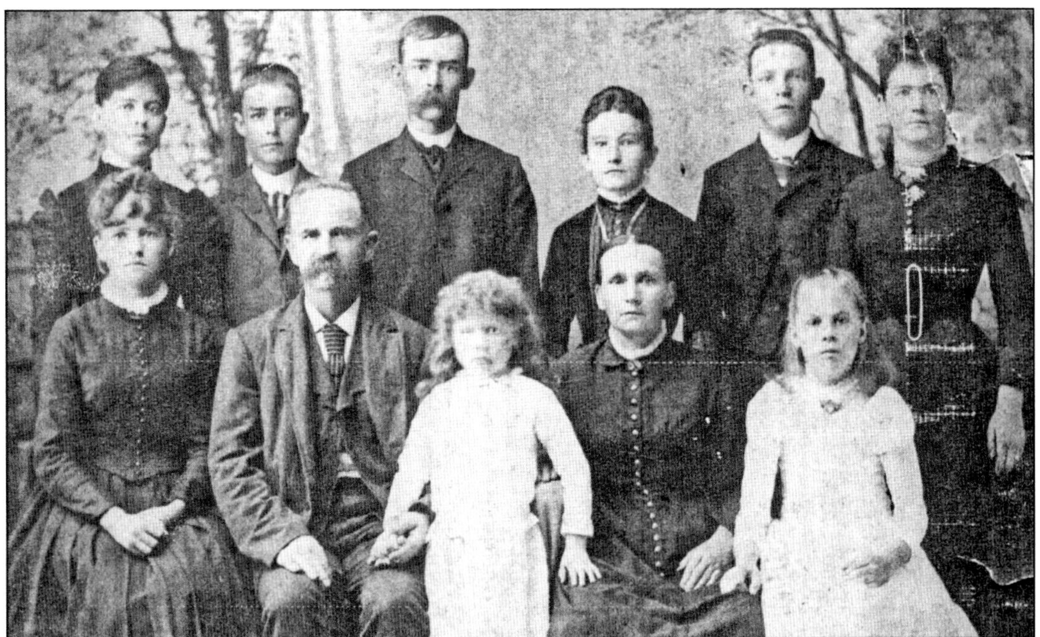

The Fritz Zedler family is pictured around the dawn of the 19th century. From left to right are (first row) Louise Zedler Gips, Fritz Zedler, Francis Zedler, Louise Zedler, and Pauline Zedler Eckhart; (second row) Jane Zedler Bunde, Carl Zedler, Berthold Zedler, Maria Zedler, Herman Zedler, and Lena Zedler Bohne. The photographer is unknown. (Courtesy Randy Engelke.)

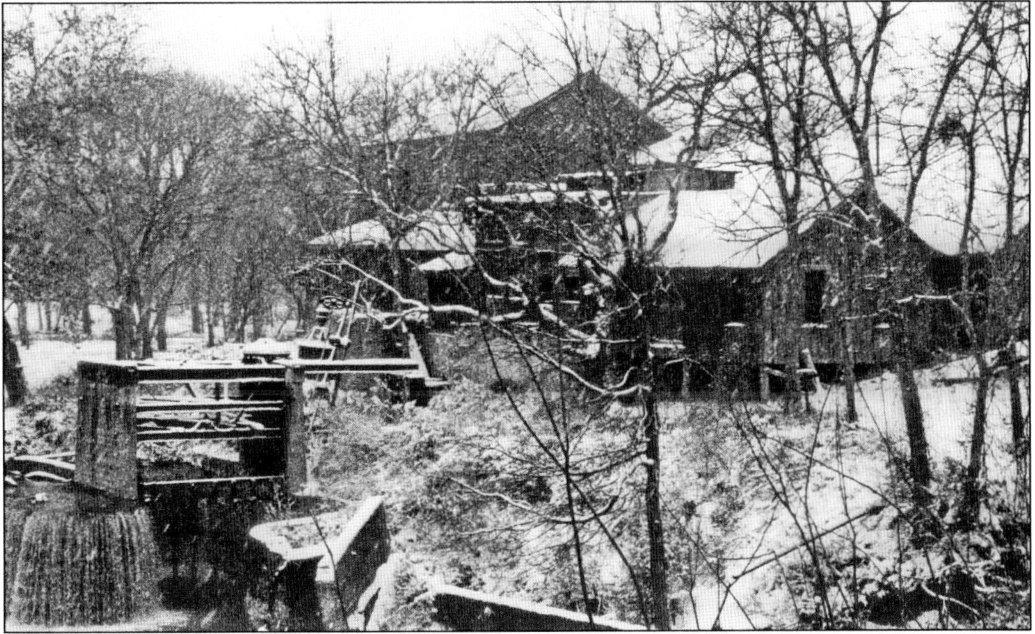

This is a rare view of Zedler's Mill in winter. Although rare, snow does fall occasionally and accumulate in Luling, as evidenced by this photograph showing a light snow on the ground and rooftops. Note the temperature has not yet reached freezing, as the San Marcos River still flows in spite of the cold. The river marks the southern boundary between Gonzales and Caldwell Counties. (Courtesy Randy Engelke.)

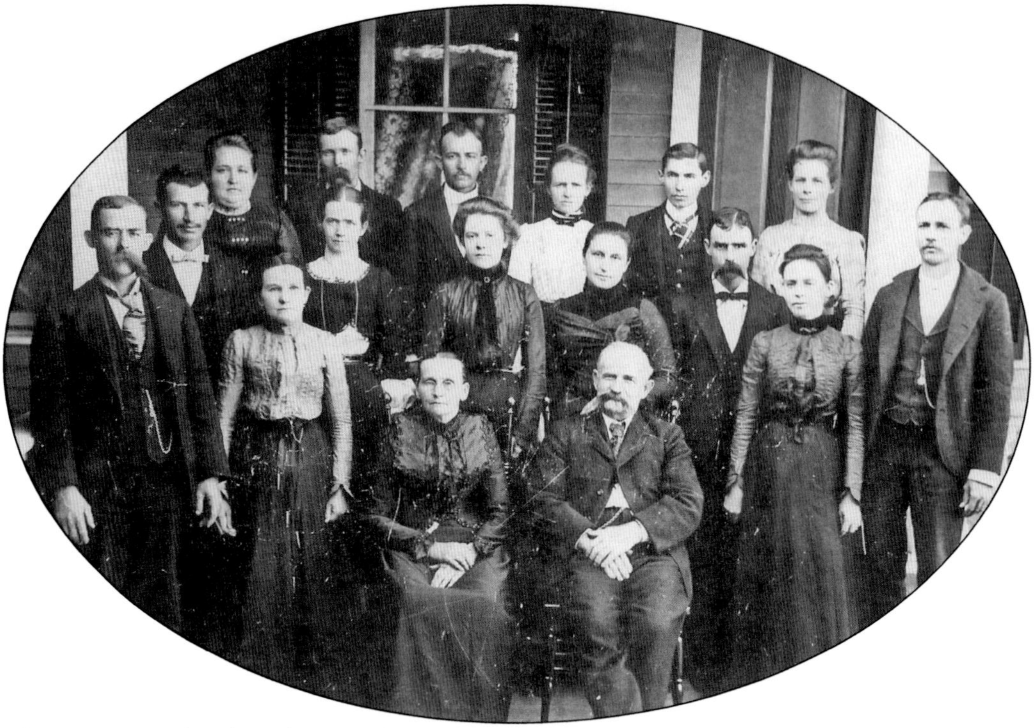

The Fritz Zedler family is shown in later years. Although undated, the image was probably made during the 1920s. From left to right are (first row) Louise and Fritz Zedler; (second row) Berthold and Marie Zedler and Jane and Caesar Bunde; (third row) Fritz and Helen Bohne, Francis Zedler, and Lottie and Charles Zedler; (fourth row) Emma and Herman Zedler, Charles and Louise Gips, and Carl and Pauline Eckhardt. (Courtesy Randy Engelke.)

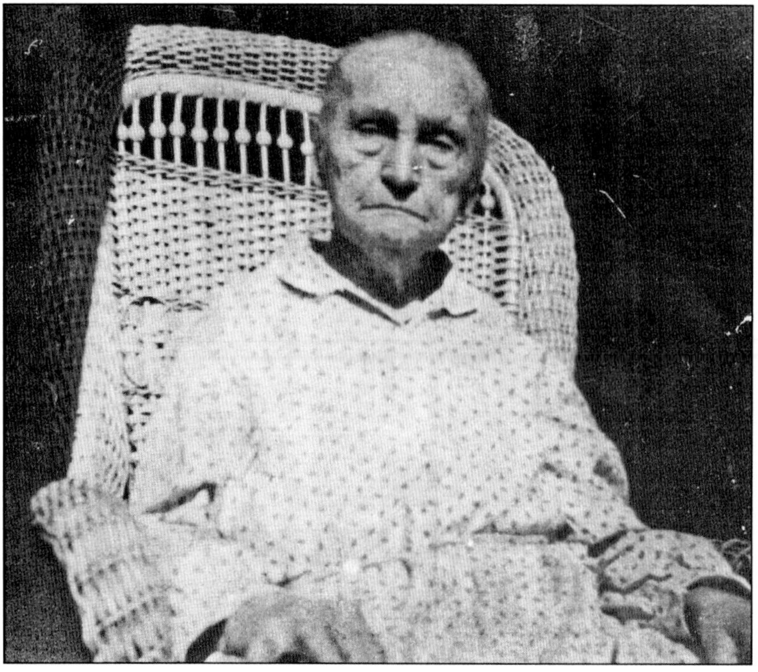

She was born Louise Fechner on January 4, 1840, in Schweinetz, Saxony, and married Frederick Christian "Fritz" Zedler on February 22, 1863, in Yorktown, DeWitt County, Texas. The couple gave 11 children to the world, all but three living to adulthood. The others, with the ages of their passing, were Berthold (88), Helen (64), Jane (101), Louise II (97), Herman (81), Carl (91), Pauline (82), and Francis (101). (Courtesy Randy Engelke.)

Charlotte Bohne Zedler, wife of Charles Zedler, is pictured with her sons, Charles Zedler at left (1903–1979) and Paul Zedler (1905–1996). Paul graduated from the University of Texas. He married Empress Young on June 5, 1928. After marriage, he and Empress moved to Luling, where they spent the remainder of their lives. The photograph is undated but appears to be from around 1920. (Courtesy Randy Engelke.)

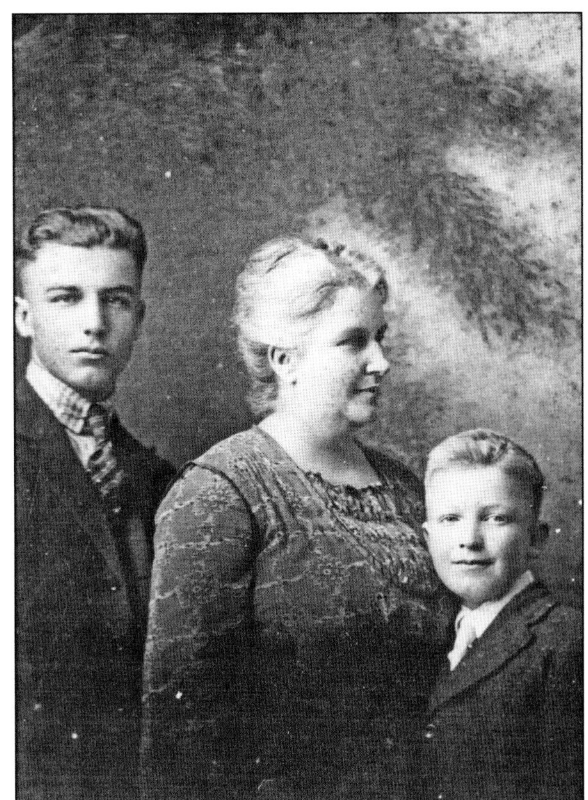

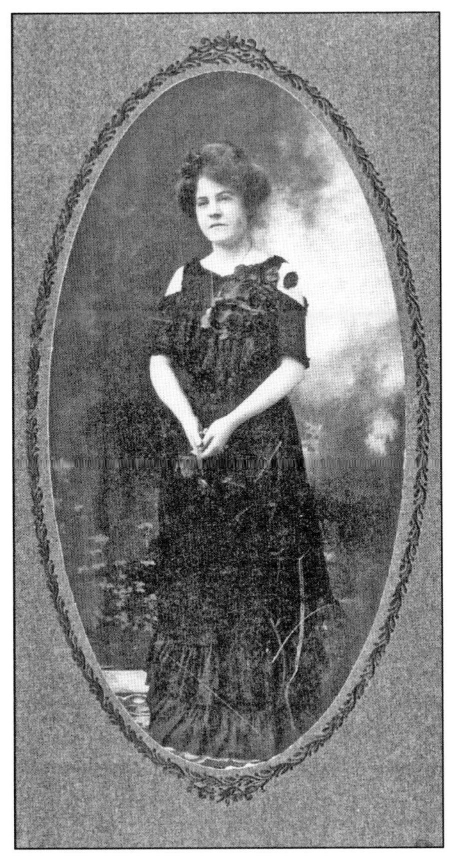

On February 3, 1984, Francis, here as a young woman, celebrated her birthday, number 101! She was then a resident of the Cartwheel Nursing Home. Today it is the Oakcreek Nursing Home, located on North Magnolia Street. (Courtesy Randy Engelke.)

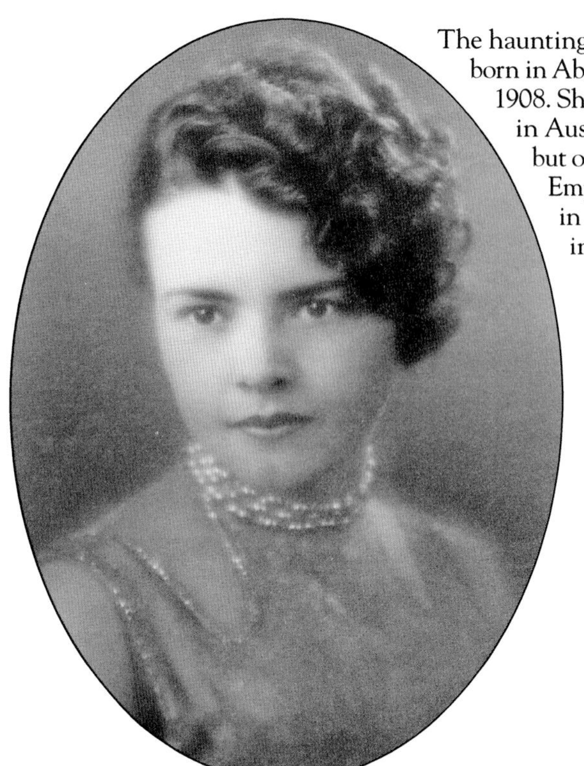

The hauntingly beautiful Empress Arlington Young was born in Abilene, Taylor County, Texas, on November 9, 1908. She married Paul Louis Zedler on June 5, 1928, in Austin, Travis County, Texas. The couple had but one child, a daughter whom they named Gay Empress Zedler. She was born March 29, 1931, in Luling, but she died young on July 21, 1966, in Luling. (Courtesy Randy Engelke.)

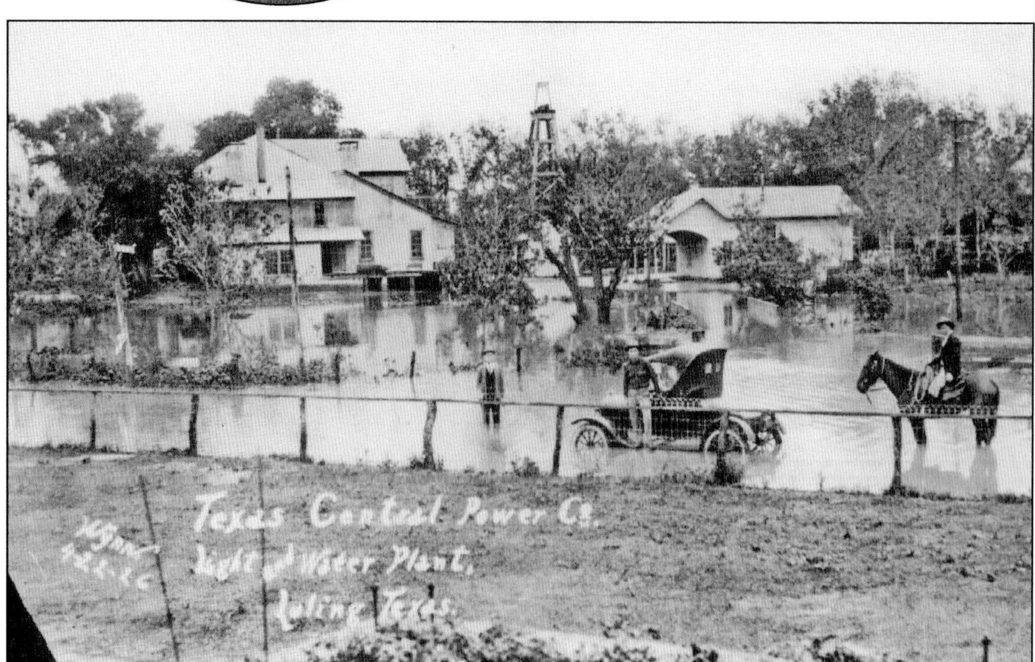

The Zedler Mill, as the Texas Power Company light and water plant, is in this image taken by photographer Wynn on April 22, 1926. The only individual identified in this unusual photograph is the young man standing center, Ernest Wilson. This photograph was obviously made during or after a heavy raining spell, unusual in Caldwell County. (Courtesy Randy Engelke.)

Five

Homes, Parks, and Hospitals

Many old and grand homes once decorated the Luling landscape but no longer exist. A few huge mansion-like homes still stand, such as the historic Francis-Ainsworth house. A number of early homes were not much more than a few boards nailed together to protect the inhabitants from the elements. Some elegant homes were dismantled in the wake of progress, such as the T. C. Greenwood home on the 200 block of North Magnolia Street, which was dismantled in the spring of 1968. From the pages of the Luling *Newsboy and Signal*, one learns that it was on land originally owned by T. W. Pierce. Frank Cross, then city secretary, bought the lot and constructed the residence, and "all inside woodwork and decorations were made by him." He lived in it a short while until selling it to G. C. and W. P. Walker in 1900. Then it was occupied by R. Maston Nixon, who sold it to T. C. Greenwood Sr. in 1904. The house remained in the Greenwood family for 63 years, when it was sold to J. M. Rabon in 1968. Another important structure still standing is the Fritz Zedler home, built in 1900 from his own plans. The original house had 10 rooms and four porches. Fritz's daughter Francis Zedler sold the house; it was used as rental property for a while until purchased in 1970 by Corine and Wesley Parker, who restored it. It was converted to the Zedler House Inn in 1983. It became a recorded Texas Historical Landmark in 1974. Today Luling residents can enjoy several parks, especially Longer Park with its play areas and Patton Park with its walking path. On the edge of Luling along the banks of the San Marcos River is South Side, which provides a beautiful golf course for a budding Tiger Woods or just a place to get away from the stress of everyday living.

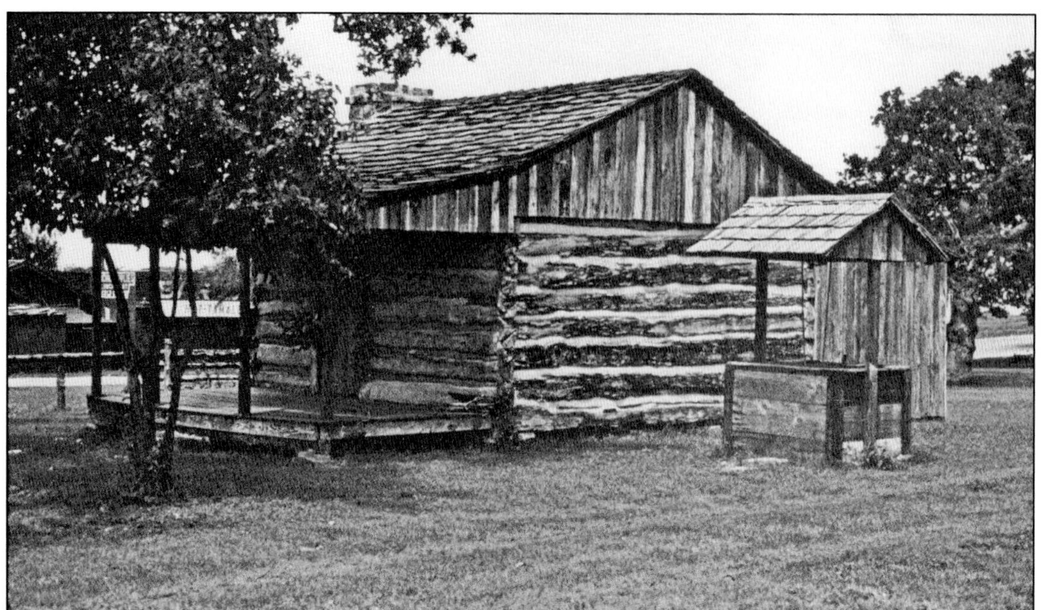

At the Blanche Square Park is preserved the shotgun house, in which all three doors are in line, so the pioneer, if necessary, could shoot from the back of the house through to the front door. This early cabin was restored by the Luling Garden Club in 1972. There are no windows; cooking was done in the fireplace. In the 1890s, Dr. T. B. Coopwood lived here. (Courtesy G&H Society.)

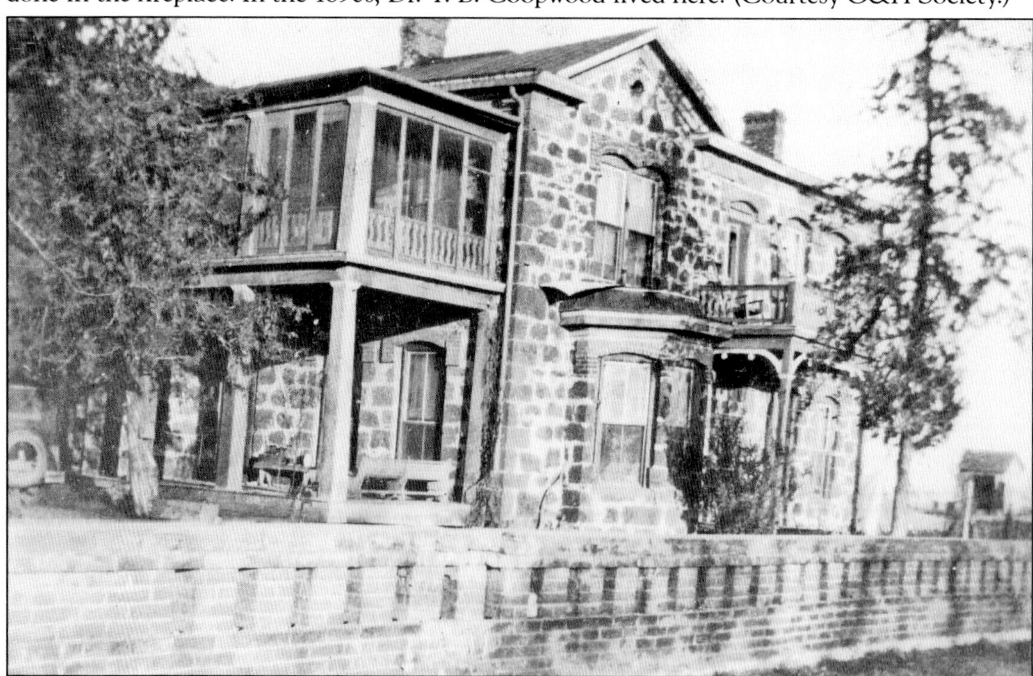

The historic Josey House was built by Joseph Josey, credited with building the first house in Luling. He was later an operator of a gin and cotton mill. The Joseys had a son, who was named Noah, born on several bales of cotton anchored together during a rise in the San Marcos River. The house today stands with some modifications at the same location at 115 West Davis Street. (Courtesy G&H Society.)

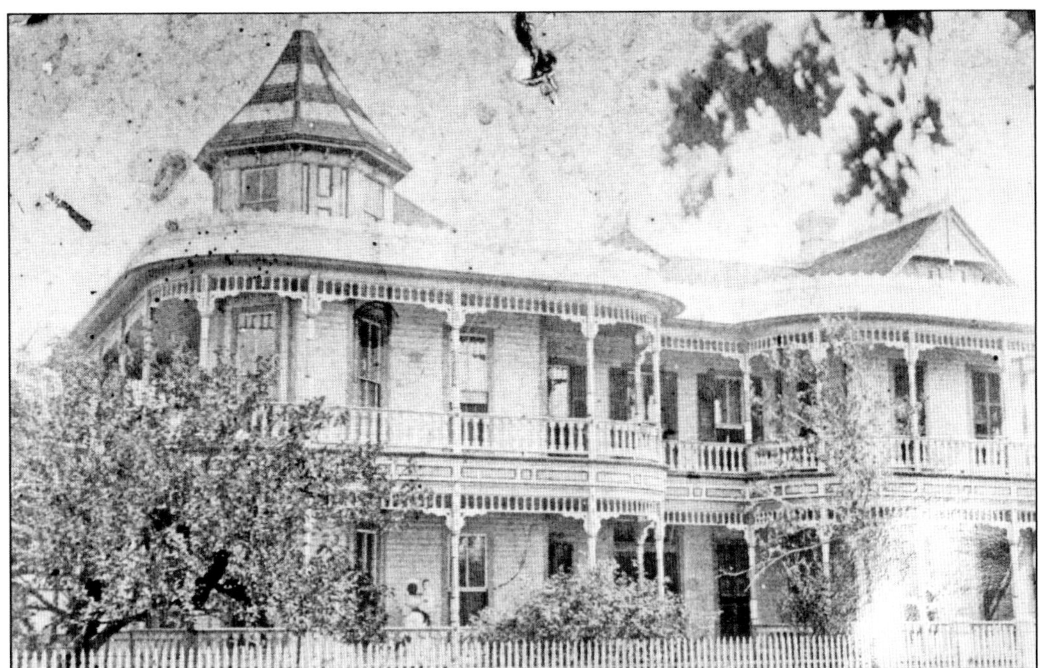

These images show the William W. Gregg home, one of the most impressive of Caldwell County's homes. It is built with the Victorian style of architecture: heavily ornamented, ornate, and large. The W. W. Gregg home was at 204 South Pecan Street, located across the street from where the J. B. Nickells library is now located. The partially visible handwritten inscription on the bottom reads in full, "Home Sweet Home—Where we spend the good old summer time of 1968." Gregg was one of Luling's first automobile dealers. When World War I broke out, he helped organize Company H, 141st Infantry. During the war, he was commanding officer of Company B, 111th Supply Train, and served in France throughout the war. (Both courtesy Don and Judy Lightsey.)

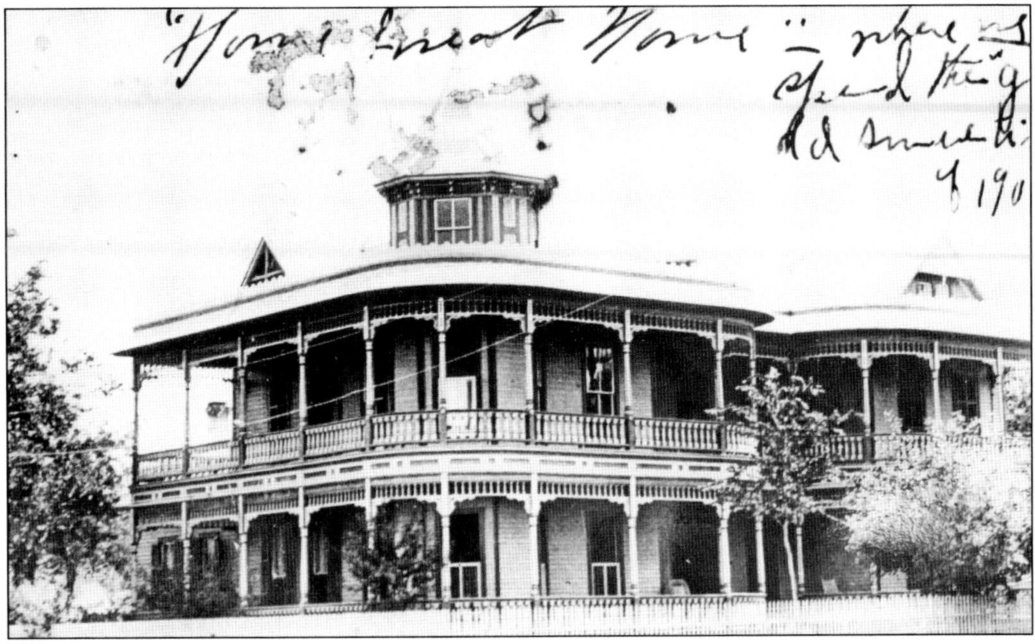

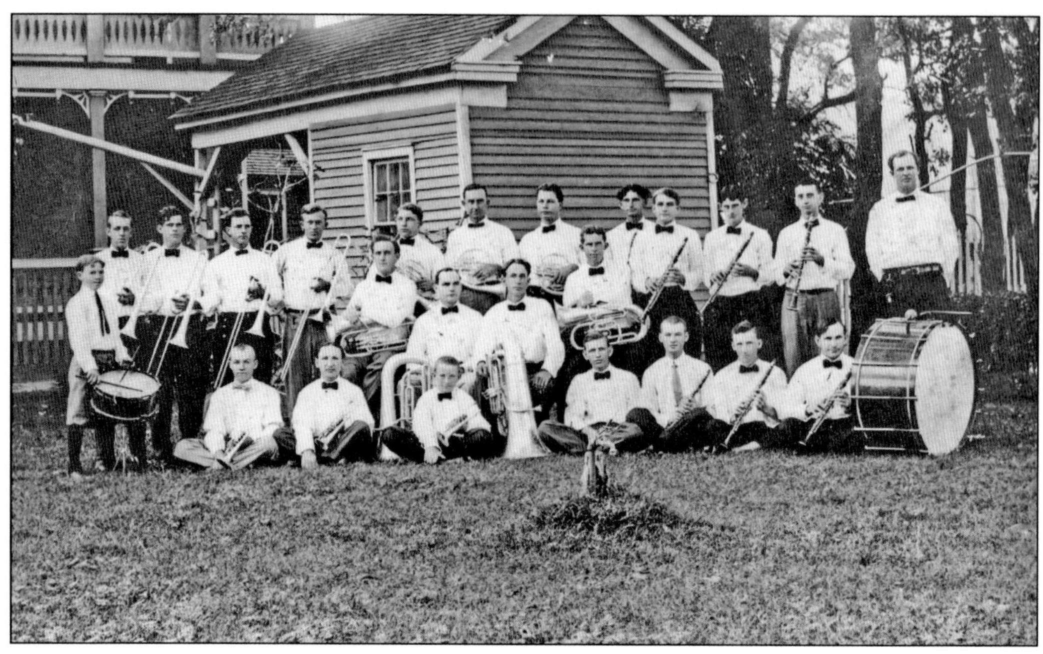

Little is known of the above group of Luling musicians, a men's only band, but the original photograph is dated 1909 and labeled as the "Luling Brass Band." The group is seated on the side lawn of the D. C. Muenster home. From left to right are (first row) Tommy Wilson, Sam Jacobs, Guy Cocreham, Hal Bridges, Linden Huff, Lewis Cocreham, and Isadore Mazur; (second row) Roland Cocreham, Will Ryan, Tom Conley, and Gene Cocreham; (third row) Will Stagner (with snare drum), Will Gregg, Sam Walcowich, Henry Beversdorff, Matt Day, Percy Walker, Adam Heise, August Beversdorff, Rube Walcowich, Otis Muenster, I. Walcowich, Lester August, and Vic French. Below is a contemporary photograph of the Muenster home. (Both courtesy G&H Society.)

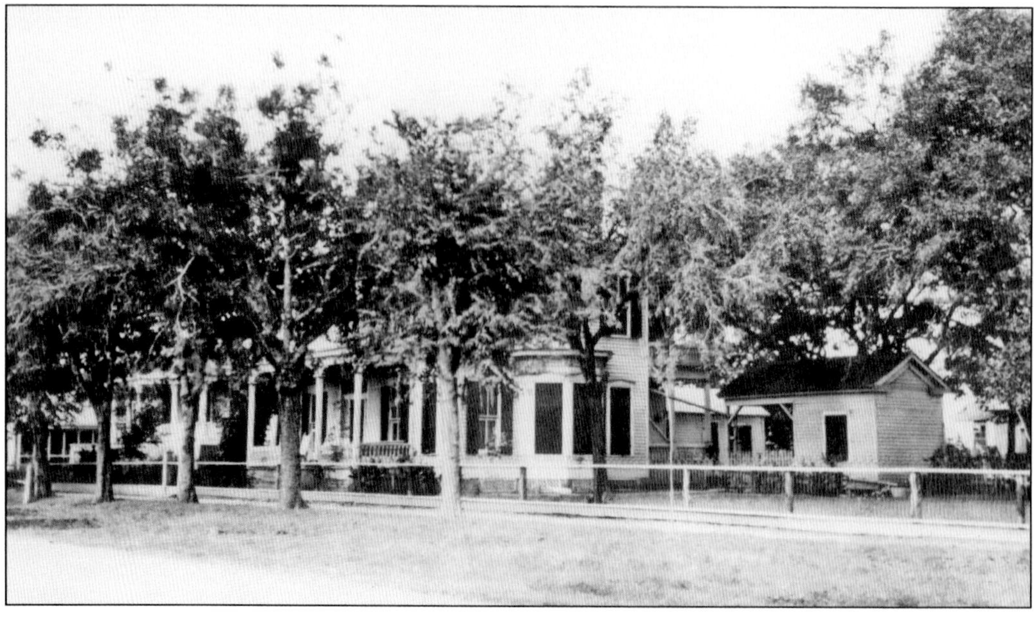

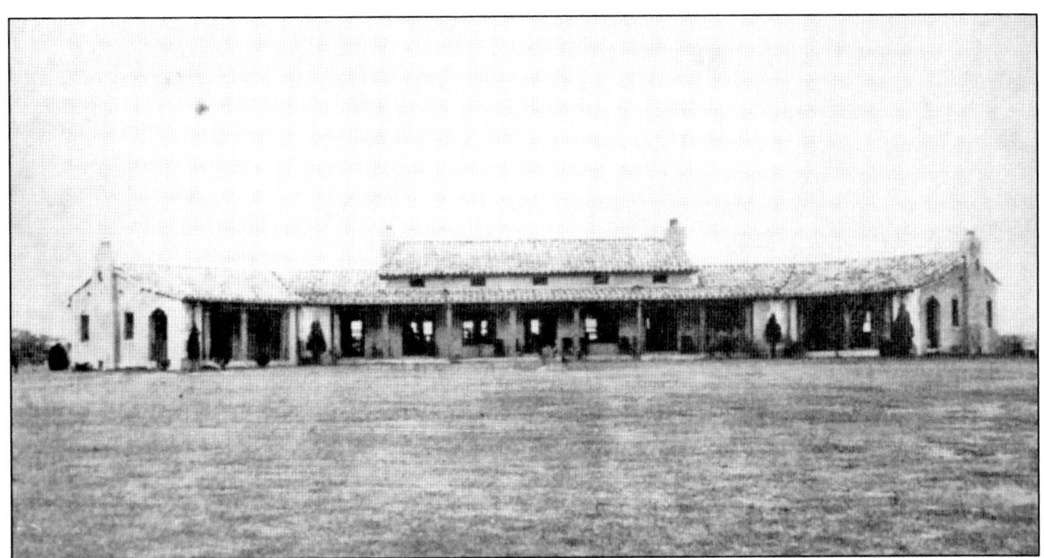

These two views of the South Side Club House, as it is most commonly known, show its usual appearance as well as how it appears after a rare winter snow. The "Southside" Park, located at 1035 South Magnolia Street, was a gift of Edgar B. Davis and is officially known today as the Edgar B. Davis Southside Park and Clubhouse. It was endowed in 1926. It is on the north bank of the San Marcos River and features an impressive golf course for local residents. On the north side of Luling, at 300 Trinity Street, is located the Edgar B. Davis North Side Park and Clubhouse, which also attracts residents for relaxation and play. Summer games include baseball and softball team competition. The North Side Park also includes a walking trail and playground equipment for younger children. (Both courtesy G&H Society.)

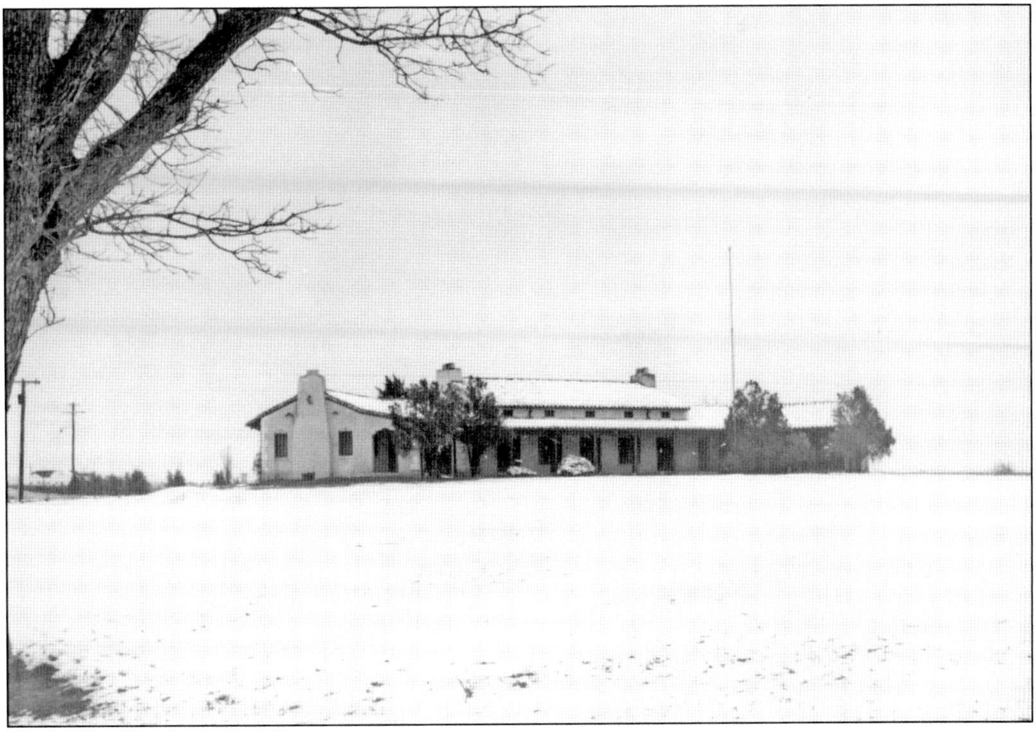

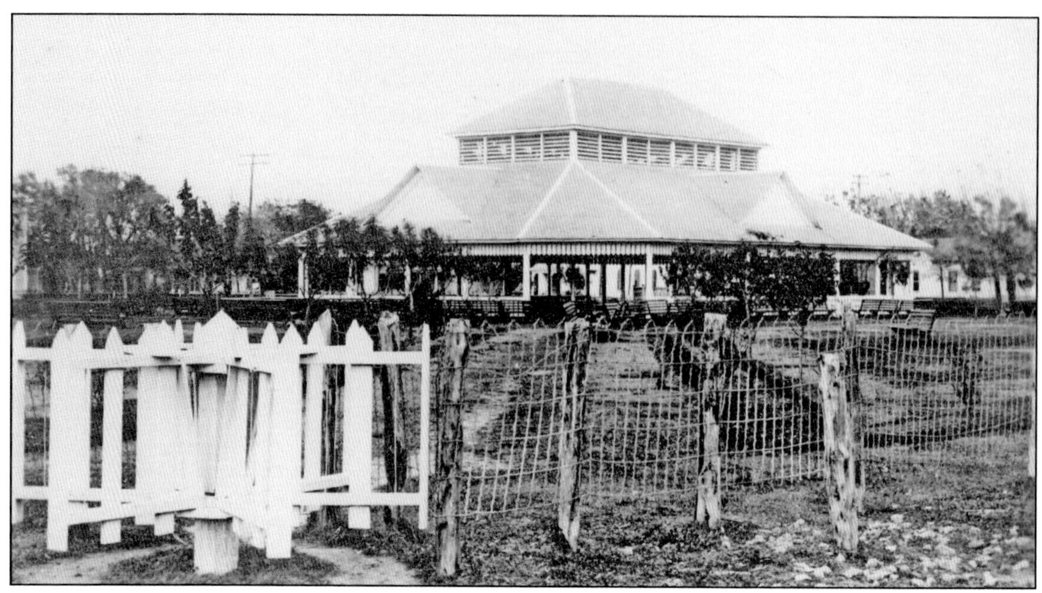

Of all the Luling city parks, Longer is the most frequently used, primarily because of the expansive "playscapes" designed for younger children. In addition, there are tennis and basketball courts for older youths. Swing sets for toddlers and elementary-age children are often in use. The playscapes were provided by funding from the Lower Colorado River Authority, the Guadalupe–Blanco River Authority, and others. Picnic tables are also provided for family gatherings. These two images show the change from the earliest years to a more modern view. The turnstile is no longer there; the pavilion remains with modern conveniences. The wire fence has also been removed. The placement of the turnstile and wire fence was intended to keep cattle out, not children in. The park itself is crossed with sidewalks lined with crepe myrtle trees. (Both courtesy G&H Society.)

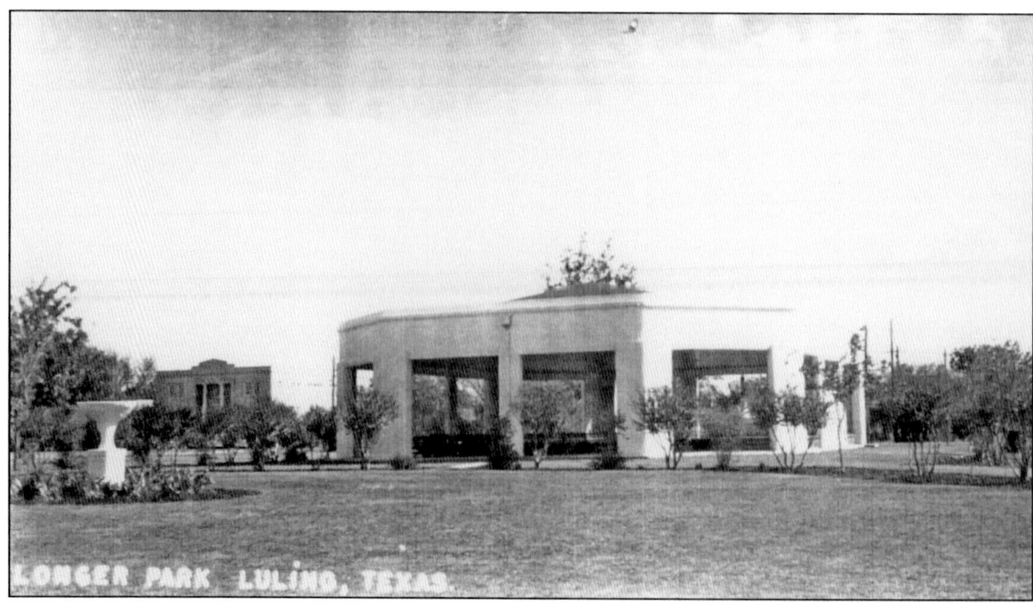

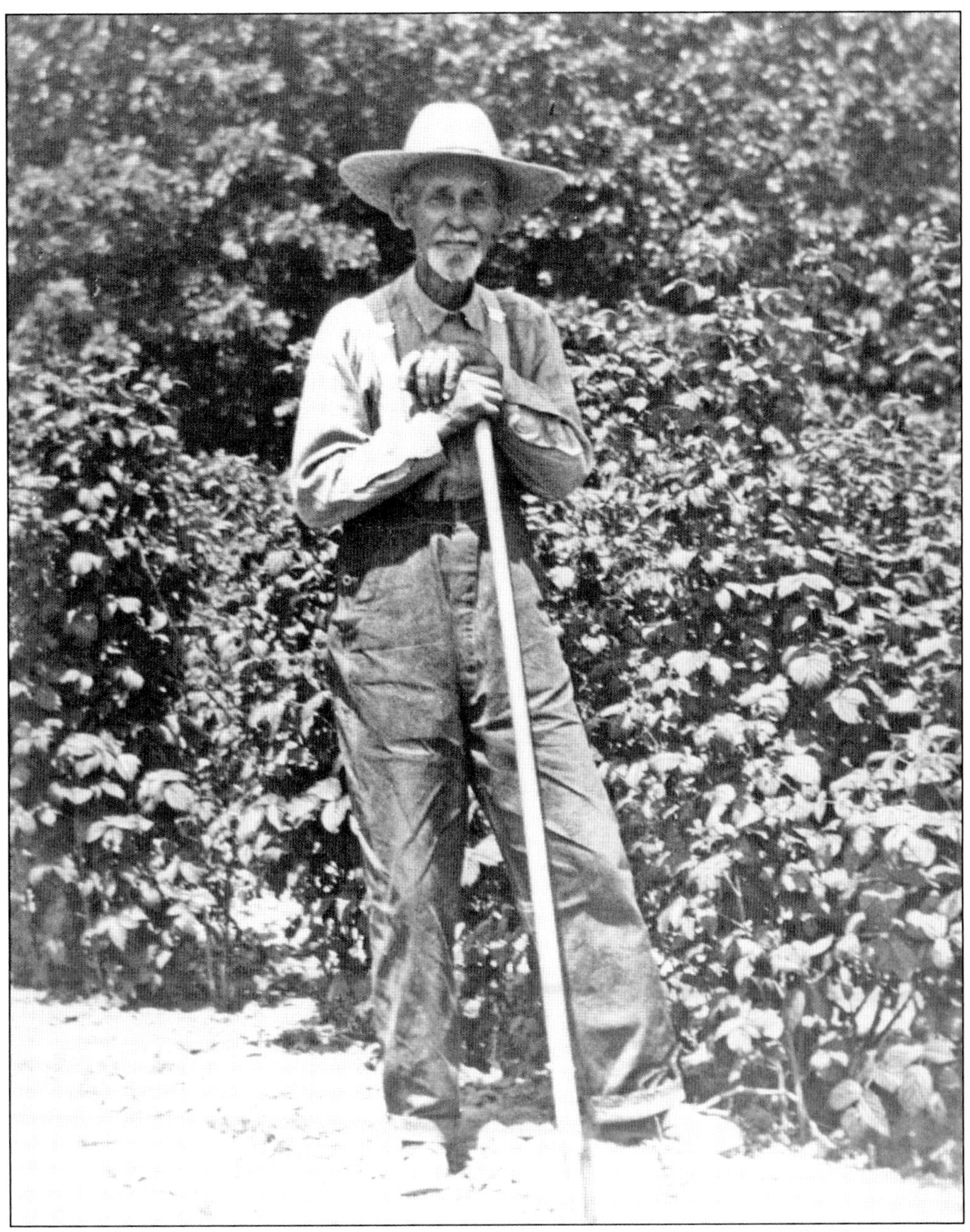

Several individuals donated land designated for parks. Patton Park was named in honor of John Dorrington "Dorn" Patton, a Mississippi native who joined the Confederate army and served in Gen. Braxton Bragg's 32nd Infantry. Patton, born June 11, 1834, married first Mary Martha Moore and second Sophronia Wrenn, a woman 23 years his junior. Dorn and Sophronia "Sofrina" Patton gave seven children to the world. He died May 25, 1913; she survived him until July 11, 1945. A portion of his land was donated to the City of Luling, and in June 1991, a red oak tree was planted in his memory by his descendants. A concrete bench was also placed, on which a plaque reads, "given in memory of our Grandpa Dorn, Jr., by his grandchildren." Patton Park today remains a popular place for walkers and joggers and has a small gazebo centrally located within its boundaries. (Courtesy G&H Society.)

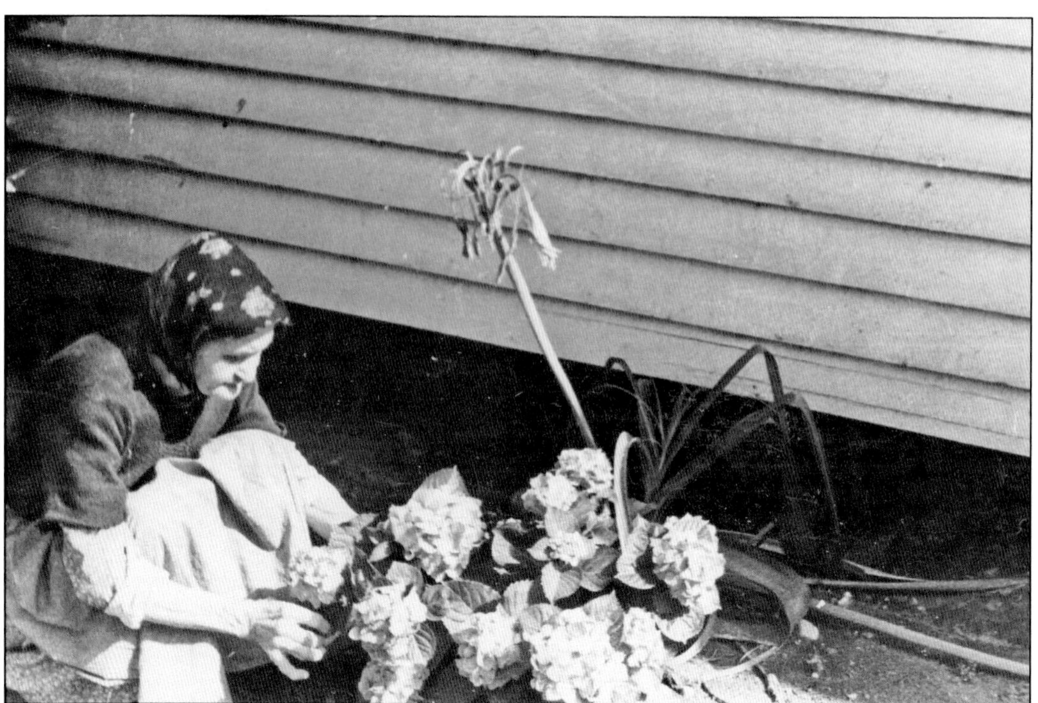

Sophronia Wrenn was born July 28, 1855, and married John Dorrington "Dorn" Patton Jr. in 1880. They had seven children. When Dorn passed away in 1913, his widow remained true to his memory, never remarrying. She died on July 11, 1945. Among other family interests, besides her children, was her garden. "Sofrina" is shown above tending some flowers and below standing at the doorway of her home. (Both courtesy G&H Society.)

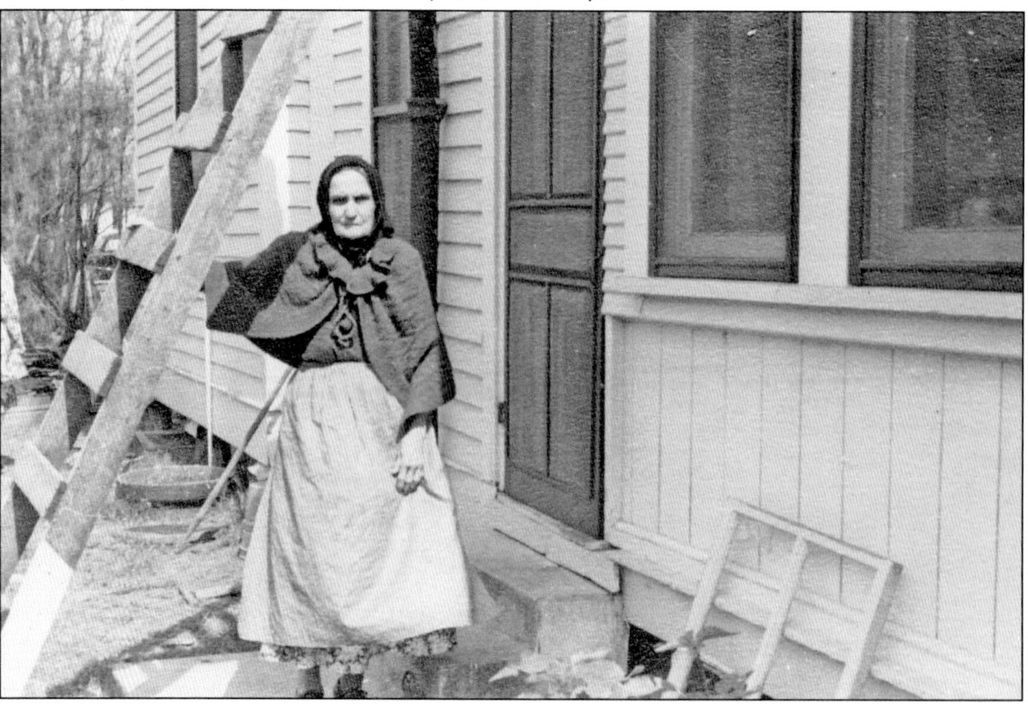

One of the seven children of John Dorrington "Dorn" Patton and his wife Sophronia was Arlie Isadora ("Dornia"). She must have realized her natural beauty judging from the pose displayed here in this undated photograph. No photographer's name is given, so it is unknown when or where this image was made. (Courtesy G&H Society.)

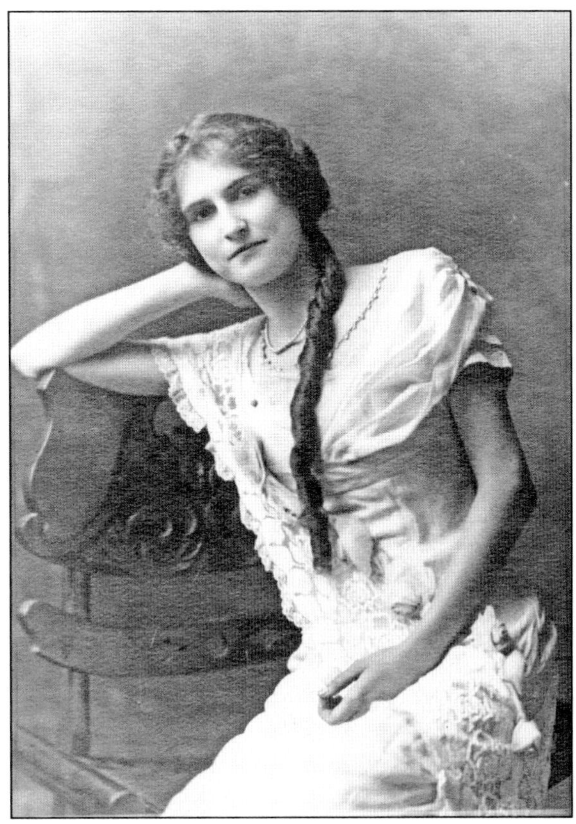

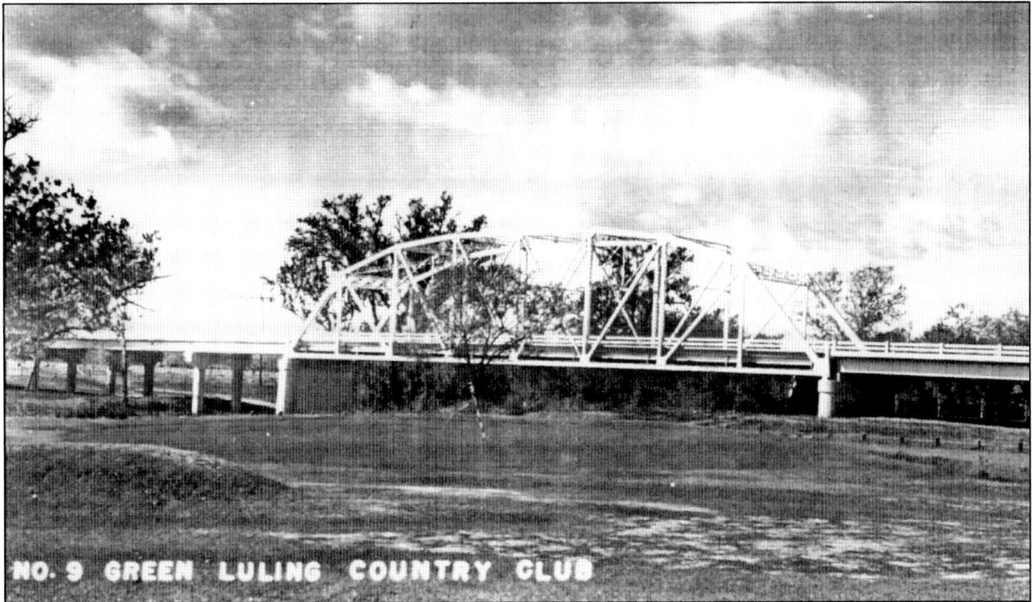

Marking the boundary line between Caldwell County and Gonzales County is the San Marcos River. This is a photograph of the "new" bridge over the river, which flows beside the grounds of the South Side Clubhouse. Today the river is popular for tubing. The bridge is opposite the golf course. (Courtesy G&H Society.)

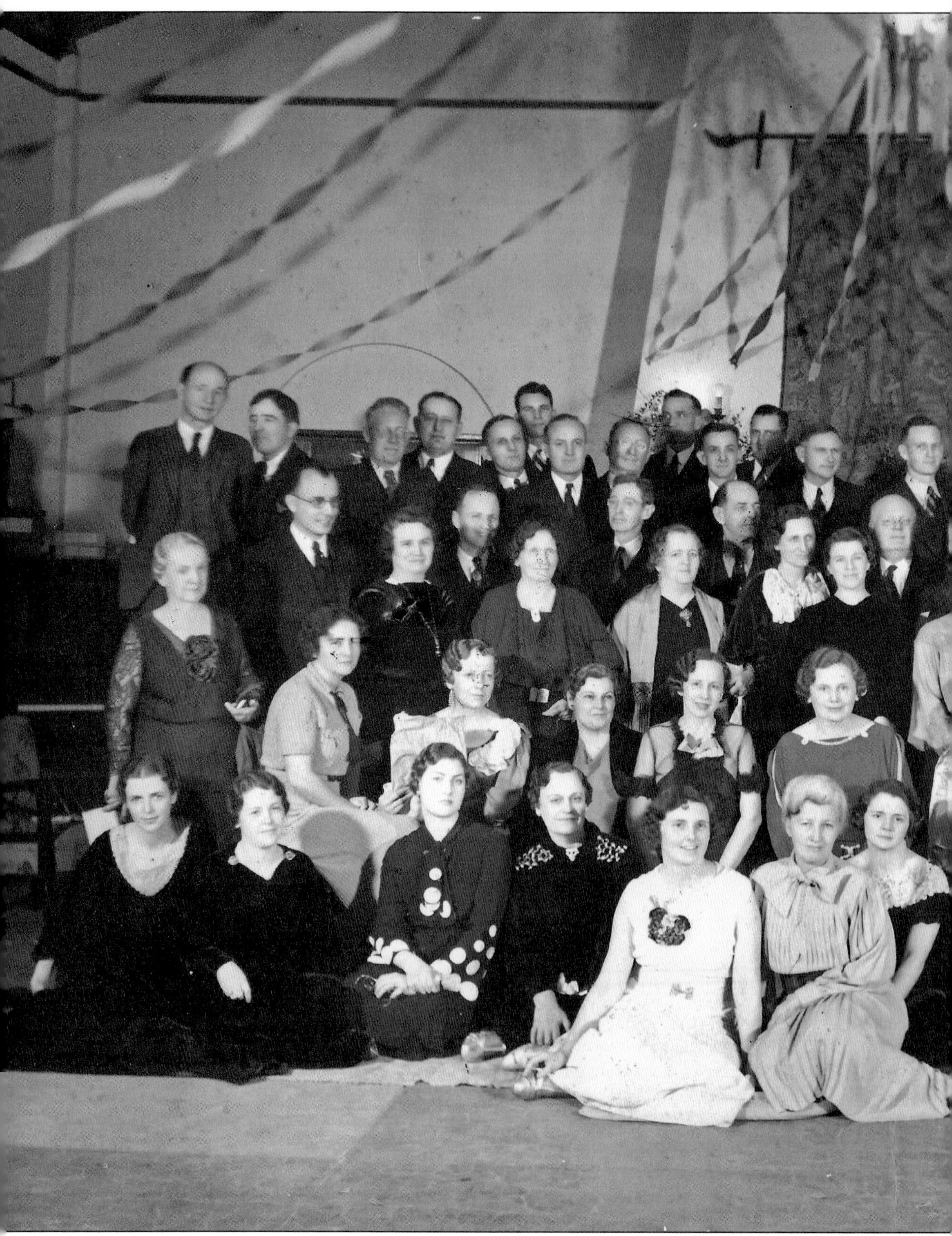

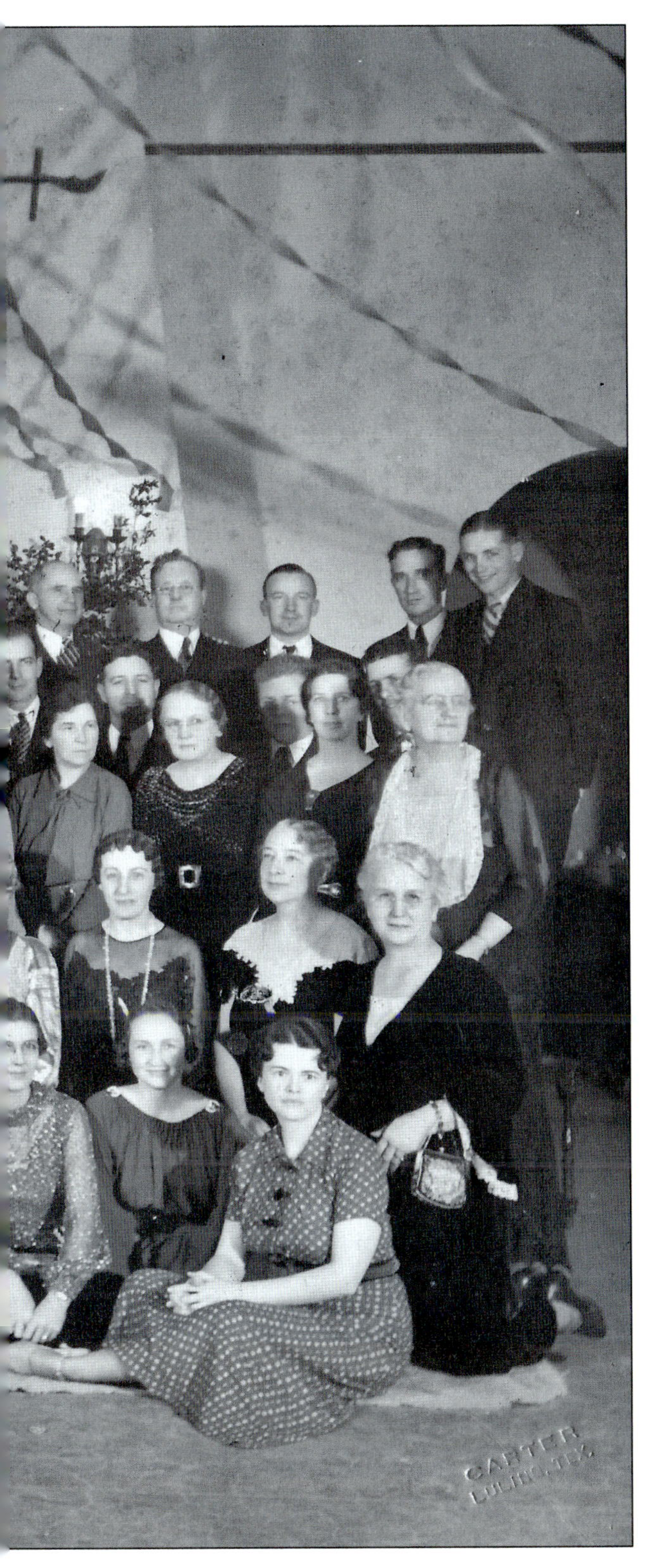

A special occasion was celebrated at the Southside Club House in 1935 or 1936. From left to right are (first row) Claire Walker, Gladys Matheny, "Gussie" McDowell, Maude Rabon, Hazel Muenster, Mrs. A. J. McKean Sr., "Honey" Pruett, Lois Carter, Dora McDonald, and Empress Zedler; (second row) Erkle Henry, Nan Colwell, Dallas Stein, Elise McKean Jr., Pinky Gregg, Callie Bouldin, Ida Walker, Mil Johnson, and Charlotte Zedler; (third row) Mrs. George Walker Sr., Dr. Harvey Henry, Anne Lawrence, Gladys Smith, Dora Pitts, Gladys Woolsey, Mrs. McKean, Dora Walker, Annie Cardwell, Hannah Walker, Kate Nugent, and Agnes Manfres; (fourth row) Dr. H. B. Henry, Robert Carter, Dr. T. R. Johnson, W. P. Walker Sr., Edgar B. Davis, W. P. Walker Jr., Walter W. Cardwell, William Temple, and "Doc" McIver; (fifth row) Zeb Nixon, Morris Dowell, Will Gregg, Luling mayor Henry Stein, C. W. Matheny, Bill Kelly, George Walker Jr., A. J. McKean, Elmo McKean, Roland McDonald, Joe Smith, Vern Woolsey, Clifton Mackey, Matthew Johnson, Nelson Pruett Sr., Arthur Lawrence, Paul Zedler, A. J. McKean Jr., and Henry Clark. (Courtesy G&H Society.)

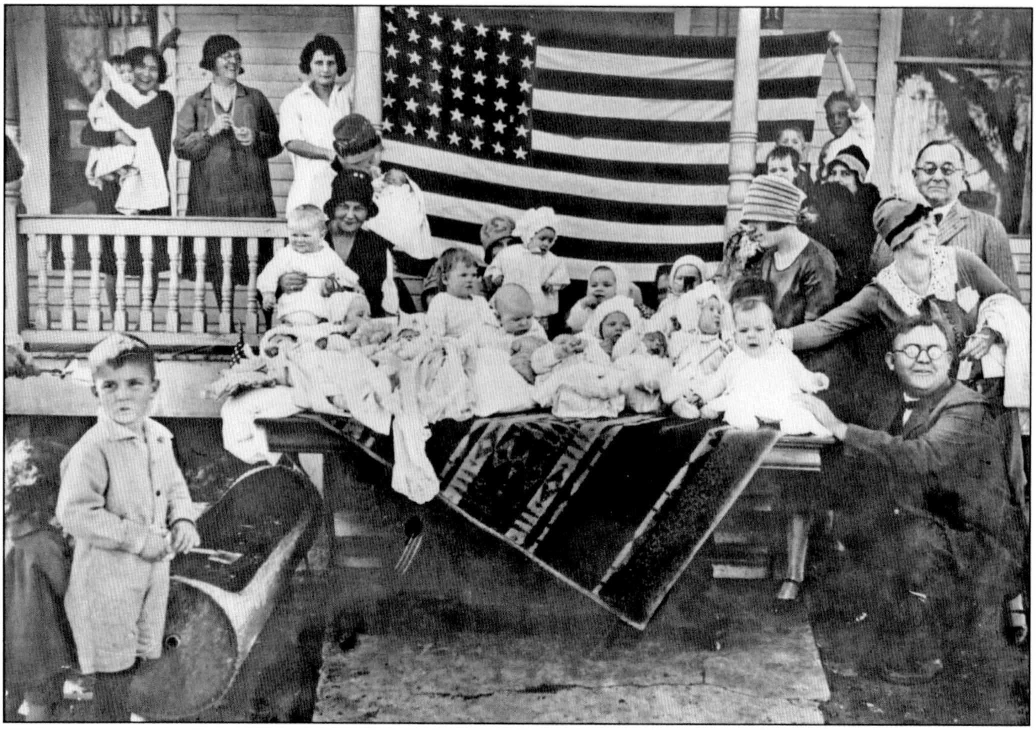

This most unusual view of Luling's hospital was taken at the time of the Texas Centennial in 1936. Shown here is Agnes Froh, owner, operator, and head nurse of the hospital, holding the American flag at left. Dr. Minor W. Pitts is standing at right, with Dr. Early A. Benbow kneeling. These are the babies delivered in the Luling Hospital during the centennial year of 1936. (Courtesy Riley Froh.)

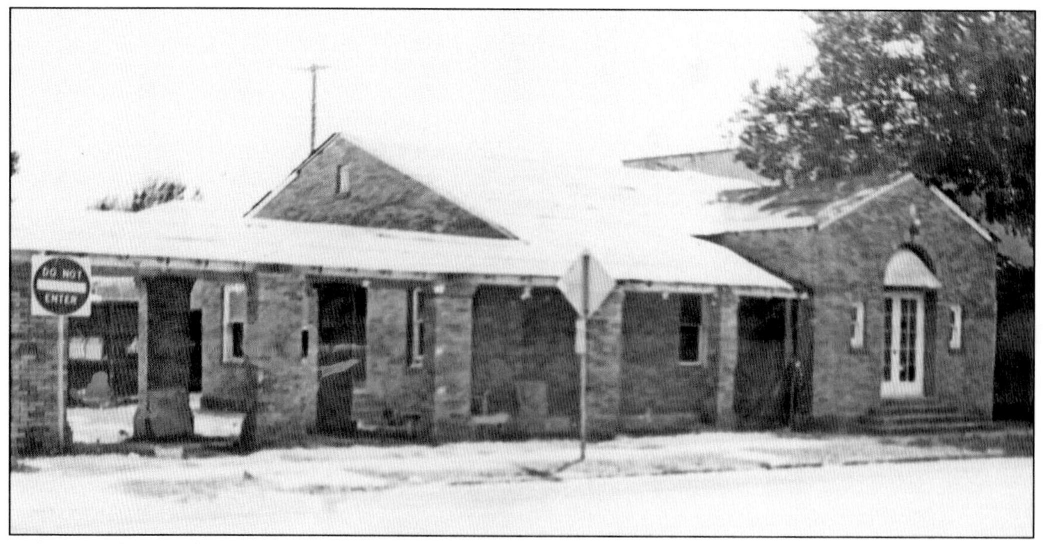

Luling's other medical facility, before Edgar B. Davis's, was the Green Cross Hospital and Pharmacy, located at 518 Pierce Street. The building remains, but today the facilities are the City of Luling Communications Municipal Court and the Caldwell County Mental Health Center–Bluebonnet Trails. The Green Cross symbol remains visible above the door. (Courtesy Riley Froh.)

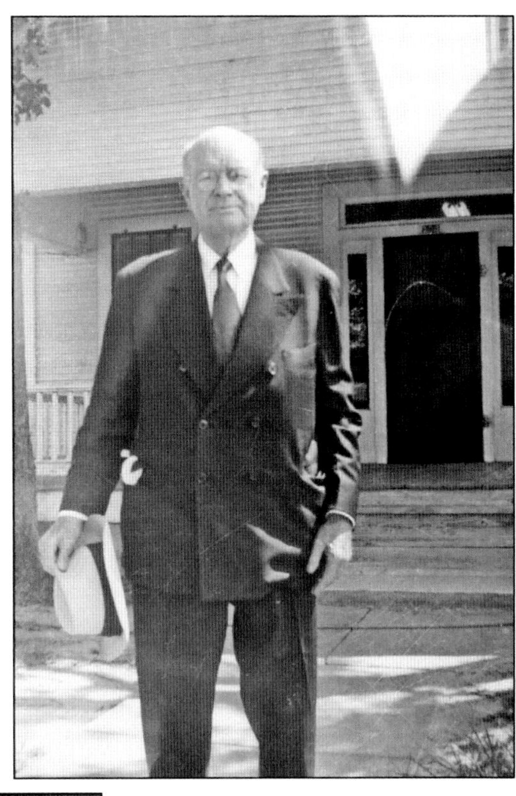

Here is an unusual photograph of Edgar B. Davis standing hat in hand at the Foundation Farm headquarters. At the Silver Jubilee of the discovery of Rios Well No. 1, Texas governor Beauford H. Jester was the principal speaker at the testimonial dinner. The Silver Jubilee was a production of the entire town of Luling; Governor Jester said the town had paid a "fitting tribute by a fine town to a great man, Mr. Edgar B. Davis." Among other events at the jubilee were a rodeo, softball games, a parade, an old fiddlers contest, the crowning of a queen, a sing-along at Longer Park, a golf tournament, a dance, and of course an address by Mayor J. M. Rabon. Davis himself conducted a thanksgiving service at Rios Well No. 1. (Right courtesy Luling Foundation Farm; below courtesy G&H Society.)

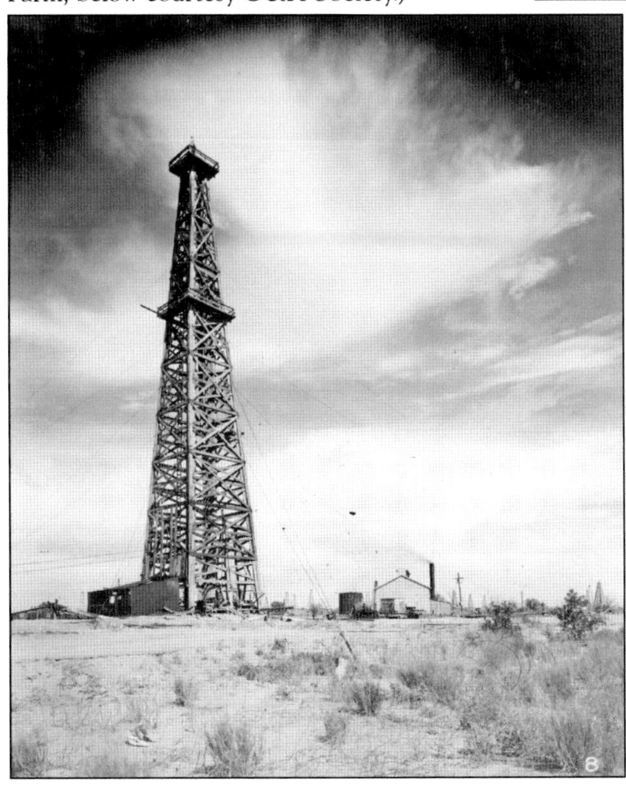

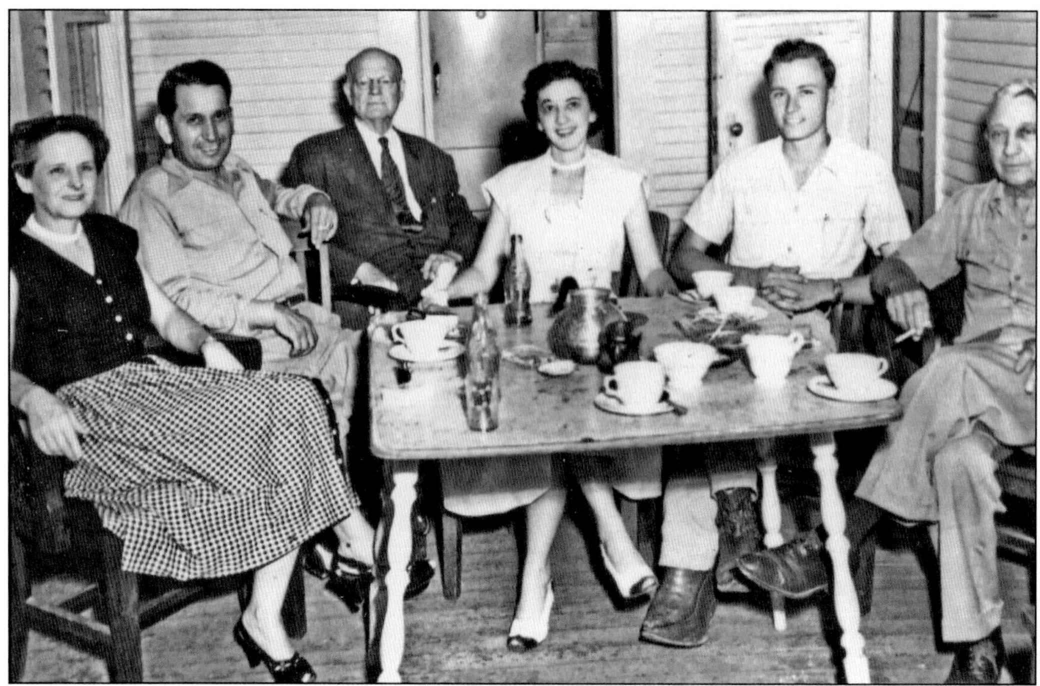

Edgar B. Davis and several key players in the success of the Luling Foundation are seated in an office of the Foundation Farm in 1950. From left to right are Lorraine Crockett; Otis Smith; Edgar B. Davis; Inez Griffin, his longtime secretary; Bruce Pipkin; and George Seybold. (Courtesy Luling Foundation Farm.)

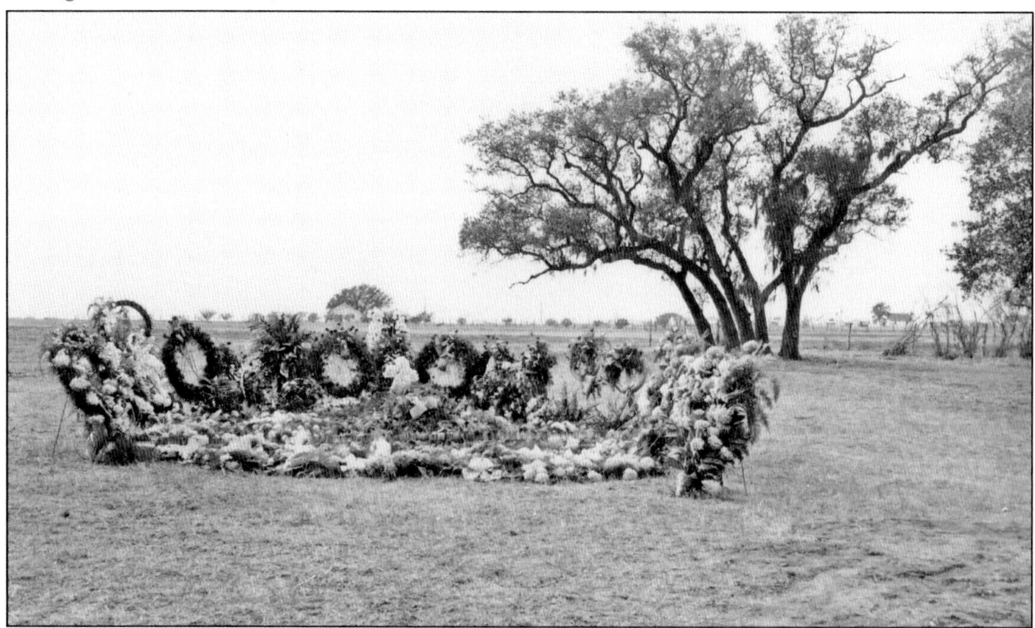

The final resting place of Edgar B. Davis, his grave is a modest mound today. After making millions in rubber and oil and agriculture, Davis chose to give much of his fortunes away. He died in Galveston on October 14, 1951, and is buried on the grounds of his former home. In 1966, the Edgar B. Davis Memorial Hospital was built on the grounds. (Courtesy Luling Foundation Farm.)

Six

EDGAR B. DAVIS AND OIL

The *New Handbook of Texas* describes him as an "oilman and philanthropist," but he was certainly "Mr. Luling." Born Edgar Byram Davis on February 2, 1873, in Brooklyn, Massachusetts, he earned his high school diploma and then went on to make his first million in the shoe business. It was 1905, and he was only 32 years of age. Davis then made another fortune in the rubber business. Thirteen years later, he sold his interest, giving much of his earnings away to friends and associates. Brother Oscar Davis had invested in oil leases in Caldwell County and in 1919 asked Davis to manage his shares. That year, Davis visited Luling for the first time. He believed that God had directed him to Luling and that his role was to convince the agriculture community leaders that the single crop of cotton was ultimately destructive to the community's economy. Davis believed oil was the answer, but the geologists insisted there was none to be found. In early 1921, Davis incorporated the United North and South Oil Company. When Oscar Davis died, Edgar bought the leases from his brother's estate. After six dry wells and deeply in debt, Davis was redeemed when Rafael Rios No. 1 gushed. It was August 9, 1922. This field was 12 miles long and 2 miles wide. By the end of 1922, the field was producing 13,000 barrels of oil every day. On June 11, 1926, Davis sold his leases to the Magnolia Petroleum Company for $12 million, then the largest oil deal in Texas history at the time. Although tremendously successful in many ventures, Davis experienced at least one failure: his Broadway play, *The Ladder*, was a disaster, even though it ran on Broadway for two years. Davis died October 14, 1951, and is buried in Luling at the site of one of his former homes. He never married. In 1966, the Edgar B. Davis Memorial Hospital was built on the site of his Luling home.

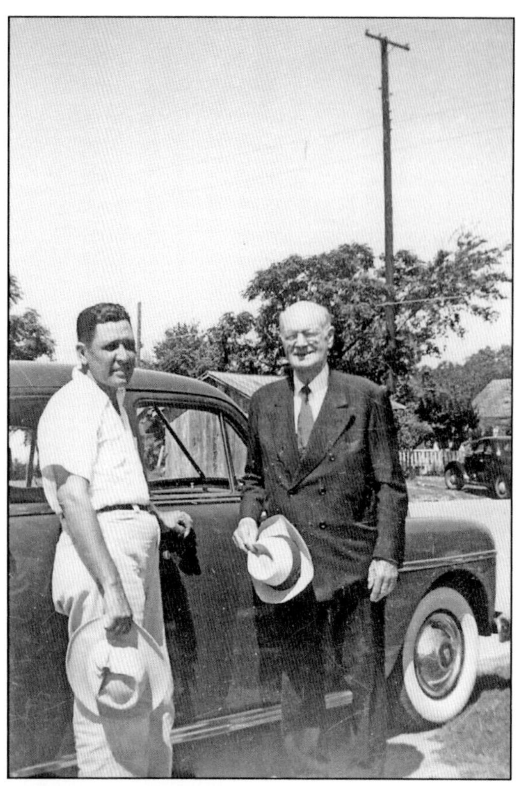

Edgar B. Davis is pictured with his chauffeur. Historian Riley Froh wrote, "Davis' distinctiveness extended to his mode of travel. Chauffeurs were . . . unheard of in Luling and the surrounding towns, with the exception of Fred Trevino. . . . The ancient and elongated eight-passenger limousine in which he rode belonged to a past era and added to the image of the celebrated character Davis had become." (Courtesy G&H Society.)

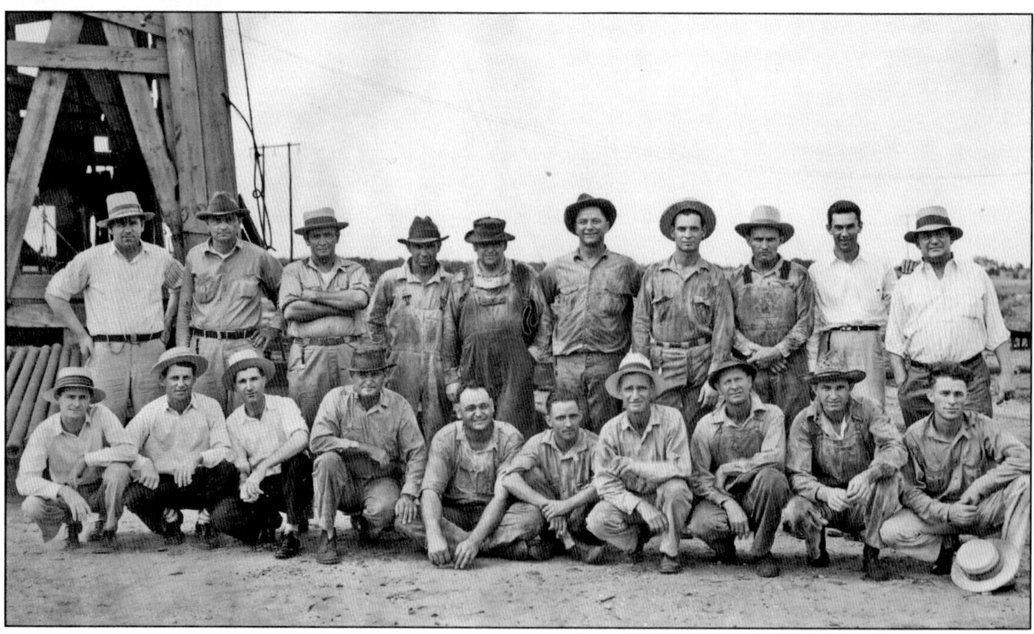

Drillers and others of the Edgar B. Davis United North and South Development Company included, from left to right, (first row) L. M. Callihan; E. Davis; R. Ross; C. F. Reeves; E. H. Lamb; J. H. Gray; C. E. Scott; R. S. Patterson; Paul Hardeman; and R. L. Miles; (second row) A. R. Hutchinson, driller; R. B. Krauskoff; J. L. Gray, driller; Charles Hall; W. D. Gallier; A. Nugent, driller; D. W. Scott; S. A. Smith; R. H. Giesey; and S. H. Rabon. (Courtesy G&H Society.)

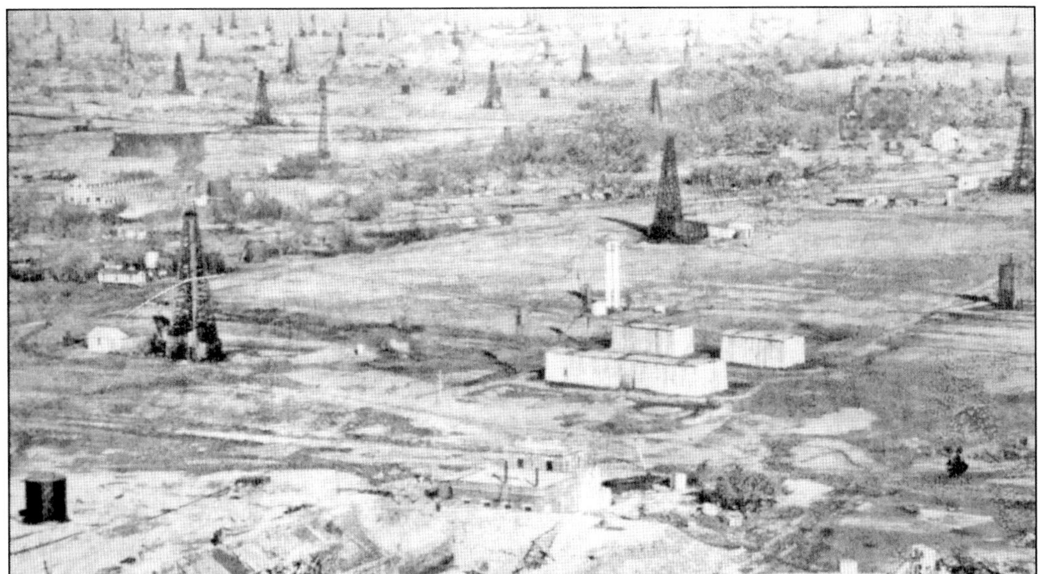

In this view of the 1928 oil field, the oil derricks appear to be "planted" like pecan trees. Credit goes to Edgar B. Davis for its discovery in 1922. The oil boom promoted rapid growth, not only in the increase of population, but also more businesses associated with oil. Luling's population grew from 1,000 to 6,000 with over 100 new businesses brought in. (Courtesy G&H Society.)

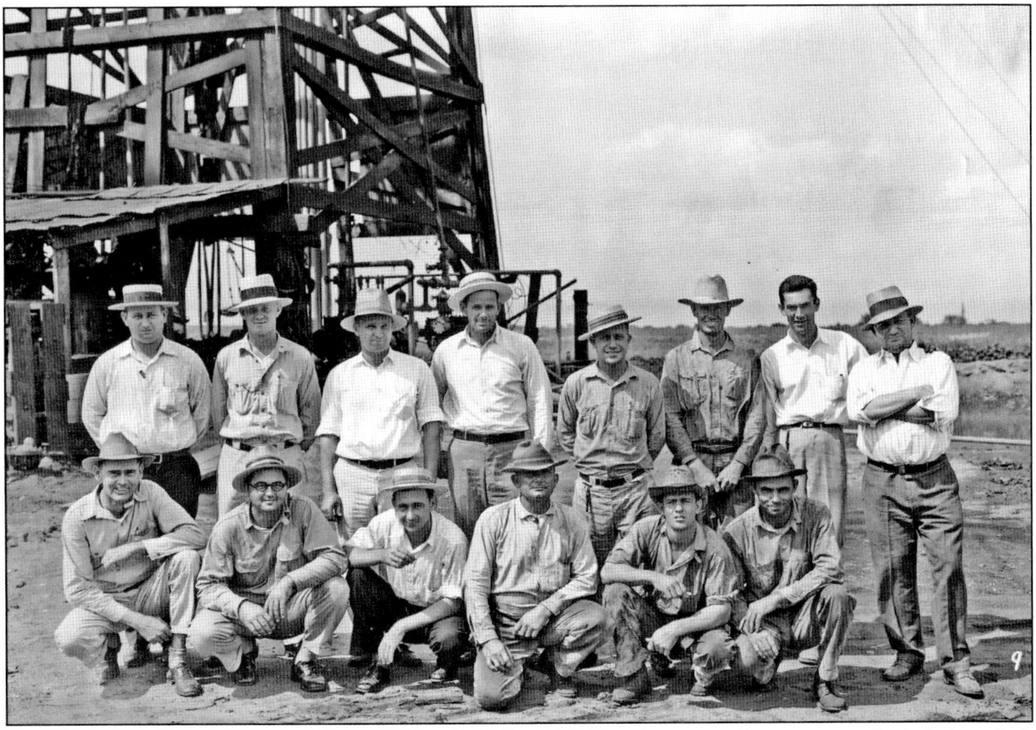

Employees of Edgar B. Davis's United North and South Development Company included, from left to right, (first row) E. Allen, driller; B. H. Chamness; Pat Fuqua; V. D. Rabon; H. D. Cullin; and W. T. McCarley; (second row) Carl Reed; Paul E. Bainbridge, driller; L. H. Sobotik; G. Hardeman; C. O. West, driller; Howard Allen; R. H. Giesey; and Sam H. Rabon. (Courtesy G&H Society.)

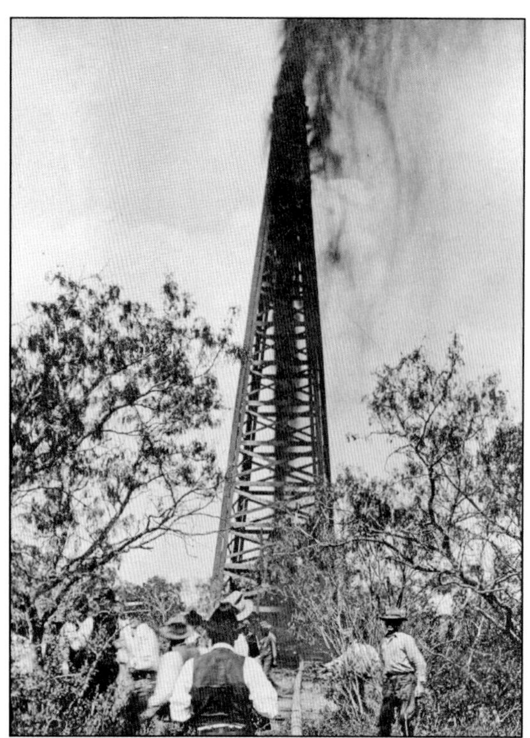

This impressive view of an oil rig is actually the first gusher on the Joseph Wilson Tract at Salt Flat Oil Field in Luling in 1927. In the foreground, with his back to the camera, wearing a vest and black hat, is Joseph Wilson. Today the tall impressive derricks are much smaller pump jacks, many of which have been decorated with comic or athletic figures. (Photograph by Robert W. Carter; courtesy Randy Engelke.)

This image of employees of the United North and South Development Company hard at work in the oil field of Edgar B. Davis reveals the excitement ever present on an oil rig. From left to right are E. H. Lamb, C. F. Reeves, and J. L. Gray. This is from the personal scrapbook of Davis. Such huge derricks are no longer visible in Luling today, replaced by decorated pump jacks. (Courtesy G&H Society.)

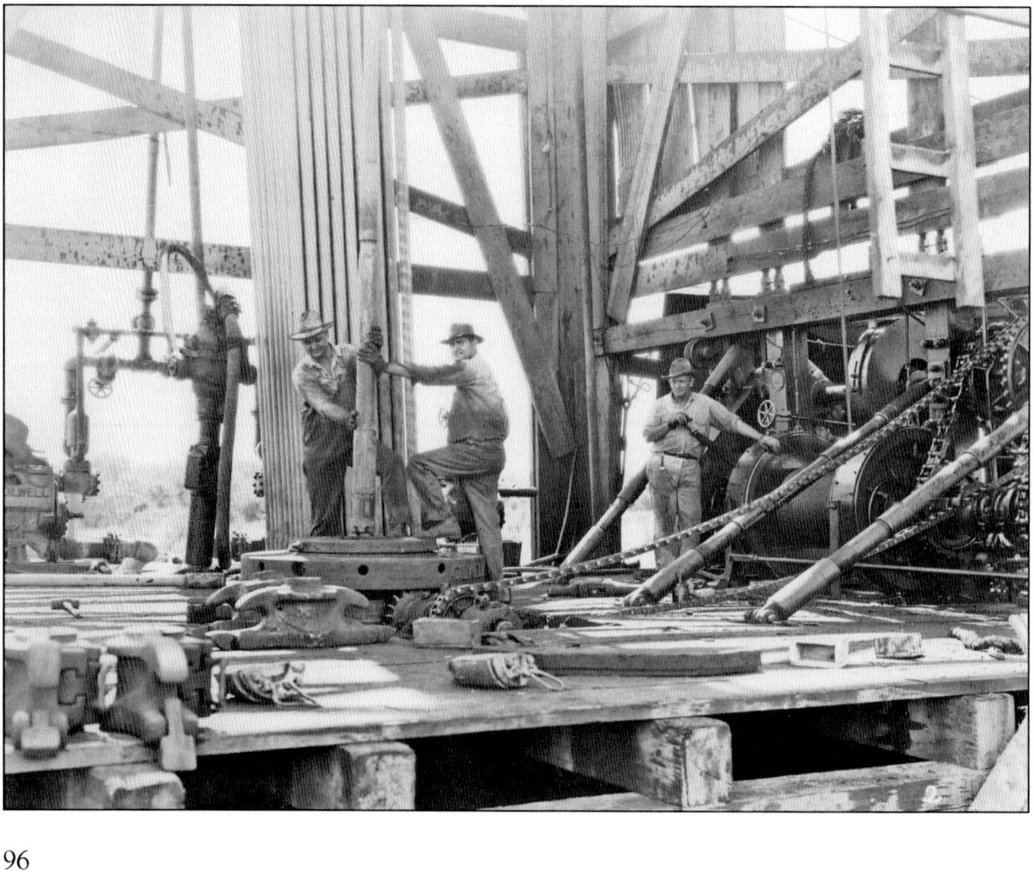

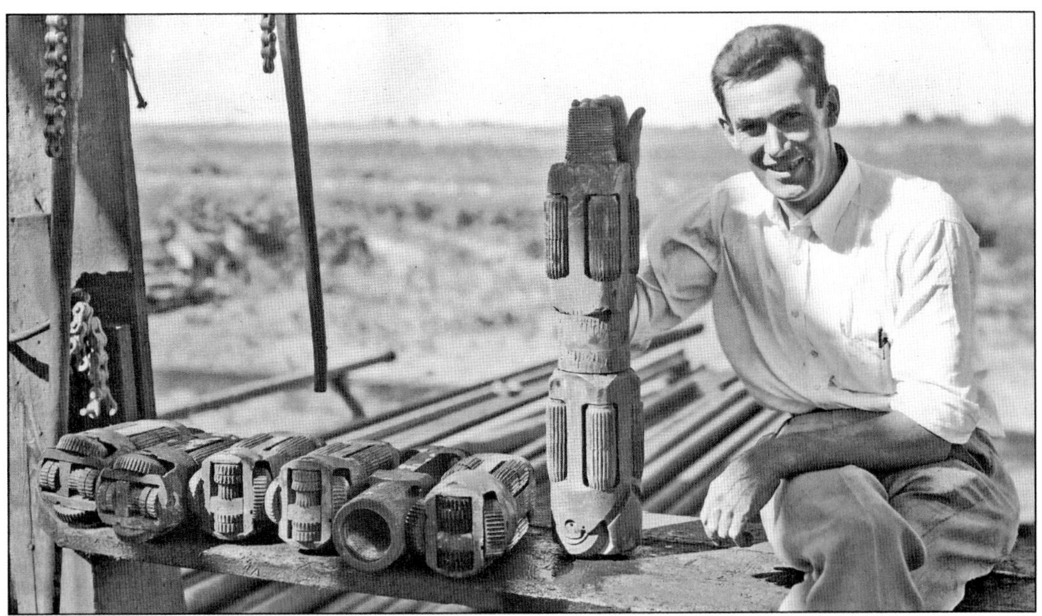

Among the many photographs in Edgar B. Davis's personal scrapbook now archived in the Caldwell County Genealogical and Historical Society Photograph Collection is this one of R. H. Giesey (above), apparently showing off or demonstrating the oil bits that brought oil to the surface. It is curious to see him wearing a white shirt and handling oil field equipment. In the photograph below are six officials of the United North and South Development Company. They take time out for the photographer. From left to right are S. H. Rabon, A. Summers, R. H. Giesey, J. E. Mowinckle, H. C. Howard, and J. I. Cadenhead. Unfortunately none of the photographs in the collection give the name of the photographer. (Both courtesy G&H Society.)

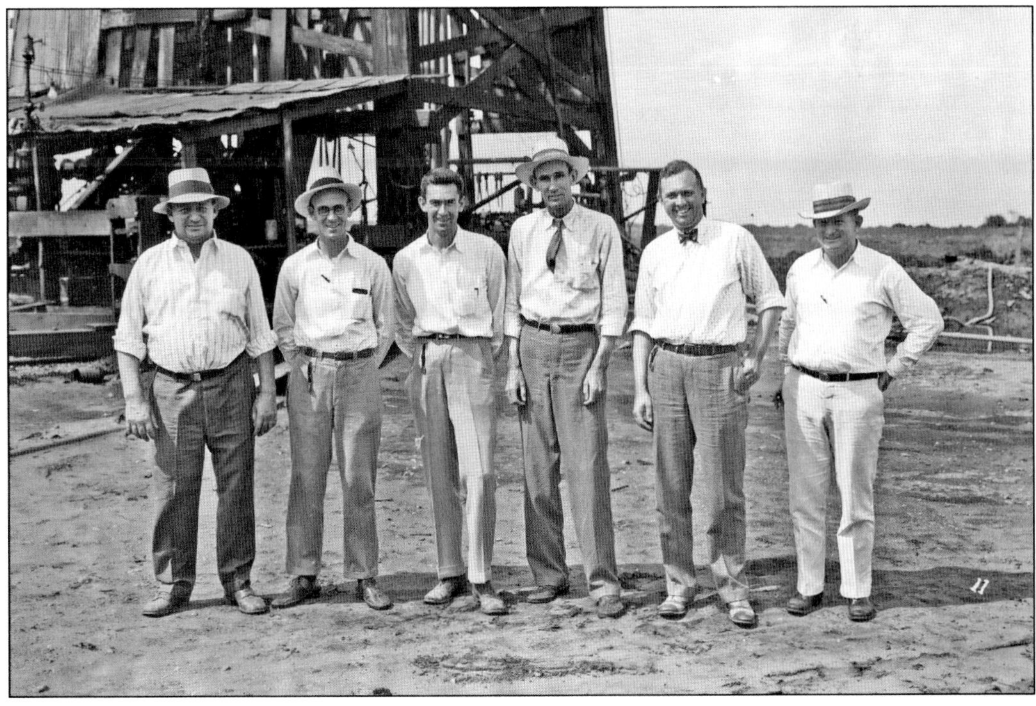

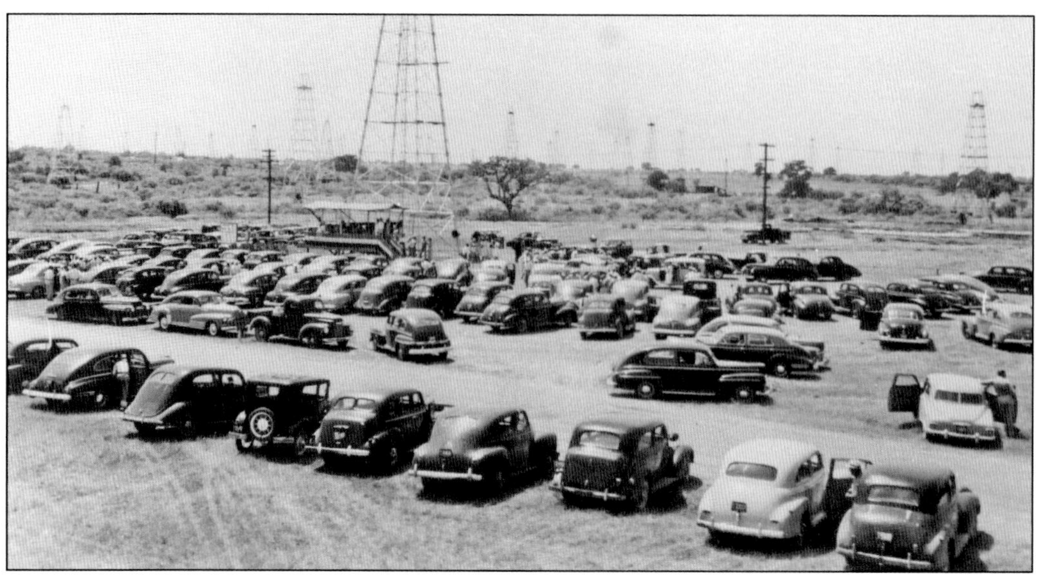

Edgar B. Davis brought in his first oil well on August 9, 1922. He controlled the oil field completely at first but later sold out to major oil companies. At its peak in 1924, the field produced had 11,134,000 barrels; by 1947, it had decreased to 1,533,000. This image records the celebration of Rios Well No. 1 at the 25th anniversary of its discovery. (Courtesy G&H Society.)

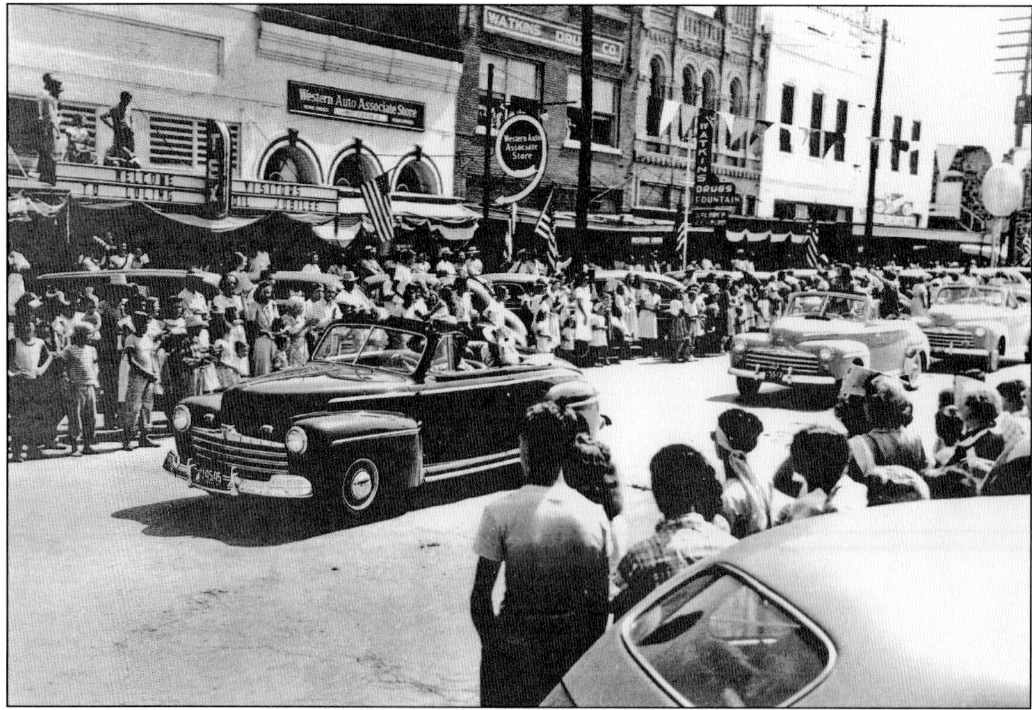

This 1947 view shows only a portion of the parade celebrating the silver anniversary of oil in Luling, but it does show how Davis (Main) Street has changed between 1947 and today. The parade is moving west on Davis Street, past the TEX Theater, the Western Auto Associate Store, and the Watkins Drug Company Store. The marquee shows "Welcome Visitors to Luling Oil Jubilee." (Courtesy G&H Society.)

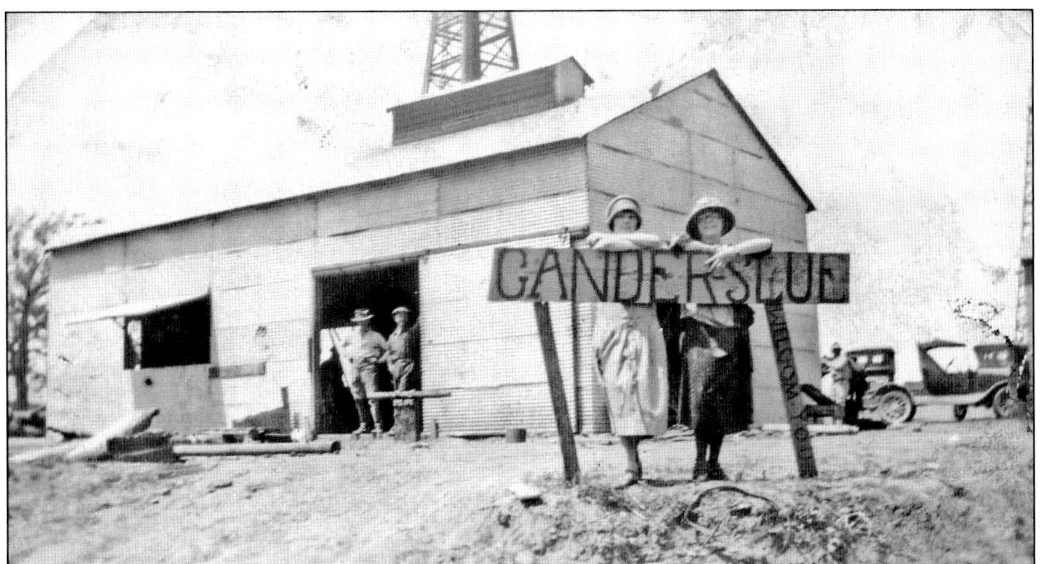

The "town" of Gander Slue is but a memory, but it existed on the eastern side of the Luling oil field for a while. "Sin flourished twenty-four hours a day," according to historian Riley Froh. Here "the disorderly elements congregated. Gamblers, bootleggers, and madams operated openly in the hastily assembled city." These two ladies remain unidentified. (CourtesySusan Allen.)

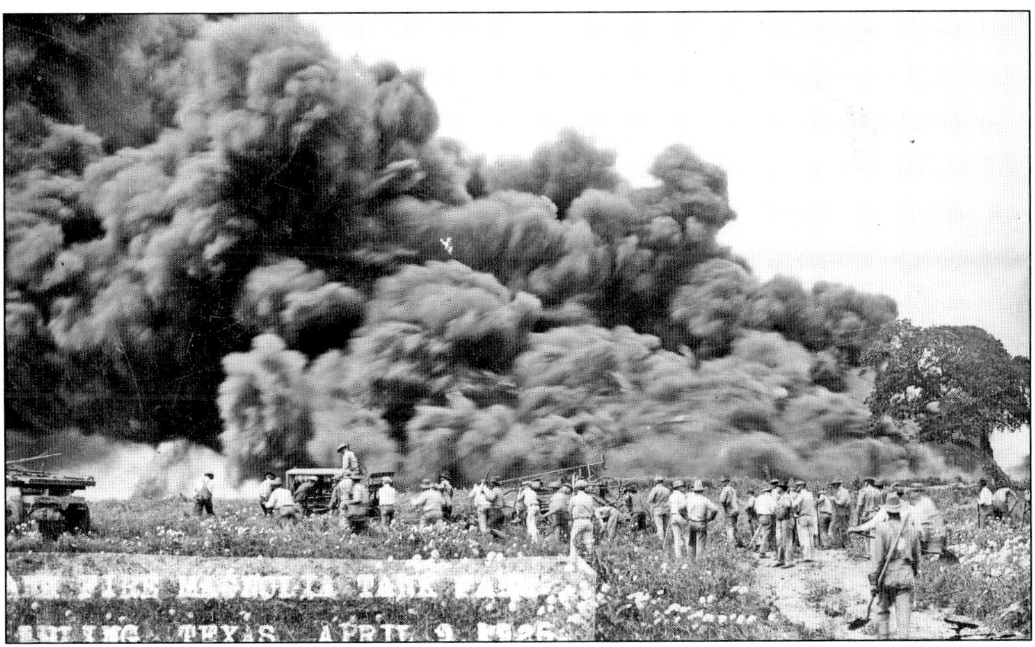

The dream of Edgar B. Davis, and his perseverance to prove oil was underneath much of Caldwell County, placed Luling on the map, resulting in many wonderful benefits for the town and surrounding area. Calamity befell the Magnolia Tank Farm Field on April 9, 1926, caused by a lightning strike. This view provides a graphic representation of the event. (Courtesy Central Texas Oil Patch Museum.)

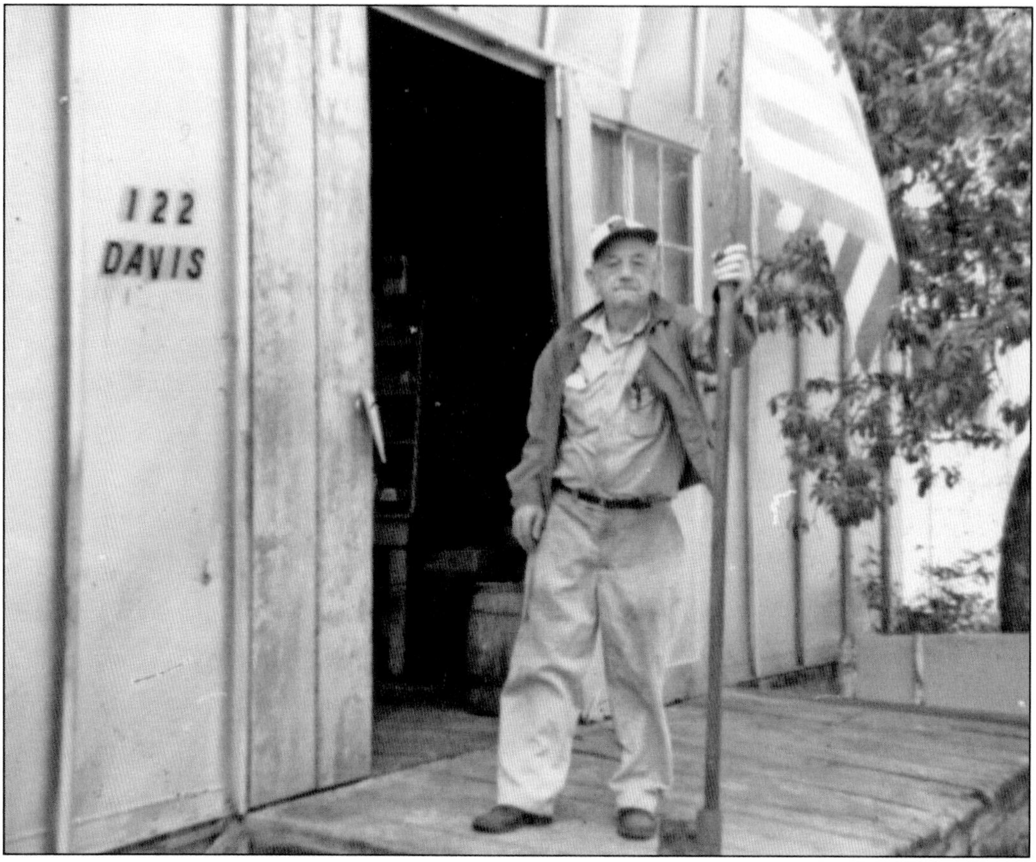

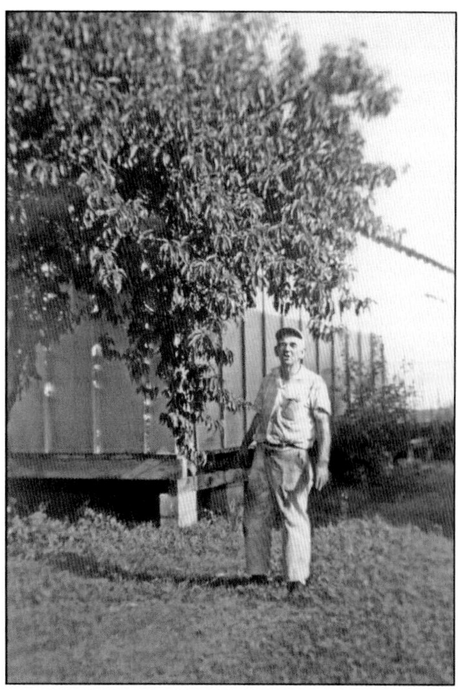

Among the many individuals who contributed to the success of the oil boom in Luling was Walter Edward Baker. Baker leased the property at 122 East Davis Street from the Southern Pacific Transportation Company of San Francisco, California, for the purpose of selling oil well equipment. Originally owned by the Marion Machine Foundry and Supply Company of Marion, Indiana, the company was transferred to Baker on February 22, 1945, and renamed the Baker Supply Company. Baker was a businessman but also an active participant in Luling's activities. He served on the Luling School Board as a member and as a president, chaplain of the American Legion, an active member of the First Baptist Church, and a Boy Scout leader. Baker continued to operate the oil well equipment business until his 1979 retirement. (Above courtesy Central Texas Oil Patch Museum; left courtesy Betty Baker Meneley.)

Seven

Agriculture and the Foundation Farm

The Luling Foundation was established in 1927 by Edgar B. Davis on 1,223 acres on the edge of Luling. According to Zona Adams Withers in *A History of the Luling Foundation 1927–1982*, it represented a "unique institution dedicated to the betterment of mankind." The Foundation Farm had a dual and difficult role, as it was "an institution of learning" and also a "farming operation." This required it to discover new practices to help Texas farmers earn a more abundant life from the soil. Edgar B. Davis endowed the Luling Foundation as a "thank offering to God" by donating $1 million. In so doing, "he sought to return to the farmers of Caldwell, Guadalupe, and Gonzales Counties a measure of his appreciation for the Divine Guidance which he knew had led him to discovery of the rich Luling oil field." The intent remained unchanged over the years. Practical things were stressed: soil improvement; terracing; proper fertilization; crop rotation; improvement of beef and dairy herds, hogs, sheep, and poultry; as well as the benefits of good seed and intensive tillage.

Dr. S. J. Francis stated the goal in simple terms: "Let's not build a showplace, but only do what any enterprising farmer can do on his own land." The motto "Plan our work and work our plans" became the Foundation's byword. Some 20 years after its creation, Davis stated that the Foundation "has developed way beyond what I expected. Through it God has given me greater riches, and I believe it will grow richer. The Farm has only started. I believe it will in a way do something for the whole agricultural world. . . . [W]e can help solve the agricultural problems not only of Caldwell, Gonzales and Guadalupe Counties, which was our primary object, but of the state of Texas and of the Nation." The original board of trustees were Dr. S. J. Francis of Luling; Clyde L. Boothe of Gonzales; Judge C. H. Donegan of Seguin; Walter W. Cardwell of Luling; Dean E. J. Kyle of Texas A&M, College Station; and A. J. McKean Sr. of Luling. Davis was the seventh member.

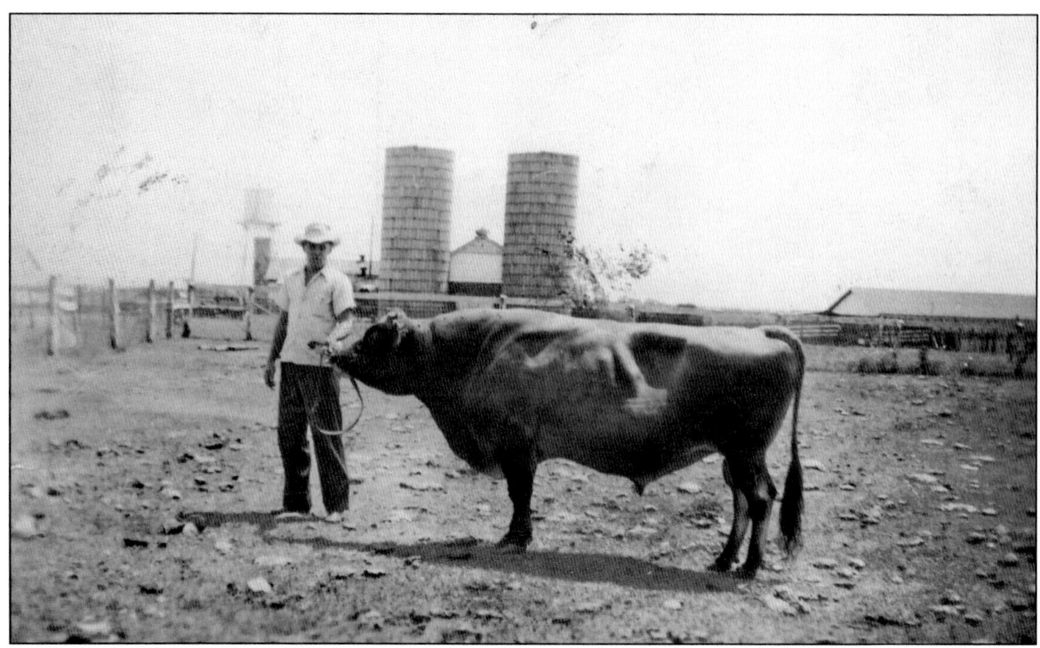

The first Santa Gertrudis cattle were two bulls purchased in 1943 for a cross-breeding experiment. Bob Kleburg of the King Ranch was pleased with the qualities exhibited. By 1946, the herd included both male and female Santa Gertrudis cattle. Heifers raised on the farm were being retained to increase the size of the herd. They were classified in 1951 by the Santa Gertrudis Breeders International. Pictured above is Bobby Matthews. (Courtesy Linda Wright.)

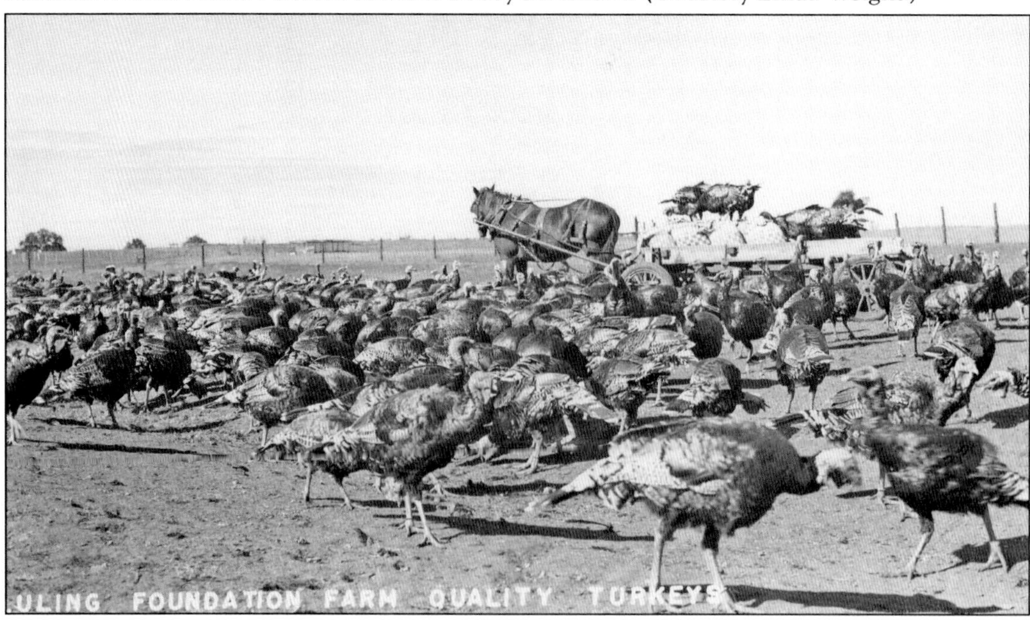

Turkeys were first placed on the Foundation Farm in 1930 as an experiment. One hundred hens and 12 toms of the best Bronze breeding stock were obtained. The experiment was met with phenomenal success, and broad-breasted turkeys became a staple. The program however was discontinued in 1957 when turkey prices were depressed, feed prices were high, and the venture ceased to be profitable. (Courtesy Randy Engelke.)

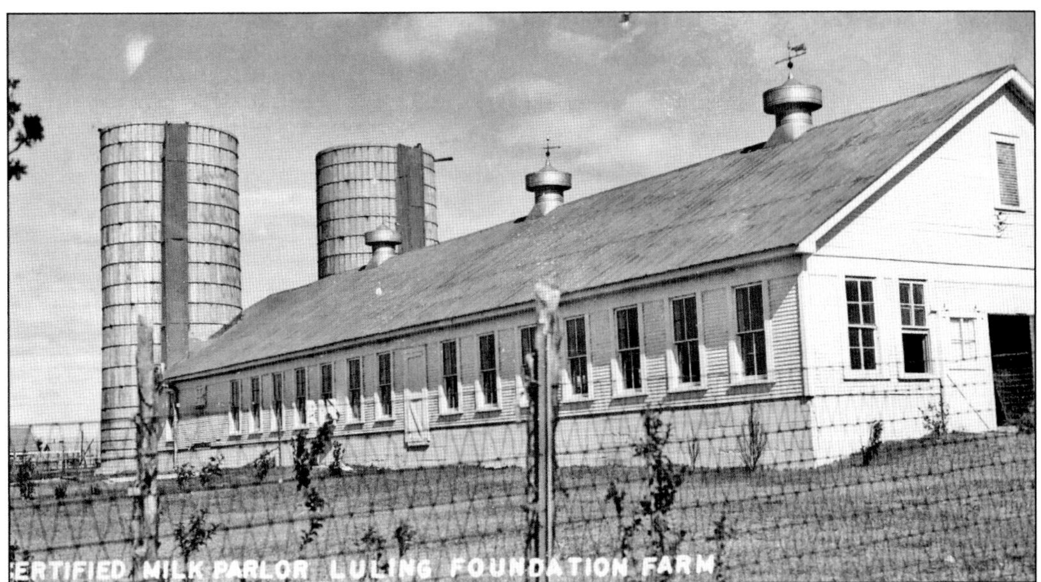

The Foundation Farm's first dairy barn was remodeled to meet changing requirements of the times. By 1928, it had been remodeled to meet requirements for the new certified milk. By 1937–1938, some 288 quarts of milk were being shipped on a daily basis to Borden's Milk of Houston, in addition to heavy sales in hometown Luling. Cows that did not produce up to expectation, or "boarders," were sold for slaughter. Awards for the Champion Jersey Herd of Texas were given to the farm in 1946, 1947, 1948, and 1949. In 1950, the farm began producing pasteurized certified milk, one of only three cities in Texas that could boast such an honor. The other two were El Paso and San Antonio. Below is an image of Caldwell County's Centennial Parade in 1948 with the Foundation Farm as its theme. Among the flowers were miniature cows. (Both courtesy Luling Foundation Farm.)

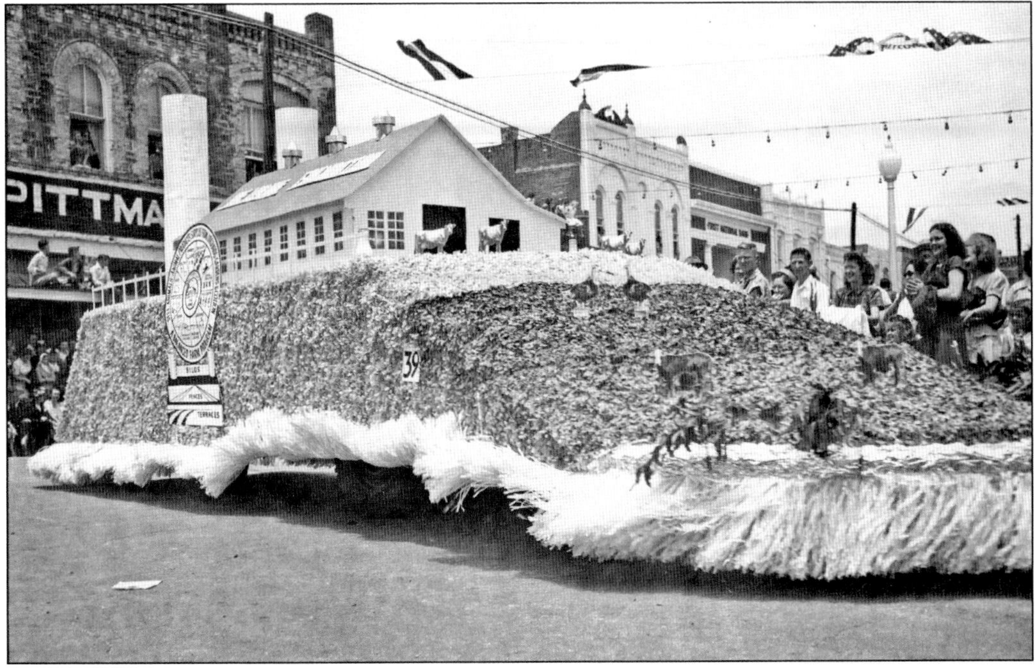

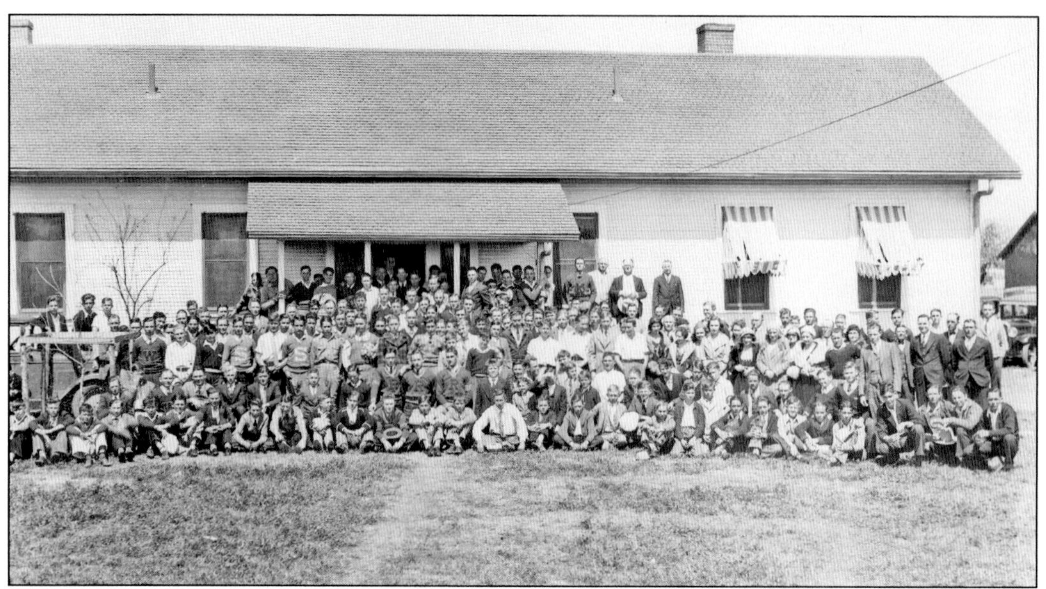

Visitors were frequent as the Foundation Farm was recognized as an important factor in successful agriculture, not only in Texas but the country over. Many countries sent representatives to study its methods. Special tours—such as the soil classes from the Pan-American College in Edinburg, Texas; geography classes from the University of Texas; and ROTC veterinary classes from Fort Sam—became frequent, as well as many high school FFA (Future Farmers of America) classes. (Courtesy Luling Foundation Farm.)

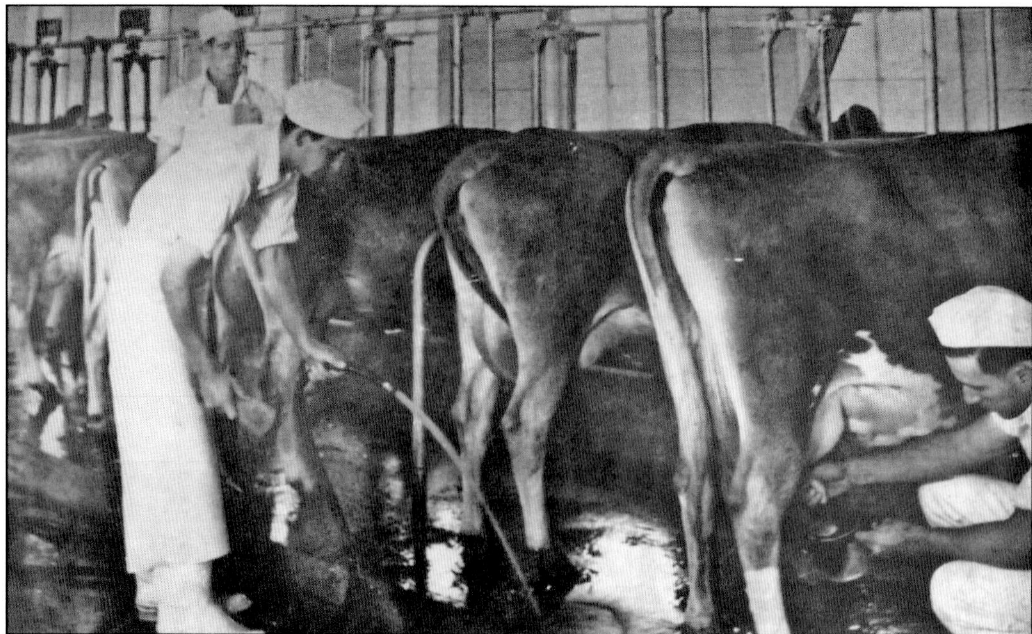

Milk production has always been a concern for all classes of people. The Foundation Farm consistently worked to improve the quality of milk and its production. The dairy farm was a model showplace in its day. Cattle from the herds proved worthy and were used to upgrade other herds in the area. The milking stalls were kept cleaner than some homes. (Courtesy Luling Foundation Farm.)

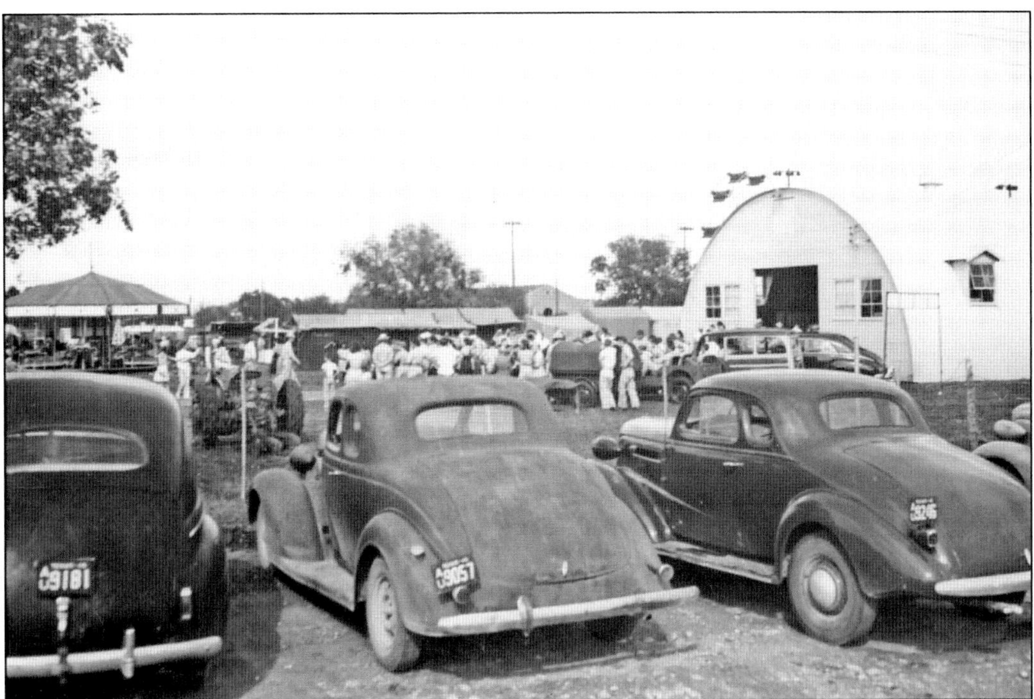

This is a busy day at the Foundation Farm's dairy barn. No specific activity is indicated with this photograph, although it was probably a demonstration dealing with cattle or milk production. The Foundation never forgot that it was established to demonstrate safe farming practices and to aid in improving home surroundings of farmers. This was accomplished by having farmers visit the farm, attend demonstrations, and observe. (Courtesy Randy Engelke.)

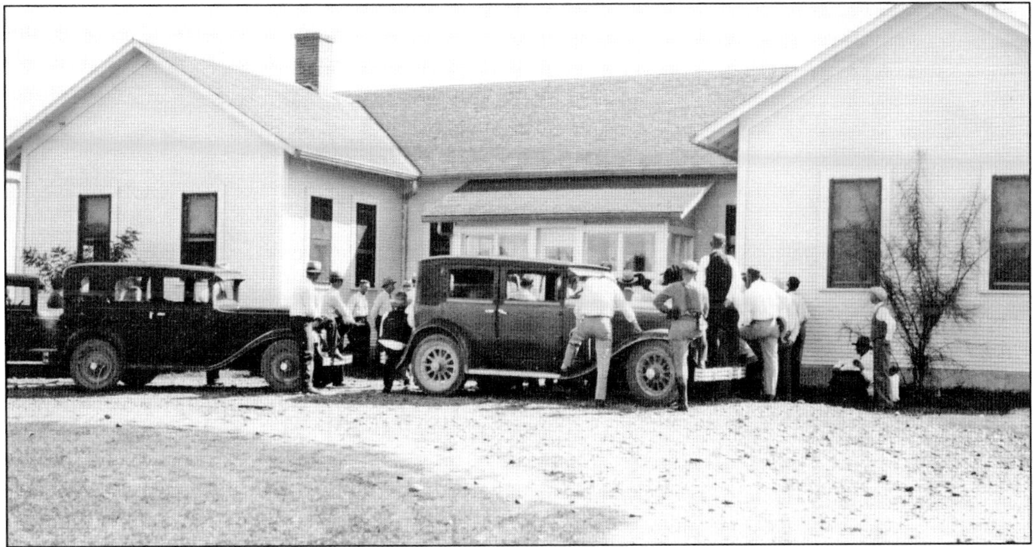

Headquarters of the Luling Foundation appear here in the 1930s. From this modest building, Edgar B. Davis controlled the most important aspects of various aspects of farming, oil production, and land development. Much of his largesse was donated to other projects and causes, such as financial gifts to aid victims of natural disasters. He also accepted significant donations, which in turn helped others. (Courtesy Randy Engelke.)

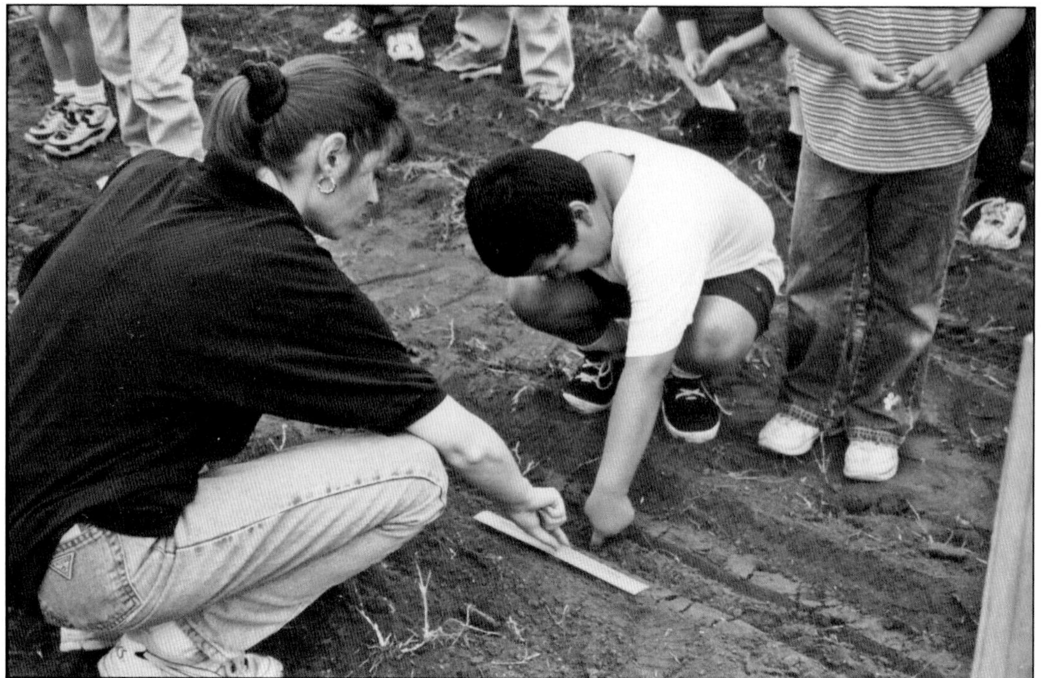

Exactly what these young lads are planting is not recorded by the photographer, but they are intent on planting something for later growth. Green and leafy vegetables perhaps? Assisted by Luling Kindergarten teacher Judy Barnett, the activity on the Foundation Farm remains part of the appeal to educators at all levels. (Courtesy Luling Foundation Farm.)

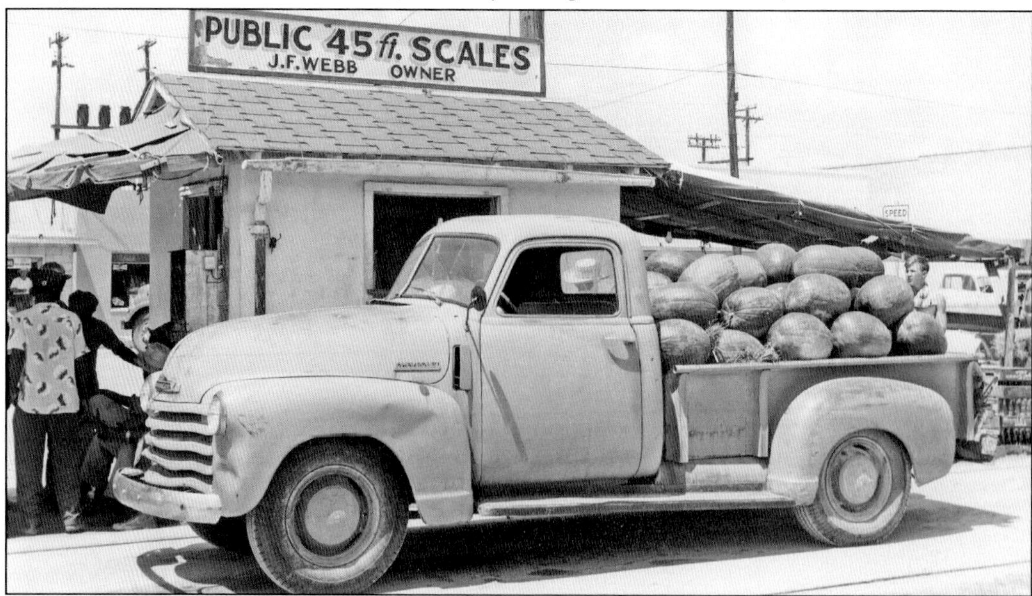

This view of a truckload of watermelons dates from the late 20th century. Traditionally one can test the ripeness of a watermelon by tapping it with the index finger; if you hear a hollow sound, then the watermelon is ripe. Locally grown watermelons begin to ripen during the first week of June, hence the Thump became an established event, taking place during the last weekend in June. (Courtesy Linda Wright.)

Eight

Watermelons, Thumping, Queens, and Parades

Few can recall the first crowning of a Watermelon Thump Queen, although everyone in Luling can name her: Bettie Sue Blackwell. She was crowned Friday night, July 2, 1954, at Eagle Field. There was a large audience witnessing the impressive coronation, which inaugurated her as the first queen to reign over the celebration. Bill Shomette "introduced the royal court as they entered the throne room which was flanked by huge baskets of coral gladioli on either side of the throne. The throne was canopied with graceful folds of pure white batiste studded with glittering white stars." Further, according to the Luling newspaper, the "colorful dresses of the royal court made a lovely summer bouquet for the queen's entrance on the arm of Prince Consort Carl Glass." Queen Blackwell was crowned by His Honor the mayor J. M. Rabon. She was presented with a check from the Watermelon Thump association and a diamond ring given by Bassett Jewelers. Soft music was provided throughout the ceremonies by Prince Lee Kohlenberg and his orchestra. Following the coronation, the royal court proceeded to the Luling club for the queen's ball. Bettie Sue Blackwell is now Mrs. Towns, and she remains a stately beauty today. Among her gifts is a large collection of photographs of each coronation preserved in large albums. They are on permanent display at the Central Texas Oil Patch Museum in Luling.

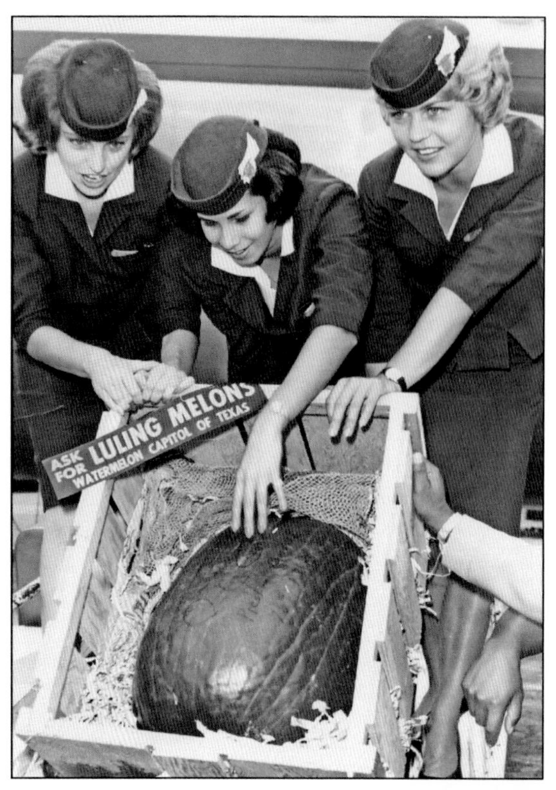

The award-winning Luling watermelons are prized the world over. Shown at left, three Braniff flight hostesses admire the melons sent to the governor of Mexico in 1963. Jim Davis, district sales manager of Braniff Airways de Mexico, S. A., arranged for the melon to be delivered to Mexico as an act of goodwill. Davis said the program of delivering the melon "was very interesting and we received good publicity, the sort of thing we need to show from time to time to boost the good neighbor relations and friendship between the U.S. and Mexico. We should have more of this." Shown also is sales manager Jim Davis (below, left), presenting the documentation verifying the melon to the deputy governor of Mexico City, Gustavo Trevino. (Both courtesy G&H Society.)

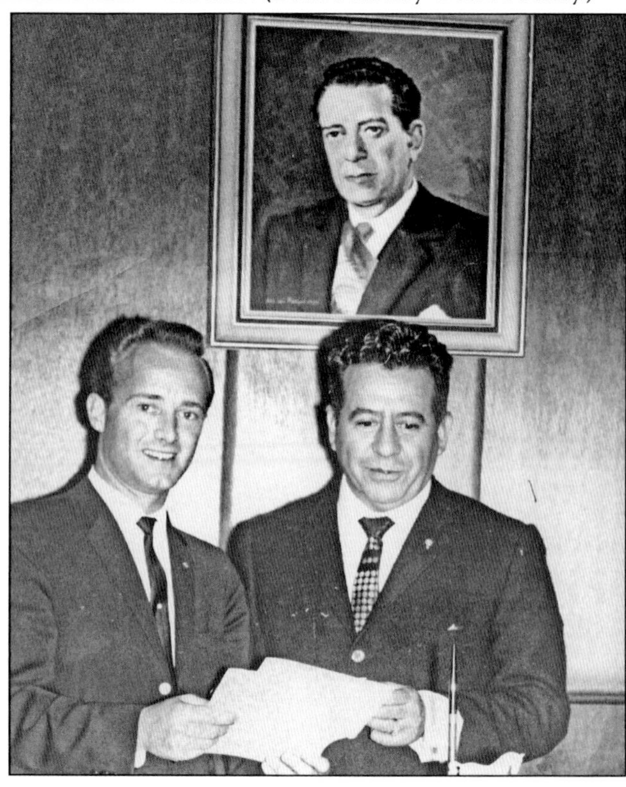

Ann Manford was secretary of the chamber of commerce when that building was located next to the Blanche Square log cabin. It stood on the northeast corner of Highway 183 and Austin Street. The building has since been replaced by an oil derrick, but the cabin remains. Manford proudly displays the Luling Watermelon Thump flag. (Courtesy Linda Wright Photograph Collection.)

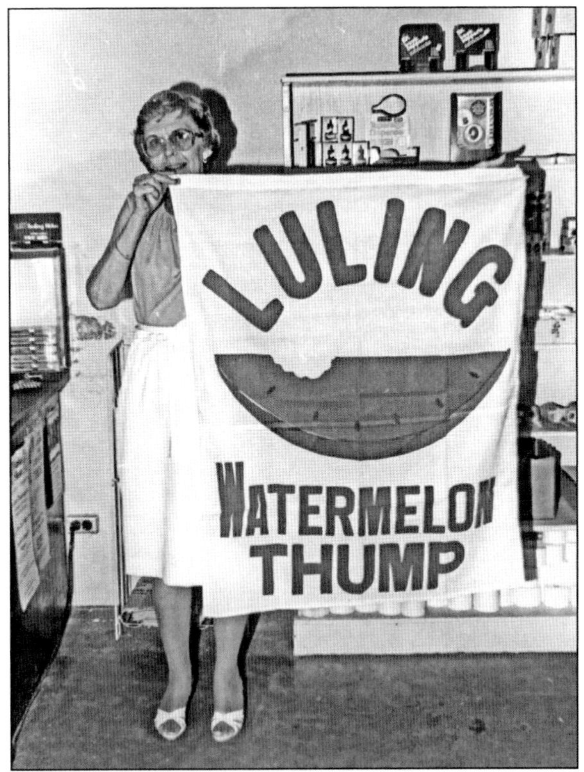

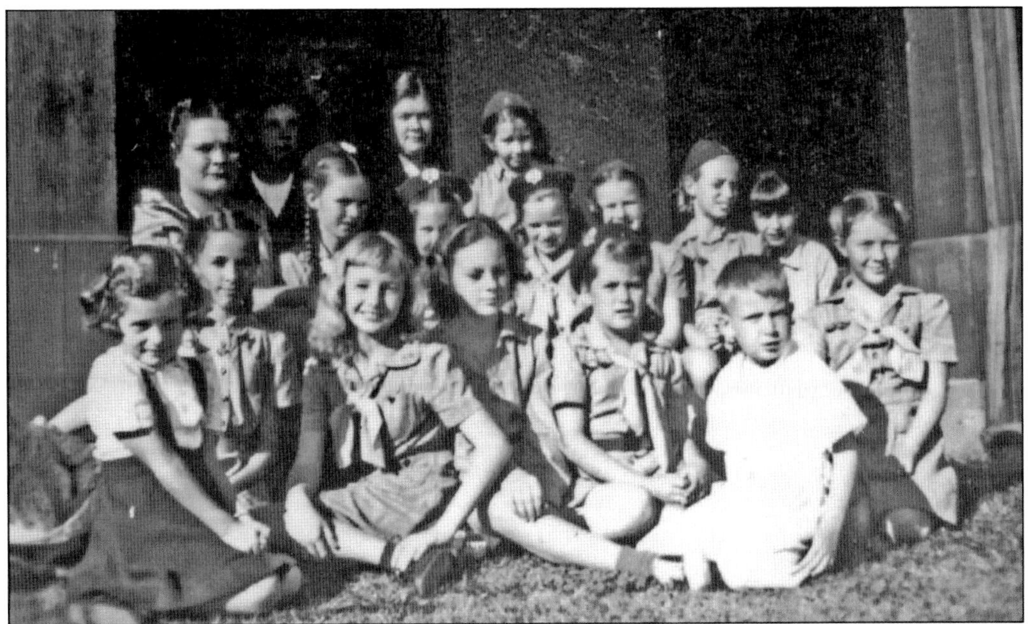

Most every little girl dreams of becoming a queen. This group of young Brownie Scouts met each week at the Southside Club House. Leaders were parents of Scout members. From this group picture, at least one Brownie became a Thump Queen. In the first row, third from left, is future Thump Queen Bettie Sue Blackwell. In the back row at right is Betty Baker Meneley. (Courtesy Betty Meneley.)

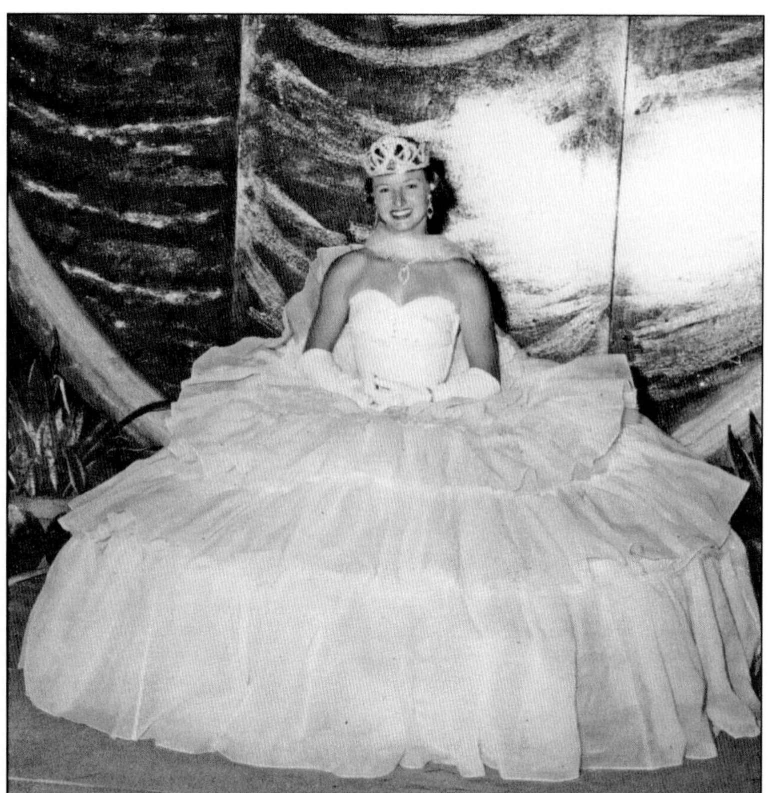

First Watermelon Thump Queen Bettie Sue Blackwell began a tradition lasting over half a century. Here she is shown in her full-length gown. Her attendants were Princess Annazelle Zedler, Mary Jo Wadlington, Bobbi Jo King, Carolyn Krauskopf, and Jacquelyn Stanwood. The historic Luling oil museum holds two large albums of photographs representing each year's event, not only of the queens but of related activities of the Thump. (Courtesy Carol Voigt.)

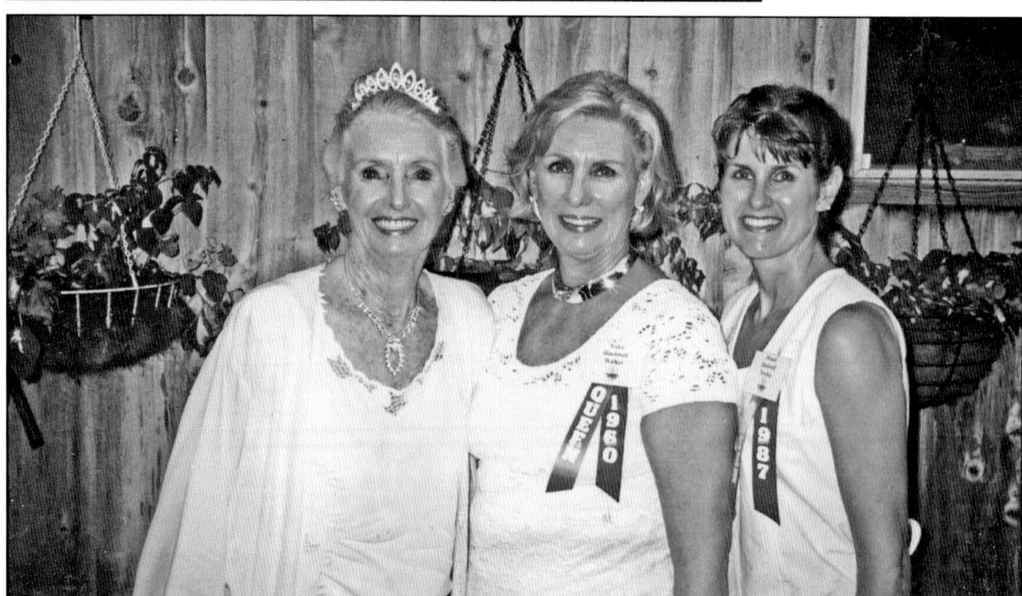

Here is a family of royalty. Bettie Sue Blackwell, now Mrs. Towns (left), was the first Thump Queen in 1954. Her younger sister, Kakai (center), followed in 1960 after the Thump Queen Phyllis Webb got married. She is now Mrs. Walker. In 1987, Brandi Blackwell, the niece of Bettie Sue Blackwell Towns, became Thump Queen. She is now Mrs. Hayden. (Courtesy Carol Voigt and Bettie Sue Towns.)

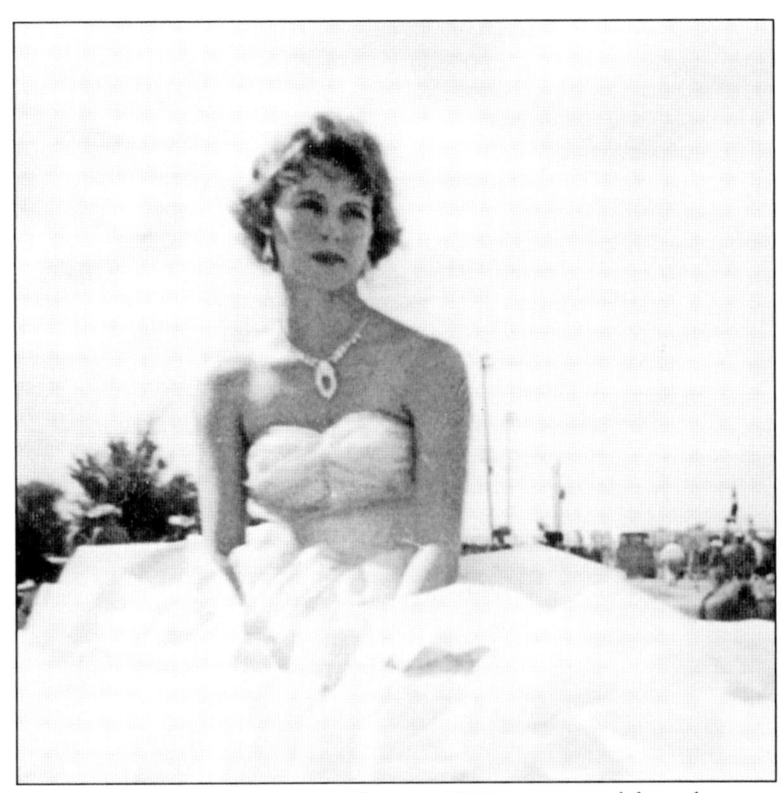

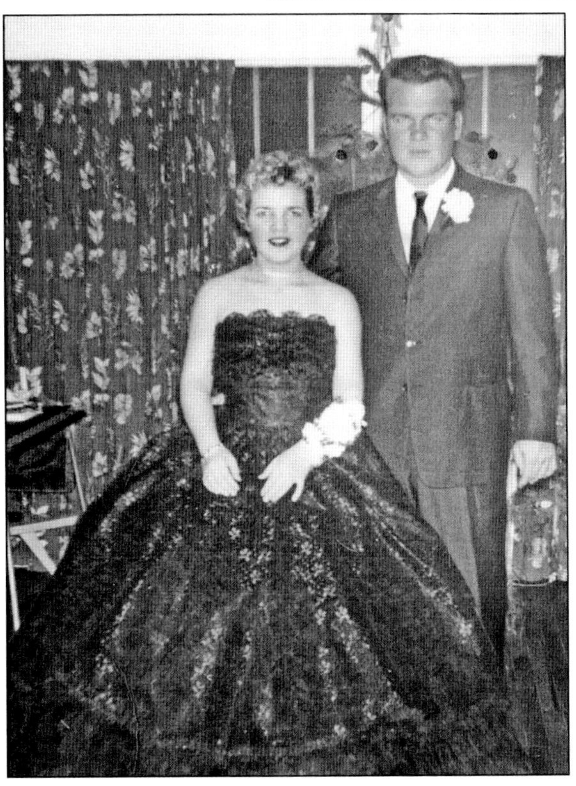

The year 1960 was special for at least two people: Watermelon Thump Queen Phyllis Webb and her escort for the evening, John Linscomb. Phyllis Webb received a majority of 214 votes with her runner-up being Kakai Blackwell. Others in the running were Merrilynn Eastwood, Dorothy Ehrig, Janice Hamilton, Kay Ogden, and Linda Stewart. The important vote counters were Herman Hoberts, chair of the Thump Association; Sonny Stair, of the chamber of commerce; Wanda McBride, chair of the election committee; Madeleine Manford, chair of the Queen's Committee; and Sally Kilgore, representing Beta Sigma Phi. The year was special because later Phyllis Webb became Mrs. John Linscomb; the couple is shown at left. The rules prevented a queen to be married, so she relinquished her crown to the runner-up, Kakai Blackwell. Thus, in 1960, there were two Thump Queens: Phyllis Webb and Kakai Blackwell. (Both courtesy the Central Texas Oil Patch Museum.)

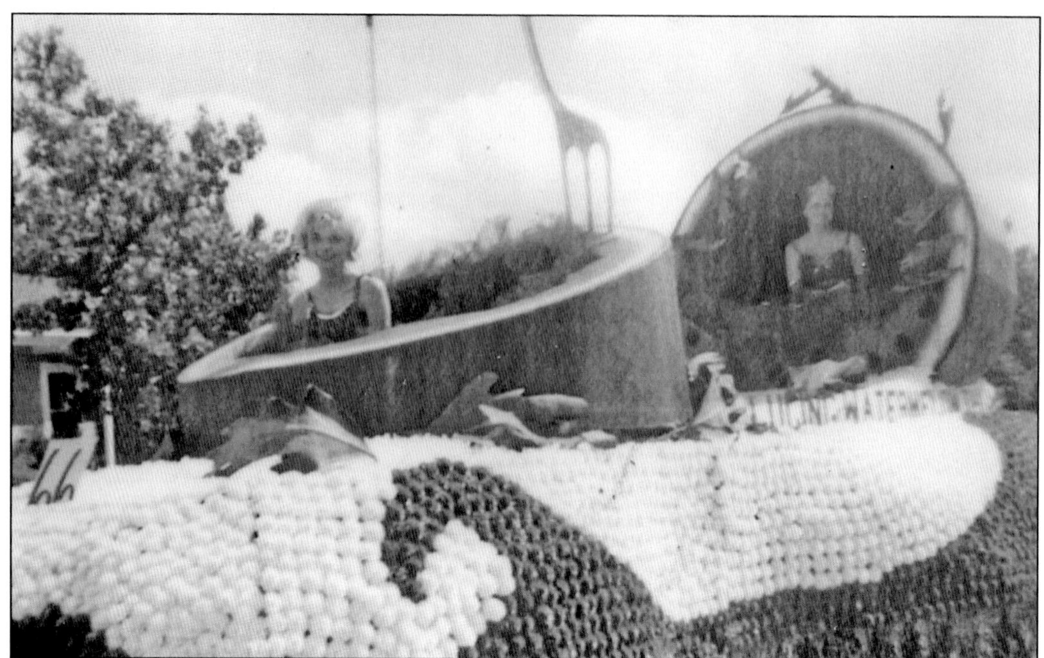

Every Watermelon Thump parade had floats that were out of this world, and this one from 1963 was no exception. Imagine an 8-foot fork stuck in a watermelon slice. The queen that year was Mary Elizabeth Carter. At the crowning ceremonies, none other than His Honor the mayor J. B. Nickells placed the crown on Carter's head. It was a memorable evening and weekend indeed. (Courtesy the Central Texas Oil Patch Museum.)

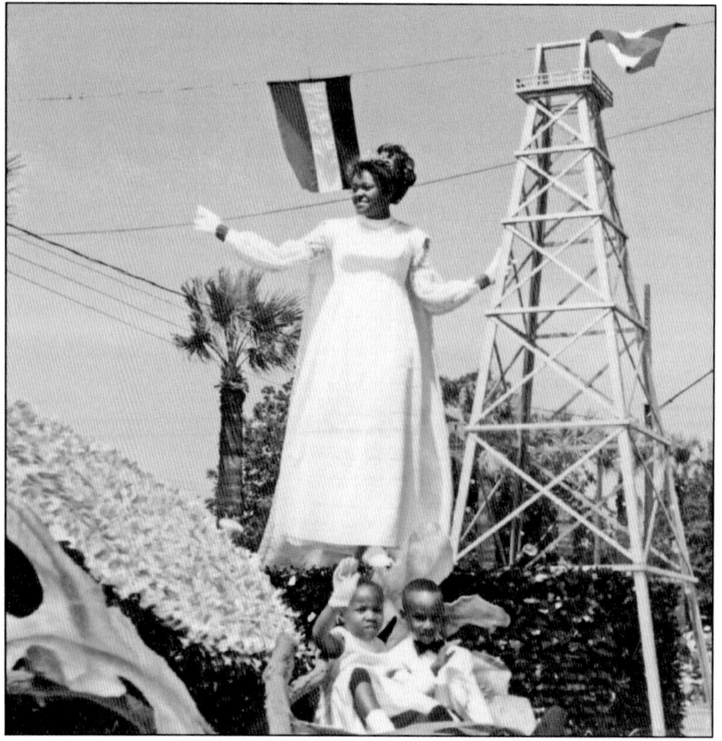

Jackie Dorn, Thump Queen in 1972, is crowned by Mayor Bryan Nickells with her escort Billy Roberts. Her train bearers were Marie Berry and Tommy Harris. Television appearances included Channel 4's *Early Evening News* to advertise the Thump and Channel 7 in Austin on the Carolyn Jackson *Women's World Show*, as well as San Antonio's Channel 5, the *Mary Denman Show*. (Courtesy the Central Texas Oil Patch Museum.)

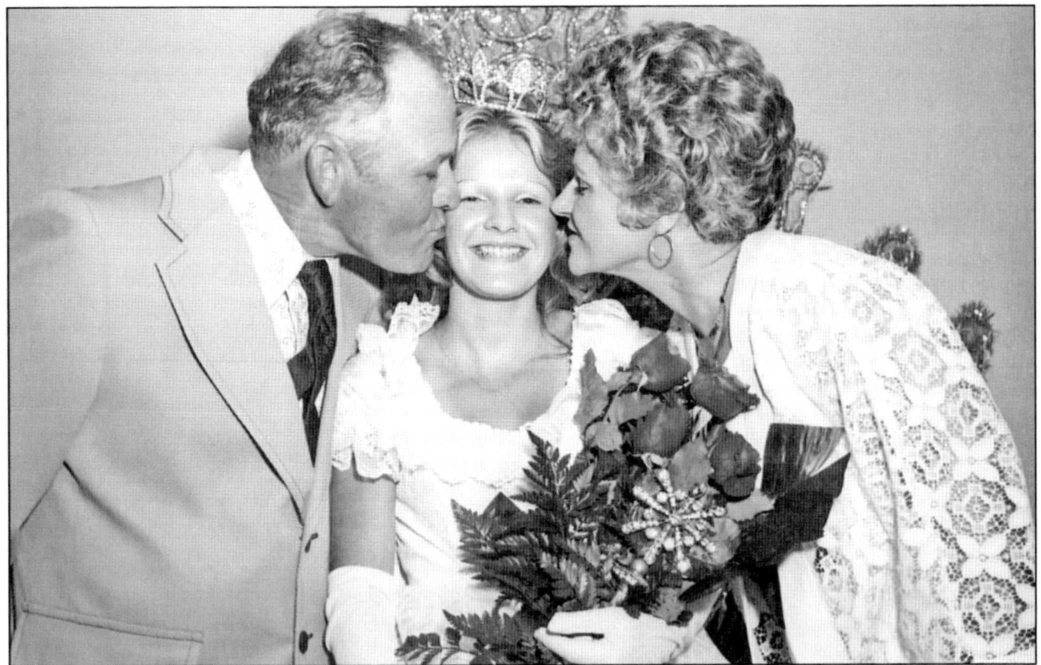

Sharon Gail Gibson, the Thump Queen in 1977, sponsored by the Kiwanis Club, is shown here receiving a kiss from her best friends, parents Aubrey and Rose Gibson. Her senior year activities included active membership in FHA, Esquires, 4-H, track, and Pep Squad. She was nominated for Miss Personality. Her hobbies included painting and swimming. The coronation was held at the Lions Club building. (Courtesy the Central Texas Oil Patch Museum.)

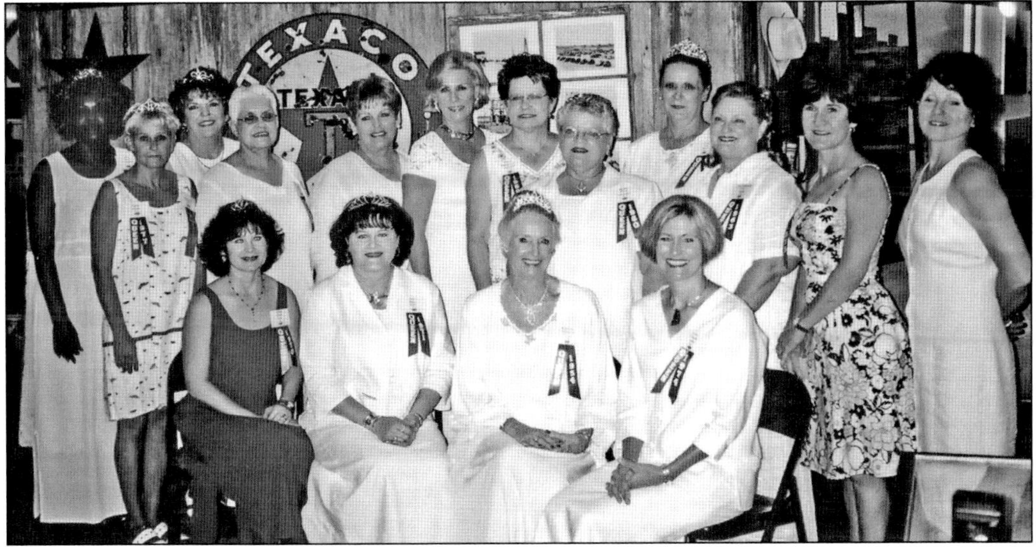

Once a queen, always a queen. Past queens gather to socialize. From left to right are (first row) Debbie Miller (1970), Pam Miller (1971), Bettie Sue Blackwell (1954), and Cathy Johnson (2003); (second row) Jackie Dorn (1972), Sharon Gibson (1977), Merilyn McGee (1959), Carolyn Frank (1962), Dorothy White (1958), Kakai Blackwell (1960), Ollie Jo Montgomery (1968), Phyllis Webb (1960), Beth Vick (1966), and Mary Elizabeth Carter Olden (1963), Karen Gleneqinkel Via (1975), and Bonnie McCrary Phillips (1976). (Courtesy the Central Texas Oil Patch Museum.)

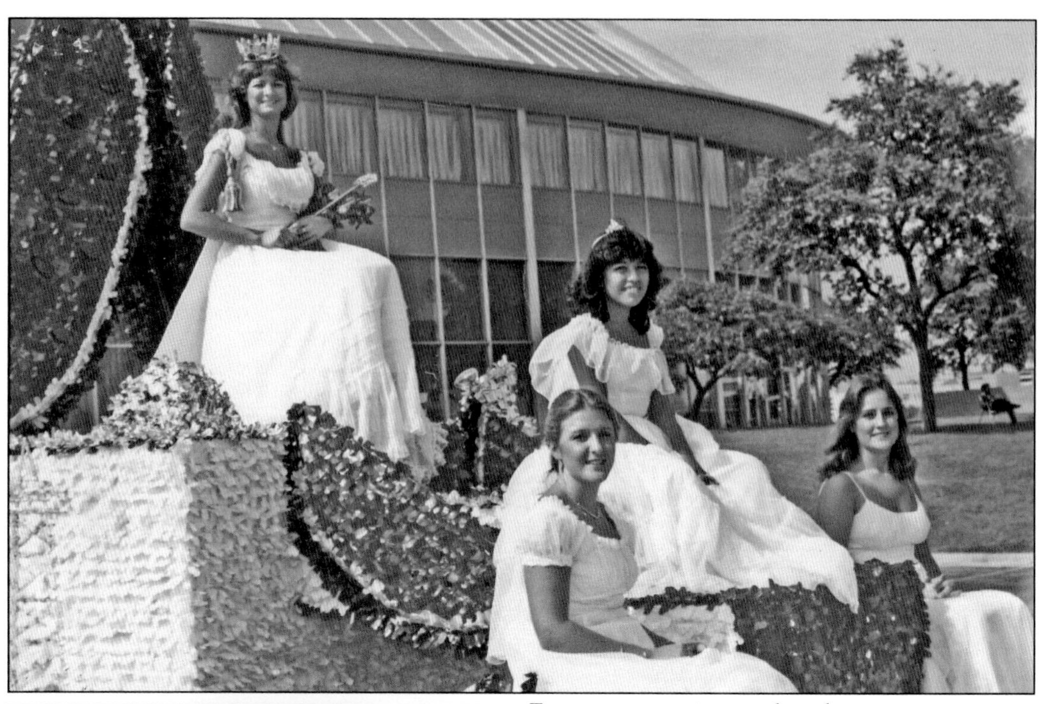

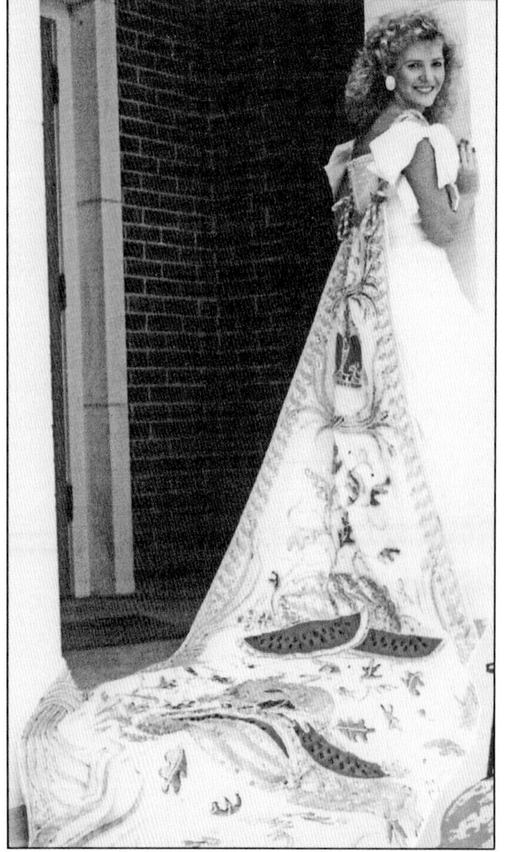

Every community needs at least one annual parade, and traditionally one of the biggest parades of central Texas remains the annual Watermelon Thump Parade, held on Saturday afternoon of the Thump weekend. Here is the queen's float of 1982. Shown here is Queen Sherry Hermann with her princess, Monica Rangel, and duchesses, Becky Gibson and Mary Nell Rightner (on the float corners). (Courtesy the Central Texas Oil Patch Museum.)

Kai Hendricks, daughter of Mr. and Mrs. Mike Hendricks, was crowned queen in 1985. She was active as a cheerleader, captain of the Flag Corps, and a participant in varsity basketball and track. She qualified in the hurdles event at the regional level in 1983 and was a member of Esquires, Student Council, annual staff, and class officer. Her hobbies included reading, skiing, running, and photography. (Courtesy the Central Texas Oil Patch Museum.)

The 1997 queen was Amanda Kidd, daughter of Mr. and Mrs. Jerry Kidd, was sponsored by the Central Texas Oil Patch Museum. The method of counting ballots was changed from hand counting to machine counting. Voting was done in the Oil Museum, but ballots were marked numerically, allowing them to be scan counted. The tabulators were an unnamed official of the Luling Independent School District and the director of the Thump. (Courtesy the Central Texas Oil Patch Museum.)

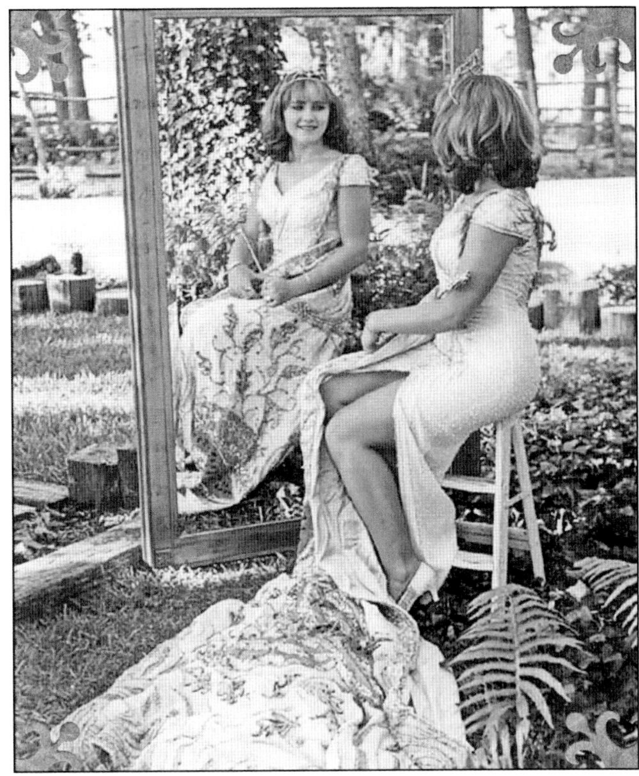

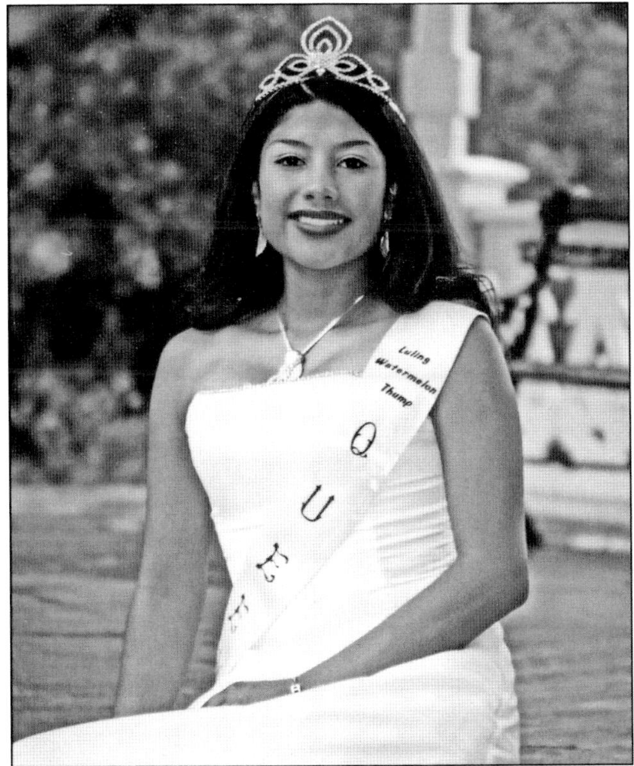

Mayra Guillen became the Thump Queen in 2001. The daughter of Esperanza Guillen-Lopez and a Luling High School senior, Mayra could look with pride on her high school activities. She had participated in 4-H, Spanish Club, Esquires Dance Team, and Catholic Church Youth Group, as well as the Rural Talent Search of Southwest Texas State University. (Courtesy the Central Texas Oil Patch Museum.)

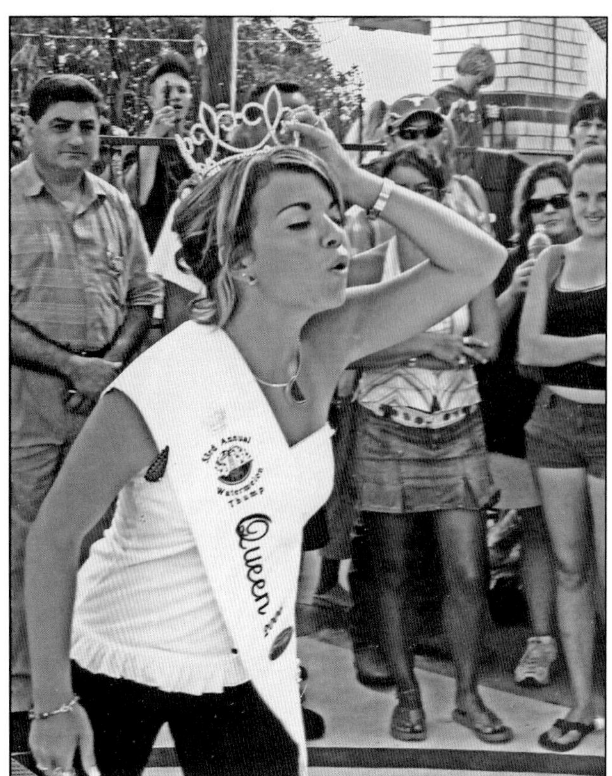

Ashley McFadin, the 2006 Watermelon Thump Queen, tries her best at winning the seed-spitting contest. Her results were not recorded, but it was a valiant effort. The all-time winner, whose name graces the pages of the *Guinness Book of World Records*, is that of Lee Wheelis. His accomplishment measured a fantastic 68 feet, 9 1/8 inches. The year was 1989. (Courtesy the Central Texas Oil Patch Museum.)

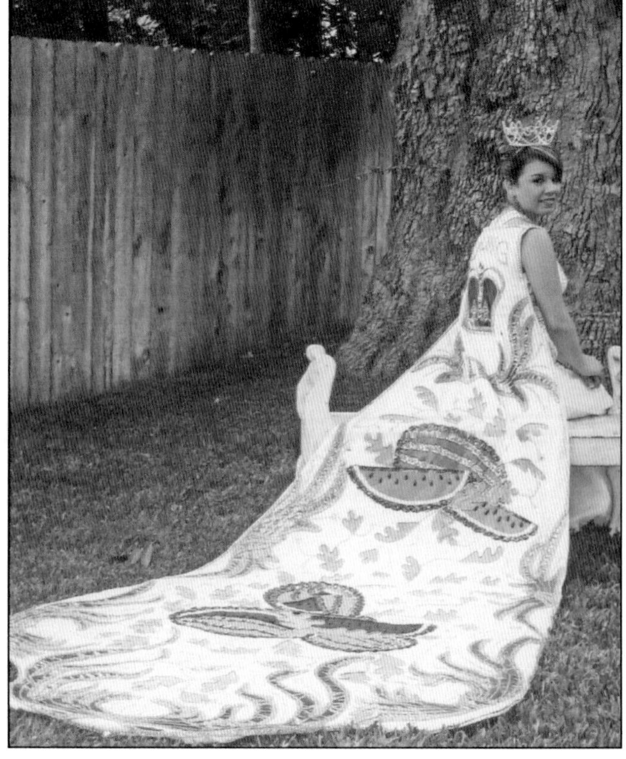

Looking much more regal in her Thump Queen costume and train (more queenly than when spitting a watermelon seed), the 57th Thump Queen Ashley McFadin poses proudly and gracefully. The white train with the watermelon motif remains traditional attire for the queen. McFadin, daughter of Janet Gonzales and Jerry McFadin, was a 2006 graduate of Luling High School. (Courtesy the Central Texas Oil Patch Museum.)

Vanessa Guerra became the Watermelon Thump Queen in 2007. Her court consisted of Princess Jade Weber and Duchesses Ashley Young, Sabrina Pearson, Amanda Collins, Yescenia Reyna, and Ciara Ingram. Most every young girl dreams of someday becoming a queen. Luling offers two opportunities, the homecoming queen during football season and the Watermelon Thump Queen in June. (Courtesy the Central Texas Oil Patch Museum.)

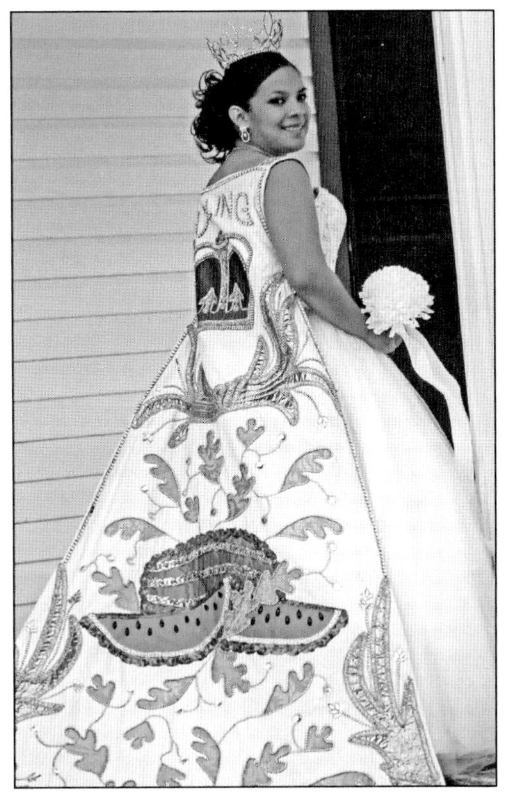

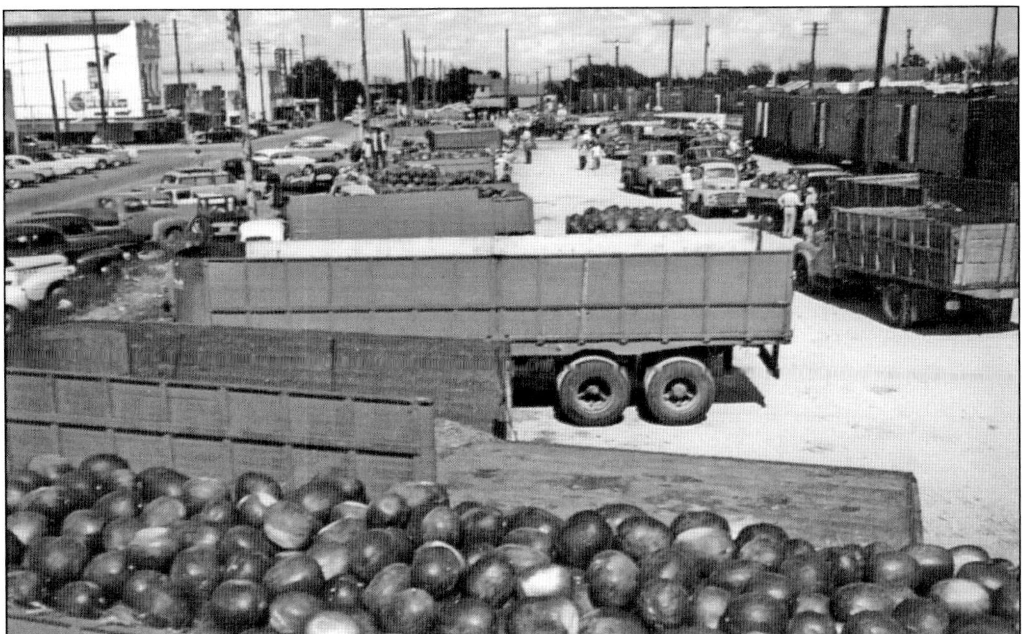

Although the year is not given, the crop appears to be bountiful as these trucks roll in filled with watermelons. In the early years, the melons were loaded by hand and placed in hay to prevent cracking and scarring. Most growers are not overly concerned with creating the biggest watermelon, just in having a sound crop. (Courtesy the Central Texas Oil Patch Museum.)

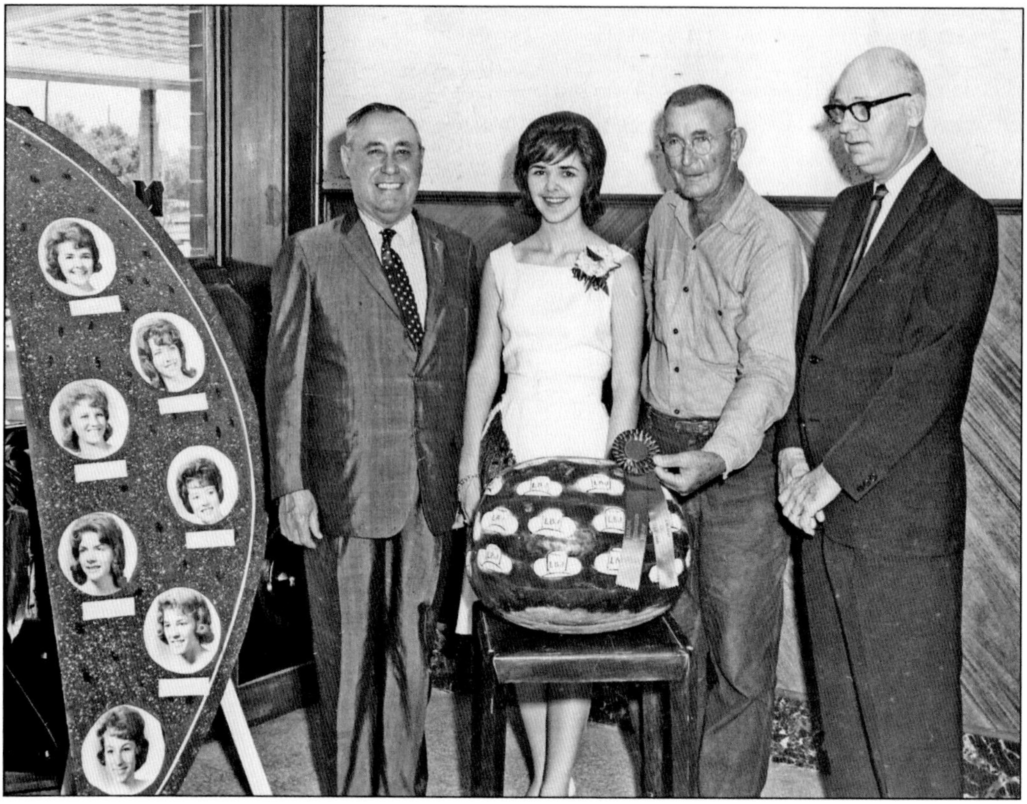

Gen. H. Miller Ainsworth paid $625 for this prize-winning watermelon. Shown here is Ainsworth; the 1964 Watermelon Thump Queen, Carmen Bassett; Louis Moore, holding the ribbon, who grew the champion melon; and Thump chairman John L. Love. The impressive watermelon was then sent to Pres. Lyndon B. Johnson. (Courtesy G&H Society.)

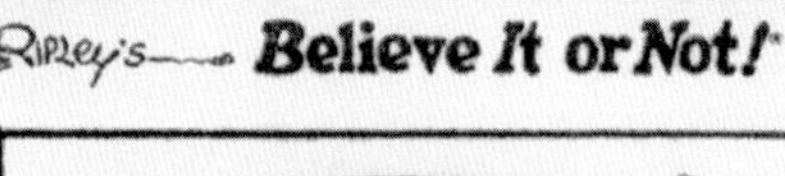

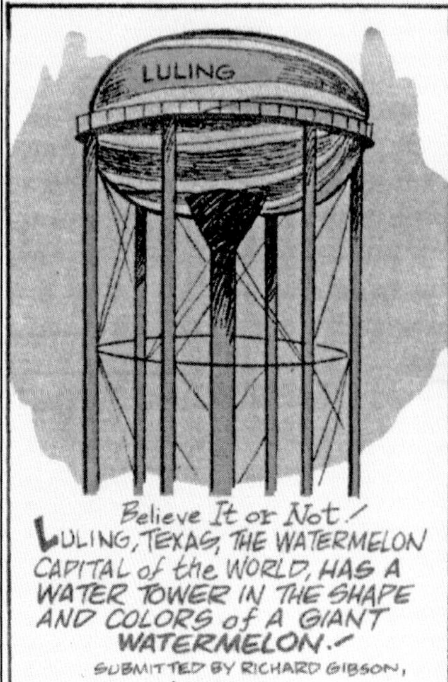

Californian Robert Leroy Ripley, born in 1893, collected odd and unusual facts from around the world. In December 1918, he began a comic strip called *Believe It Or Not!*, and among the thousands of items he recognized was Luling's 154-foot-tall water tower with a 56-foot-diameter storage tank. This drawing appeared in countless newspapers, providing positive publicity for Luling. (Courtesy the Central Texas Oil Patch Museum.)

Nine

Past Heroes and Looking to the Future

Every community has its past heroes, and Luling is no exception. One can wander the county's cemeteries and point out heroes of various sorts: men who fought and died in the Civil War, the Spanish-American War, and those more recent. During World War I, Luling's own Benton McCarley gave the supreme sacrifice for freedom. The American Legion Post No. 177 is named in his memory. During World War II, James M. Logan hit the beach at Salerno and within a short time advanced, took out a machine gun nest, killed several of the enemy, and took prisoners. His action earned him the Congressional Medal of Honor.

Edgar B. Davis became a hero to many, although not in such dramatic fashion as Logan. His name is seen frequently, on hospitals and clinics and on street signs. His influence is still felt on a daily basis. Also in a much less dramatic fashion, many people have contributed significantly to the success of Luling as a community, and their influence will continue. In the 20th century, efforts were made to improve the intellectual level of Luling with the organization of a study club. A small library began in a private home, and now Luling can rightfully boast of an impressive small-town library and an important genealogical and historical society, both in the J. B. Nickells Memorial Library. A Friends of the Library group has been organized and participates or sponsors various events throughout the year. Meet the Authors is held in late March in the historic oil museum, which brings in various authors from communities throughout Texas and attracts hundreds of visitors. The Thump will continue; the Meet the Authors will continue; the oil museum will continue—all bringing in thousands of visitors annually. The future of Luling is bright indeed.

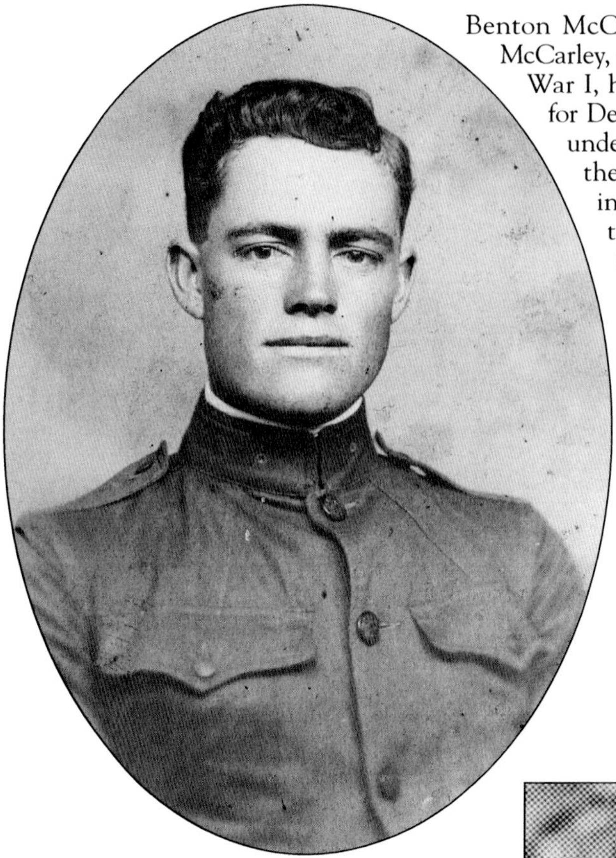

Benton McCarley, son of Rev. Tom and Emma McCarley, was born December 18, 1895. In World War I, he was killed in action, having "died for Democracy and for mankind in France, under the colors of the United States," as the local newspaper described his death in a fitting funeral service. His last letter to his parents was read at his funeral. (Courtesy Riley Froh and the American Legion Post.)

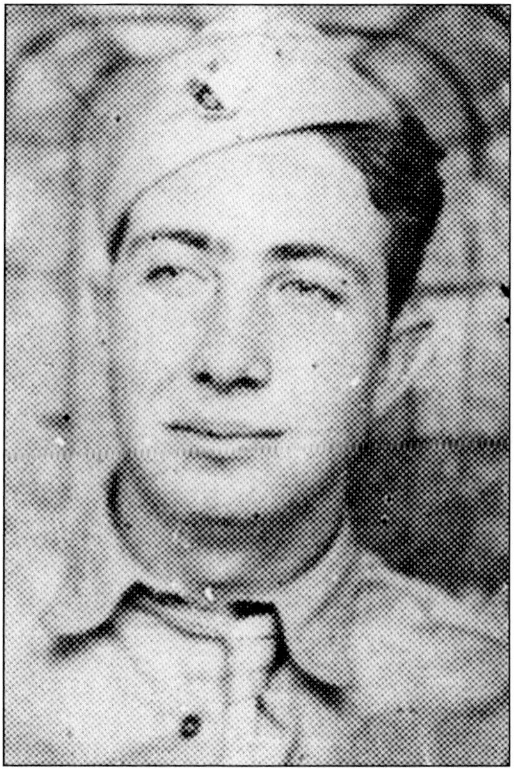

James Marion Logan was in the first wave of the 36th Infantry Division to land at Salerno in 1943. Under heavy fire, Sergeant Logan jumped from his place in the ditch and ran 200 yards to the machine gunners' "nest" behind a wall. He leaped the wall, killed two gunners, and turned the gun on the fleeing enemy. He marched his prisoners back to his lines. (Courtesy Riley Froh.)

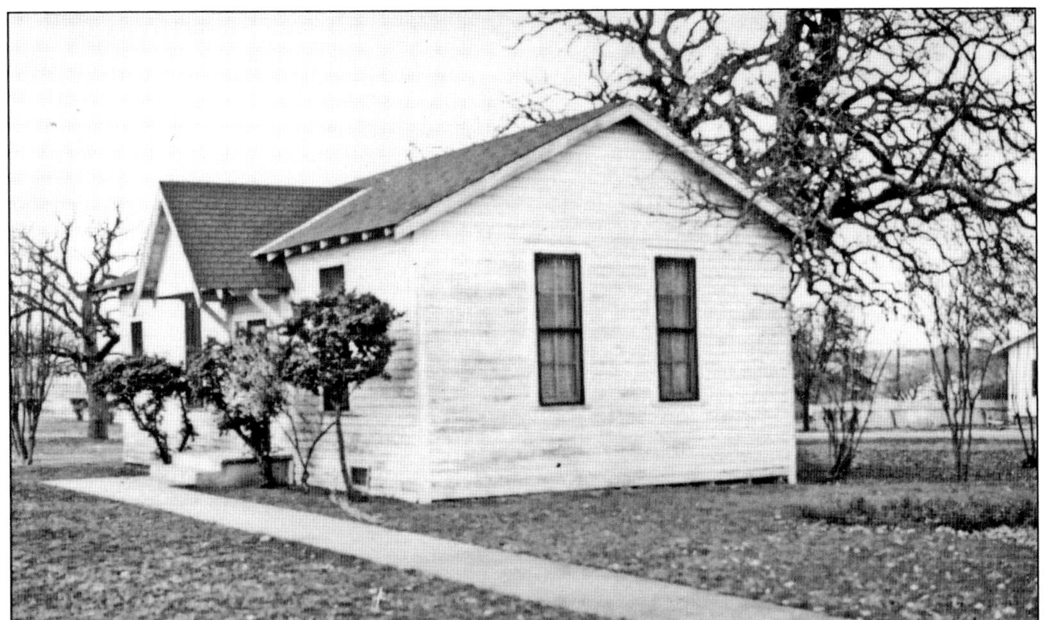

This building, built for the Luling Study Club or Civic Club, was placed in the Blanche Square Park and later became the chamber of commerce office. The charter members of the Civic Club were Annie C. Bridges, Louise Bridges, Blanche Bridges, Willie J. Zedler, Annie Van Gasken, and Anna Bishop. The group was disbanded about 1917. (Courtesy G&H Society.)

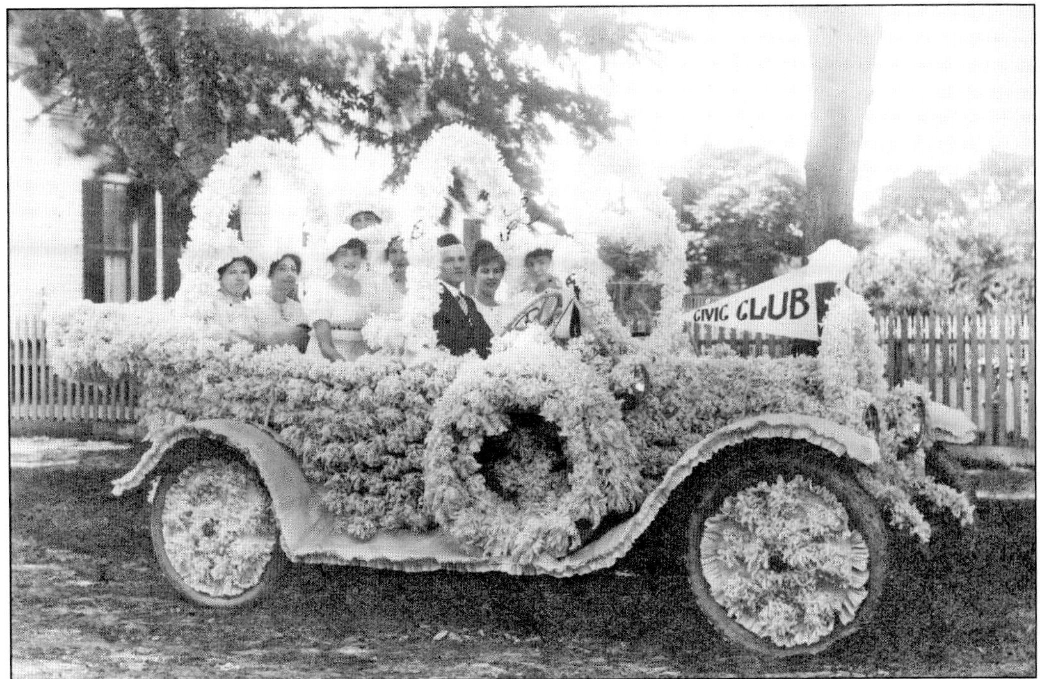

The year is not given for this photograph of a Civic or Study Club float, but perhaps it dates from the 1920s. At the wheel is Robert W. Carter. To his left are Louis Jennings and Josie Gambrell. In the back seat are, from left to right, Blanche Bridges, Josephine Johnson Van Gasken, Maceil Millican, and Louise Zedler Bronson. (Courtesy G&H Society.)

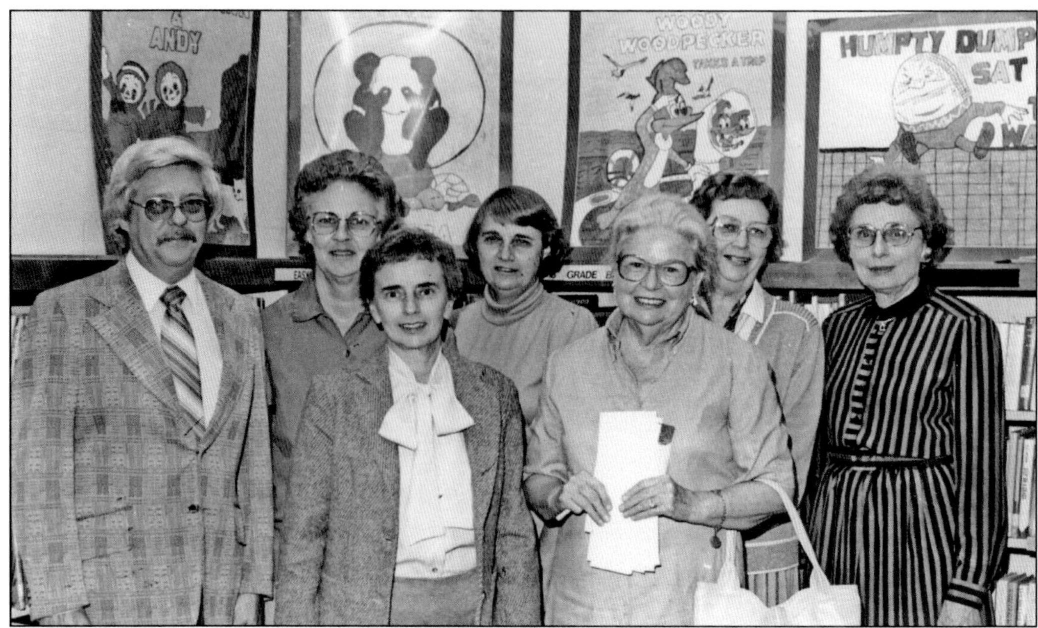

Building up resources for a genealogy library has not been an easy task. This group, shown in an early executive committee meeting, perhaps formed the basis for much of the Luling Genealogical and Historical Society's success. From left to right are Donaly E. Brice, Opel Crowell, Rosalie Roberts, Katie McMillian, Erma Hiltpold, Eva Wilson, and Mary Wanda Harp. (Courtesy G&H Society.)

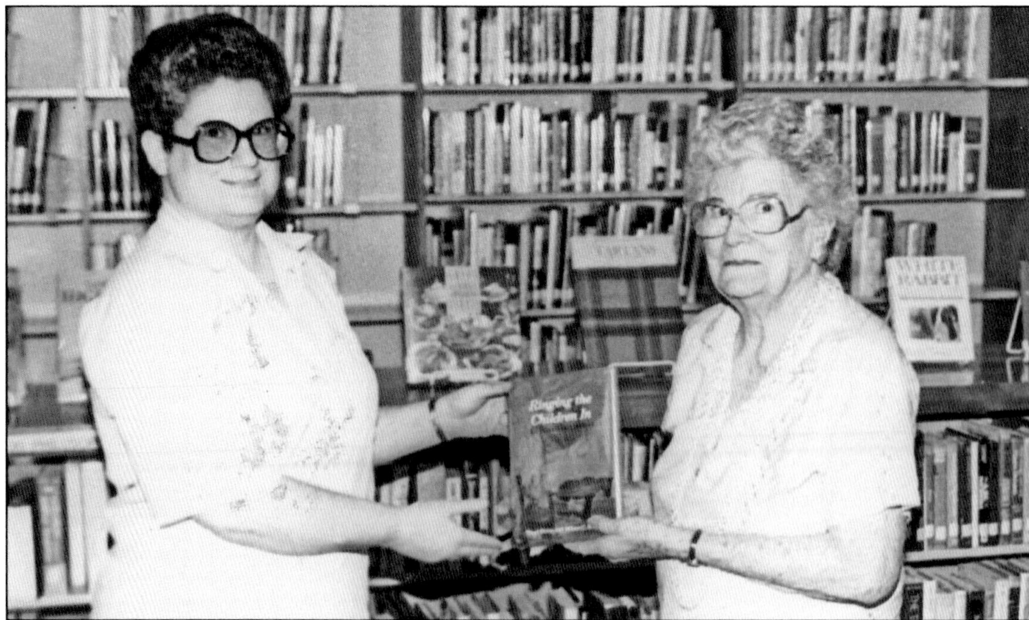

Head librarian Nancy Gilchrist accepts a presentation copy of the book *Ringing the Children In*, authored by Susie Anderson. The library has consistently provided books, newspapers, periodicals, and audio-visual materials to the public of Caldwell, Gonzales, and Guadalupe Counties. Usually busy are the state-of-the-art computers. The genealogical and historical society is housed within the main library and is staffed by volunteers. (Courtesy G&H Society.)

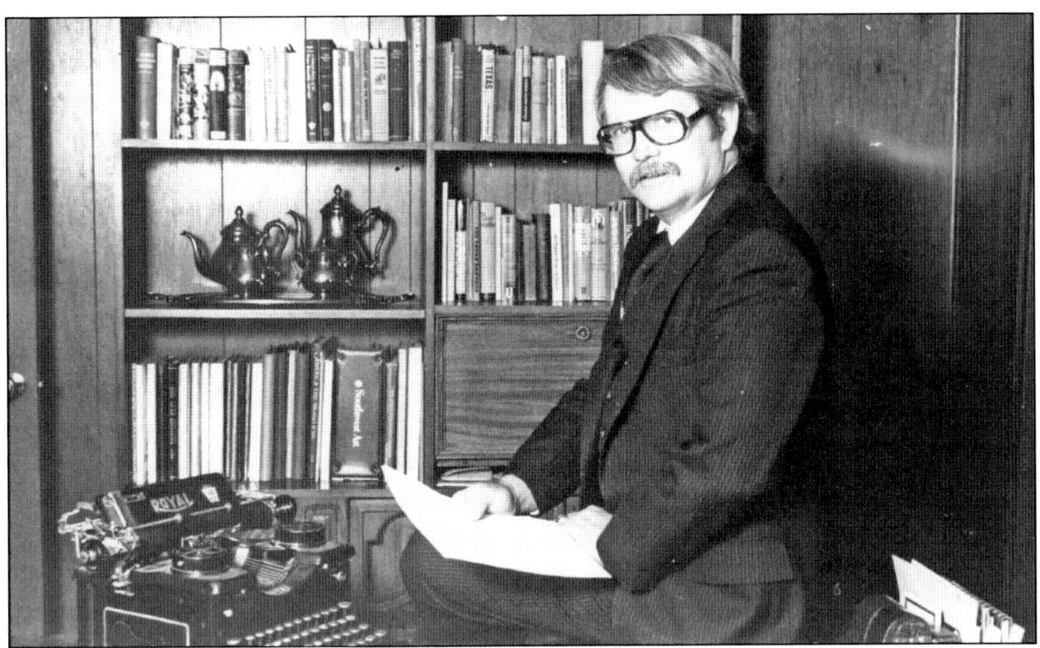

Within the past few years, the Friends of the Library and the oil museum have cosponsored the annual Meet the Authors event, attracting writers whose books cover a wide variety of subject matter. One of the most popular authors remains Riley Froh (above), a descendant of original settlers of Luling. His early interest in the people, legends, and folklore of Luling fascinated him. Froh attended college in San Marcos and then relocated to teach Texas and American history at San Jacinto College. Shown below is Froh at a book signing when his biography, *Edgar B. Davis: Wildcatter Extraordinary*, first appeared. In 1903, his *Edgar B. Davis and Sequences in Business Capitalism: From Shoes to Rubber to Oil* appeared. Froh is currently working on a multi-volume history of Luling, chronicling its story from the mid-19th century to the present. (Both courtesy G&H Society.)

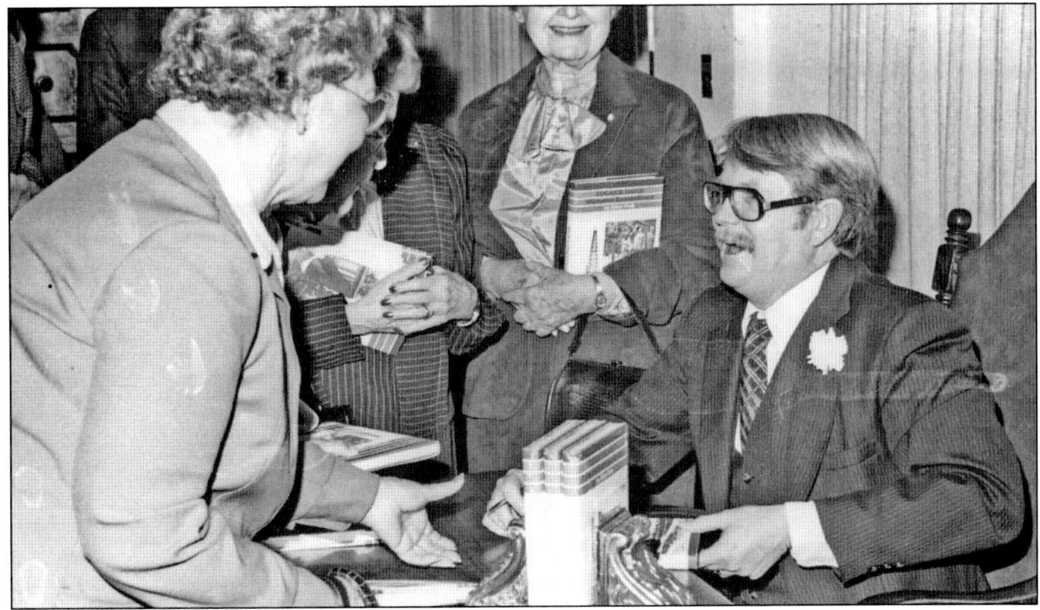

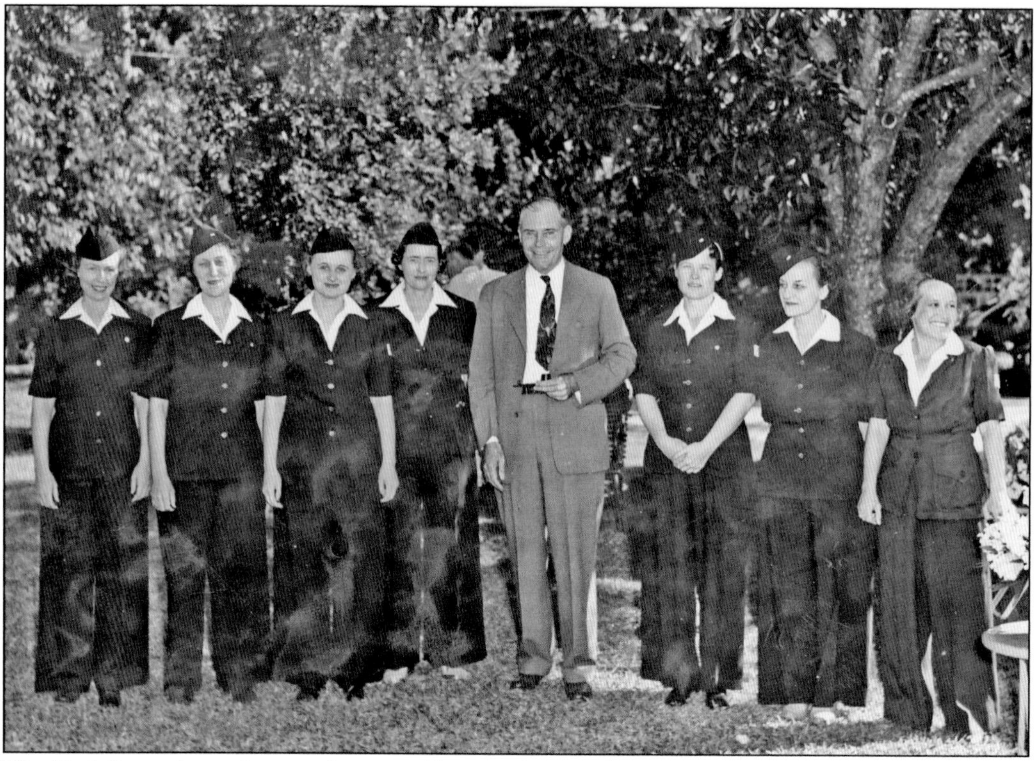

The Red Cross depends on volunteers. During Gov. Coke Stevenson's term (1941–1947), these seven ladies were volunteers who gave up time with their own interests and "went into towns to teach first aid." They are, from left to right, Lillian Conley, Bertha Mehner, Eva Pearl Carter, Willie Watson, Governor Stevenson, Margaret Miller, Lillie Howerts, and Dora Walker. (Courtesy G&H Society.)

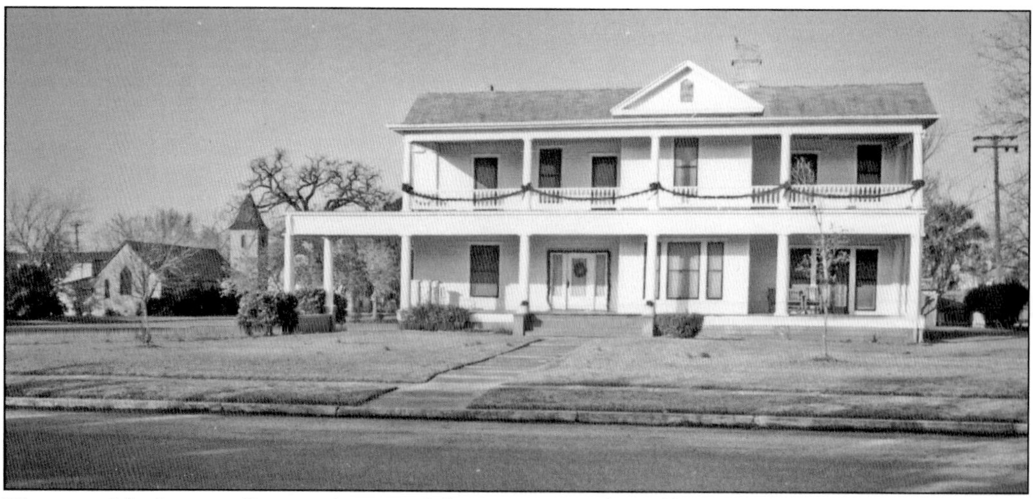

The site of the historic Francis-Ainsworth house was purchased by Dr. Sidney Francis (1867–1935) in October 1895. After his marriage to Annie Gregg, a modest house was built, enlarged in 1916. Their youngest daughter and her husband, H. Miller Ainsworth, moved into the house in the 1930s. The house is now owned by Ada Potts and is Luling's premier bed-and-breakfast. (Courtesy G&H Society.)

The Watermelon Thump Queens

1954—Bettie Sue Blackwell
1955—Janice O'Banion
1956—Margaret Ann Leazer
1957—Dianne Rabon
1958—Dorothy Watkins White
1959—Merilyn McGee
1960—Phyllis Webb, replaced by Kakai Blackwell
1961—Ellen Kay Webb
1962—Carolyn Frank, replaced by Ann Colwell
1963—Mary Elizabeth Carter
1964—Carmen Bassett and Becky Seay
1965—Di Anne Thorp
1966—Beth Vick
1967—Molly Shelton
1968—Ollie Jo Montgomery
1969—Nora Ann Webb
1970—Debbie Miller
1971—Pam Miller and Sherry Janca
1972—Jackie Dorn
1973—Sue McBride
1974—Kathy Folsom
1975—Karen Glenewinkel
1976—Bonnie McCrary
1977—Sharon Gibson
1978—Denise Gonzales
1979—Vicki Mohr
1980—Darla Franks
1981—Susie Rollert
1982—Sherry Hermann
1983—Roxanna Ivey
1984—Jennifer Otto
1985—Kai Hendricks
1986—Sherry Saur
1987—Brandi Blackwell

1988—Tandra Lewis
1989—Catherine Farmer
1990—Tamera Watts
1991—Kelly Ward
1992—Monica Kidd
1993—Meghan Allen
1994—Veronica Suarez
1995—Ashley Bassett
1996—Aurora Guillen
1997—Amanda Kidd
1998—Shannon Zamora
1999—Ginny Robbins
2000—Kelsey Bassett
2001—Mayra Guillen
2002—Raven Robbins
2003—Cathi Johnson
2004—Rebekah McClure
2005—Megan Cox
2006—Ashley McFadin
2007—Vanessa Guerrero
2008—Michelle Levesque

Bibliography

Catalog of the Photograph Collection Archives, Caldwell County Genealogical and Historical Society, Luling.

Duncan, Dawson. *The Luling Foundation, 1927–1948*. Luling: The Luling Foundation, 1948.

Engelke, Randy. Collection of photographs, artifacts and clippings relating to the history of Luling.

Froh, Riley. *Edgar B. Davis: Wildcatter Extraordinary*. Luling: The Luling Foundation, 1984.

———. *Edgar B. Davis and Sequences in Business Capitalism*. New York: Garland Publishers, Inc., 1993.

The Luling Newsboy and Signal. Microfilm reels archived in the Caldwell County Genealogical and Historical Society.

The Plum Creek Almanac. Complete files archived in the Caldwell County Genealogical and Historical Society, Luling.

Vertical Files. Newspaper clippings and obituaries archived in the Caldwell County Genealogical and Historical Society.

"The Watermelon Thump." Two scrapbooks of photographs and clippings prepared by Bettie Sue (Blackwell) Towns archived in the Central Texas Oil Patch Museum.

Withers, Zona Adams. *A History of the Luling Foundation 1927–1982*. Luling: The Luling Foundation, 1982.

Wright, Charles and Linda. Collection of photographs and clippings relating to the history of Luling.

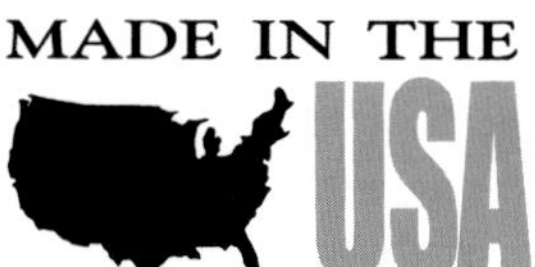
MADE IN THE
USA